T0325074

Game AI Uncovered

Game AI Uncovered: Volume Two continues the series with the collected wisdom, ideas, tricks and cutting-edge techniques from 22 of the top game AI professionals and researchers from around the world.

The techniques discussed in these pages cover the underlying development of a wide array of published titles, including *The Survivalists, Wheelman, Plants vs. Zombies: Battle for Neighborville, Dead Space, Zombie Army 4, Evil Genius 2, Sniper Elite 5, Sonic & All-Stars Racing Transformed, DiRT: Showdown*, and more.

Contained within this volume are overviews and insights covering a host of different areas within game AI, including generalised planners, player imitation, awareness, dynamic behaviour trees, decision-making architectures, agent learning for automated playthroughs, utility systems, machine learning for cinematography, directed acyclic graphs, environment steering, difficulty scenarios, environmental cues through voxels, automated testing approaches, dumbing down your AI, synchronised path following, and much more.

Beginners to the area of game AI, along with professional developers, will find a wealth of knowledge that will not only help in the development of your own games but also spark ideas for new approaches.

This volume includes chapters written by Nuno Vicente Barreto, Steve Bilton, Andy Brown, Dr Allan Bruce, Richard Bull, Phil Carlisle, Sarah Cook, Michele Condò, Steven Dalton, Rodolfo Fava, Jonas Gillberg, Dominik Gotojuch, Dale Green, Tobias Karlsson, Jonathan Keslake, Fernando Penousal Machado, Ivan Mateev, Dr Nic Melder, Dr Bram Ridder, Paul Roberts, Licínio Roque, and Andrea Schiel.

Game AI Uncovered
Volume Two

Edited by
Paul Roberts

Illustrations by
Nicholas Dent

CRC Press
Taylor & Francis Group
Boca Raton London New York

CRC Press is an imprint of the
Taylor & Francis Group, an **informa** business

Designed cover image: Team17 Digital

First edition published 2024
by CRC Press
2385 NW Executive Center Drive, Suite 320, Boca Raton FL 33431

and by CRC Press
4 Park Square, Milton Park, Abingdon, Oxon, OX14 4RN

CRC Press is an imprint of Taylor & Francis Group, LLC

ISBN: 978-1-032-34729-5 (hbk)
ISBN: 978-1-032-34317-4 (pbk)
ISBN: 978-1-003-32354-9 (ebk)

DOI: 10.1201/9781003323549

Typeset in Times
by codeMantra

Contents

Preface

When we began, *Game AI Uncovered* was only going to be a single volume, but it quickly became evident that there was a lot of interest from the game AI community to get involved and to make this into something bigger. So, to ensure each and every one of these amazing AI professionals could share this platform, we decided to keep going and create a second volume. This all happened while volume one was being developed, so trust me when I say the workload increased significantly. And it didn't stop there. Spoiler alert, there will be a third volume next year, such was the interest.

For me, this demonstrates how amazing the games industry is, and more specifically the game AI portion of it. There are so many extremely talented people in this industry, and their constant push to share knowledge, allow others to build upon their ideas, and continually move the field to better places, is astounding. Anyone who has worked in a games studio will know this happens daily, but reaching out to share new approaches and advances with the wider world is awe inspiring. It would be so easy to keep advances secret and to not share, but that's not who we are.

Paul Roberts

Acknowledgements

Game AI Uncovered (Volume Two) was quite an undertaking to bring together. Starting from scratch and reaching out to the game AI community to see if there was even any interest in such a project was a monumental undertaking. As it turned out, there was a great deal of interest. And a huge thanks to all those people (some of whom did not end up contributing a chapter themselves) who suggested colleagues, or friends that would be interested in getting involved.

A special thanks to my wife, the amazing Emma Roberts who proofread this entire volume and, as she did with volume one, pointed out a plethora of inconsistencies and mistakes.

The artwork throughout this volume was once again done by the super talented Nicholas Dent. He took our programmer art and not only made them look professional but also added a lot of character as well. Thanks Nick.

The amazing cover artwork for this volume was provided by Team17 Digital from the game *The Survivalists*. Four chapters covering techniques from this game appear in this book: *Low Bandwidth, Synchronised Path Following in Team17's The Survivalists, Going Stateless: An Evolution of Behaviour Trees in Team17's The Survivalists and Beyond, Monkey Business: NPC Player Imitation in Team17's The Survivalists,* and *Dynamic Behaviour Trees: Building for Scalability.*

Thanks to the guys at CRC Press who have supported this project from the start. A special call out to Will Bateman, who supported the idea of a second volume right away (before volume one was published), such was his confidence in this series. And a huge thanks to Sathya Devi who spends hours turning my manuscripts into the amazing final product you see before you. I'd be remiss if I didn't call out the excellent work that Simran Kaur does in the background. Thanks Simran. And to Shamayita Dey who took over the reins from Simran for Volume Two. Thanks Shamayita.

A huge thanks to all those studios who supported their staff and allowed for this information to be shared.

Projects of this kind are a labour of love. And I think each and every contributor in this series has shown an undeniable passion for the field of game AI. Sharing expertise and knowledge takes time. This is time outside of our day-to-day jobs of game development, meaning weekends and evenings over many months were filled with the development of this volume. This includes the writing, editing, drawing, rewriting, organising permissions, and much more. So, a final huge thank you goes to all our families who have both supported us and allowed us to take the time to work on this project.

Editor

Paul Roberts is the Technical Director of the independent game studio Grinning Cat. Prior to this, he worked in a variety of Principal /Lead AI Programmer roles for a range of studios in the UK including Sumo Digital, Team17, Traveller's Tales, Activision, and some smaller indie studios. For several years, Paul also led the Games Programming department at Staffordshire University, where he taught Game AI and programming principles. He has a Master's degree in Computer Science with Artificial Intelligence, which focused on pathfinding, the development of the DRS algorithm and ways to test the believability of generated paths. Paul has written a number of books, some fiction, others academic, the latest of which is *Artificial Intelligence in Games* published by CRC Press in 2022 and is also the editor for this Game AI Uncovered series.

Contributors

Dr Nuno Vicente Barreto works as a Principal AI Programmer at DR Studios, Ltd. He has a PhD in Information Sciences and Technologies, focusing on Video Game Creature Believability, from the University of Coimbra. While taking his PhD, he co-founded Titan Forged Games where he developed *Slinki* and *Tanks Meet Zombies* and worked as a freelance Gameplay Programmer for other companies. He really enjoys developing and studying Gameplay/AI systems and is very fond of A-Life, and Life-Sim games, ever since he played *Creatures 3*, back in 1999.

Steve Bilton is currently a Principal Programmer at Firesprite and has been a game developer throughout his working life. Much of that time has been spent working on high-level AI behaviour for both friendly and enemy NPCs, in a variety of different genres and games of varying scope, but tends to dig his fingers in almost any player-facing pie given half a chance. He cares most about the psychology of game AI and how it is perceived by players, preferring to put the intended game experience above all other considerations. He holds an MEng in Computing with Artificial Intelligence from Imperial College London from a long time ago, which was the last time he did any actual AI that wasn't smoke and mirrors.

Andy Brown began his career in 1997 at Gremlin Interactive where he worked on several sports titles, the last of which being a soccer game which was his first taste of AI programming in a commercial game. Following that he spent 5 years at Eurocom, where he was part of the core gameplay team on *Spyro: A Hero's Tail* along with *Pirates of the Caribbean* where he focused on player mechanics as well as core AI systems. In 2008, he moved to Sumo Digital where amongst other things he helped develop AI systems for several of the studios driving titles, in particular *Sonic & All Stars Racing Transformed,* as well as AI technology to support the development of *Crackdown 3*. His current role involves leading the gameplay team on an unannounced AAA title.

Dr Allan Bruce holds a PhD from the University of Aberdeen, in the field of AI known as qualitative reasoning. He has a comprehensive background in the video games industry, beginning with Midway Games in 2006, moving to CCP Games in 2009, and joining Sumo Digital in 2018. Throughout this time, he has worked on AI and AI Systems for a number of games, including *Wheelman*, *EVE: Valkyrie*, *Hood: Outlaws and Legends*, and *Call of Duty: Vanguard*. He currently resides in County Durham, UK, with his wife, two sons, three cats, and dog, Bowser.

Richard Bull has been a full-time professional programmer in the games industry since late 2000, following a short stint coding industrial software, after graduating a couple of years previous. He has specialised in architecting AI and gameplay systems, working as a lead AI programmer on *Empire: Total War* for The Creative Assembly, and on titles such as *Grand Theft Auto: Chinatown Wars* and *L.A. Noire* for Rockstar Games. Among his other previous employers he counts Software Creations, Acclaim, Kuju, and Activision, and is credited on numerous other titles including *Dungeons & Dragons: Tactics, Call of Duty: Strike Team, Nom Nom Galaxy*, and the *Lego Harry Potter* remasters. Since 2014, he has been working on various original and co-developed projects through his own company Gentlemen Of Science, with co-founder and fellow veteran games industry programmer Ash Henstock. They are currently assisting development on an unannounced cross platform title with Ice Beam Games, for Secret Mode.

Phil Carlisle is a Senior Lecturer for Games and Computer Science at the University of Lincoln in the UK and runs a small consultancy firm called Generative Machines specialising in machine learning enabled procedural content generation tools for game developers. Phil has been a senior programmer in the games industry and has shipped multiple games for the likes of Team17, Hasbro, Microprose, Ubisoft, and others under varying programming roles including AI programmer. Phil has spoken widely about AI in games, including at GDC and other conferences. Phil's research uses computer vision to empower procedural content generation for AI behaviour and cinematography by learning from films.

Michele Condò has been programming in the video games industry for 10 years. He started in the mobile gaming sector before moving across to AAA games, working for high-profile games companies Ubisoft and IO Interactive. Although he specialises in AI, he also has a wide range of games programming experience. His work on open world, stealth, and action games has gained him credits on the hugely popular games *Ghost Recon Wildlands* and *Watch Dogs: Legion*. When not programming, he enjoys spending quality time with his family and 2 cats and playing video games of course.

Sarah Cook is currently a Lead Programmer at Sumo Digital Sheffield. She began programming at age 8, extending games such as *Space Invaders* in BBC Basic, and has gone on to have a career in the games industry spanning over 15 years, of which 7 have been spent as an AI programmer. Sarah has degrees in Electrical and Electronic Engineering (BEng/MEng), and Artificial Intelligence (MSc), and has a PhD focusing on computer-generated routes for pedestrian navigation. She has a range of published titles including *Strange Brigade, Sniper Elite 4, Sonic & All-Stars Racing Transformed, Virtua Tennis 2009*, and *Sensible Soccer 2006*.

Steven Dalton has spent the last 13 years at various UK-based studios including several years as Team17's AI specialist, a stint as a freelance AI programmer, and presently leads the AI team at a relatively new studio, Steel City Interactive working on their inaugural project *Undisputed*, a competitive boxing game. After developing an interest in video-game AI in the final year of a Computer Game Programming degree at Teesside University, Steven undertook a variety of different programming roles in industry before landing at Team17 and pursuing a definitive AI role. He hasn't looked back since!

Nicholas Dent is an experienced Game Designer with over 30 years games industry experience in various creative roles from Artist and Animator to Producer through to his current role for over 18 years as a Game Designer (Senior, Lead, Creative Director). He has worked with some of the biggest names in the entertainment industry such as Disney, EA, Bandai Namco, Konami, SEGA, and Square Enix, as well as developing many original Sports IP's.

Rodolfo Fava is an AI Programmer that has worked on indie and AAA game titles, most notably *Returnal* (PS5), doing contract work from Climax Studios. Currently, a happy AI coder at indie company Jaw Drop Games since 2021. He did an undergraduate internship at Mechamania, Nijmegen, and graduated from his degree in Games Programming from the Breda University of Applied Sciences, The Netherlands.

Jonas Gillberg is a Principal AI Engineer at EA helping game and research teams push game testing further using game AI and machine learning. He presented early results of this work at the GDC AI Summit in 2019 (AI for Testing: The Development of Bots that Play *Battlefield V*). Before joining EA, he worked at Ubisoft for many years and was fortunate enough to work on the Snowdrop engine from a very early stage. He shipped Tom Clancy's *The Division* as the Technical Lead AI Programmer and gave a talk on some of it at the GDC AI Summit 2016 (Tom Clancy's *The Division*: AI Behavior Editing and Debugging). He is also the creator of Magic CardSpotter, an open-source Chrome Extension that detects cards on live streams of *Magic: The Gathering*, perhaps more notably forked by VirtualEDH which became SpellTable (Wizards of the Coast).

Dominik Gotojuch is the creative and technical director of the independent game studio Robot Gentleman. He began his game development journey in 2009 programming AI for AAA games, including *Fable III* and *Witcher 3: The Wild Hunt*. In pursuit of creative freedom, he co-founded Robot Gentleman, whose dark comedy debut, *60 Seconds!*, sold over 4 million copies. Dominik oversaw the studio's transition from a garage duo to a sustainable team while continuing to code, write, and design games. Meanwhile, he has also been giving conference talks and university lectures, spearheading investments into fellow indie studios, and even running an art gallery. Most recently, he established an R&D group at Robot Gentleman and has been conducting research into learning agents at the University of Glasgow.

Dale Green is a software engineer who has worked in a range of disciplines, settling within AAA video games. Dale has worked on multiple AAA titles for both PC and console, focusing mainly on AI systems. He has self-published a PC title, authored a book on Procedural Content Generation for C++ Game Development, and is working on a game library for x64 assembly. Dale currently works for Red Kite Games.

Tobias Karlsson is an industry veteran who started his career as an AI programmer in 2000. He has made AI for games for EA, Disney, Lucas Arts, Microsoft, and Sony, where he worked on franchises such as *Battlefield*, *Star Wars*, *Lord of the Rings*, *Mirror's Edge*, and *Days Gone*, and has also presented talks on game AI at the Game Developer Conference. He is currently working as a lead AI programmer at Blizzard Entertainment.

Jonathan Keslake has worked in the AA games industry for four years. In this time he has worked for Team 17 and Sumo Digital on such projects as *The Survivalists*, *My Time at Portia* and *Golf with Your Friends*.

Dr Fernando Penousal Machado is Associate Professor in the Department of Informatics of the University of Coimbra in Portugal. He is the Deputy Director of the Centre for Informatics and Systems of the University of Coimbra (CISUC), the Coordinator of the Cognitive and Media Systems group, and the Scientific Director of the Computational Design and Visualization Lab at CISUC. His research interests include Evolutionary Computation, Computational Creativity, Artificial Intelligence, and Information Visualization. He is the author of more than 200 refereed journal and conference papers in these areas, and his peer-reviewed publications have been nominated and awarded multiple times as best paper. He is the recipient of several scientific awards, including the prestigious EvoStar Award for outstanding Contribution to Evolutionary Computation in Europe, and the award for Excellence and Merit in Artificial Intelligence granted by the Portuguese Association for Artificial Intelligence. His work was featured in the *Leonardo* journal, Wired magazine and presented in venues such as the National Museum of Contemporary Art (Portugal) and the "Talk to me" exhibition of the Museum of Modern Art, in New York (MoMA).

Ivan Mateev is an AI Software Engineer, specialising in Vehicle AI. Ivan comes from a background in Theoretical Computer Science at Sofia University "St Kliment Ohridski" and graduated from the University of Abertay in 2014 with a BSc in Computer Games Technology. Over Ivan's career, he's worked on various racing game titles by Electronic Arts and Codemasters in the *GRiD*, *DiRT* and *Need for Speed* franchises. Ivan's primary interests lie in the applications of Computer Science concepts to video games technology – a venture he's enjoyed in multiple contexts of game AI programming, including Gameplay, Tools, and Software Architecture.

Dr Nic Melder has over 15 years' experience developing vehicle AI systems. Previously, he was the Lead Vehicle AI Programmer on *Watch Dogs: Legion* where he was responsible for developing the traffic AI and the felony (chase) systems, as well as maintaining and enhancing the level design and build tools for creating the road network. He also worked on the Vehicle AI systems for *Watch Dogs 2* and *Far Cry 6*. Prior to that he worked at Codemasters on the *DiRT, GRiD* and *F1* series of racing games, where he released 10 titles. In a previous life he spent 5 years working in academia and obtained a PhD in Multi-Finger Haptics.

Dr Bram Ridder earned his PhD in Computer Science at King's College London where he researched AI Planning. During his post-doc, he worked on various robotic projects where he used AI Planning to create autonomous robots, including the EU Project PANDORA creating Autonomous Underwater Vehicles that can maintain and inspect subsea infrastructure; The EU Project SQUIRREL creating autonomous robots using an underlying cognitive model to interact and play games with children. In addition, he worked with various industrial partners to investigate applications for detecting and clearing mines in oceans and how to deploy instruments to search for water on Mars Rovers. After leaving academia, he joined Rebellion to work as an AI Programmer on *Zombie Army 4*. After that game shipped, he focused on replacing the automated testing suite that Rebellion used internally and switched from a record/replay system to an autonomous system. In his free time, he creates games using his own 3D engine and creates AI systems that play games autonomously.

Paul Roberts is the Technical Director of the independent game studio Grinning Cat. Prior to this, he worked in a variety of Principal/Lead AI Programmer roles for a range of studios in the UK, including Sumo Digital, Team17, Traveller's Tales, Activision, and some smaller indie studios. For several years, Paul also led the Games Programming department at Staffordshire University, where he taught Game AI and programming principles. He has a Master's degree in Computer Science with Artificial Intelligence, which focused on pathfinding, the development of the DRS algorithm, and ways to test the believability of generated paths. Paul has written a number of books, some fiction, others academic, the latest of which is *Artificial Intelligence in Games* published by CRC Press in 2022 and is also the editor for this Game AI Uncovered series.

Dr Licínio Roque obtained a PhD in Informatics Engineering from the University of Coimbra while developing "Context Engineering", a socio-technical approach to information systems development. He is Assistant Professor at the University of Coimbra where he teaches postgraduate courses on Human-Computer Interaction, Game Studies and Development, Software Engineering, and Information Systems Development. He is Adjunct Professor at Carnegie Mellon University Master on Software Engineering Programs. Over the past 10 years, he has done research and development on diverse forms of participatory media in several application fields such as e-government, decision support systems, online learning, and multiplayer online games. He currently advises PhD students in the fields of Information Systems Research, Human-Computer Interaction, and Digital Games Research. He is co-founder of Tapestry Software and the Portuguese Society for the Science of Video Games.

Andrea Schiel is currently an AI Technical Lead for the Assassin's Creed franchise at Ubisoft. Formerly a principal AI architect at Worlds Edge (Microsoft, *Age of Empires*), she's been working in game AI for over 25 years. She's worked on a wide variety of titles, including *EA Sports FIFA*, *Medal of Honor*, and *Mass Effect*. Her academic work includes Genetics, Archaeology, and partial order planners in the field of AI. She has a vague dream of somehow combining all three fields someday.

1 Low Bandwidth, Synchronised Path Following in Team17's *The Survivalists*

Steven Dalton

1.1 INTRODUCTION

The Survivalists is a survival sandbox game set in Team17's *Escapists* universe in which up to four players can play online to cooperate in exploring a vast, procedurally generated island filled with friends and foes alike. The fast-paced and frenetic gameplay means that fast, efficient, and precise non-player character (NPC) replication between online players is a priority to ensure a rich experience for all, regardless of connection quality. With up to 60 NPCs active and interacting with players at any one time, replication of their movement and actions is a constant concern with regard to both bandwidth consumption and connection speed and must be considered throughout development. This chapter will discuss in detail the measures put in place specifically to handle NPC replication.

1.2 NETWORK MODEL

The client-server network communication model adopted in *The Survivalists* saw the host (the player whose island is being explored) acting as the server for up to three additional players. The server acts as the sole authority when it comes to character movement and interactions by being the only instance of the game hosting a *logical world* as well as a *cosmetic world,* whereas each client has only an instance of a *cosmetic world*. This structure is depicted in Image 1.1.

DOI: 10.1201/9781003323549-1

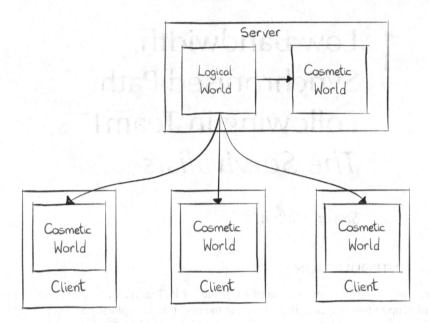

IMAGE 1.1   *The Survivalists'* two-world, client-server architecture.

1.2.1 THE LOGICAL WORLD

The logical world is the single acting authority of *The Survivalists* responsible for every logical operation. This includes collision detection and correction, authorising interactions between characters and objects or other characters, spawning objects, movement, and more. When the game begins, either in a single-player game or in a multiplayer game when a client joins, the logical world's data is replicated to its cosmetic-world counterpart. This is done by taking the locations, orientations, and types of each entity and streaming them to the corresponding cosmetic world which is responsible for displaying the entities. This can be done in two ways depending on the type of game. A single-player game requires only that the data be sent locally to the sibling cosmetic world within the same game instance, whereas a multiplayer game requires that the server's logical world is replicated in another player's cosmetic world over the wire. In multiplayer games, only the server has an instance of both the logical world and the cosmetic world. All clients will have an instance of a cosmetic world with the server's logical world controlling it.

1.2.2 THE COSMETIC WORLD

As discussed previously, the cosmetic world is responsible for representing the state of the game, or rather the state of the corresponding logical world, to the player. As entities are updated in the logical world, their counterparts or puppets are updated accordingly in the linked cosmetic world(s). Using this model, it is required that each entity in the world be represented in both a logical and a cosmetic form. A simple example of this would be a bush or a tree entity that can be destroyed by a character. Image 1.2 shows a simplified version of the logical and cosmetic components required to represent a single tree in both worlds.

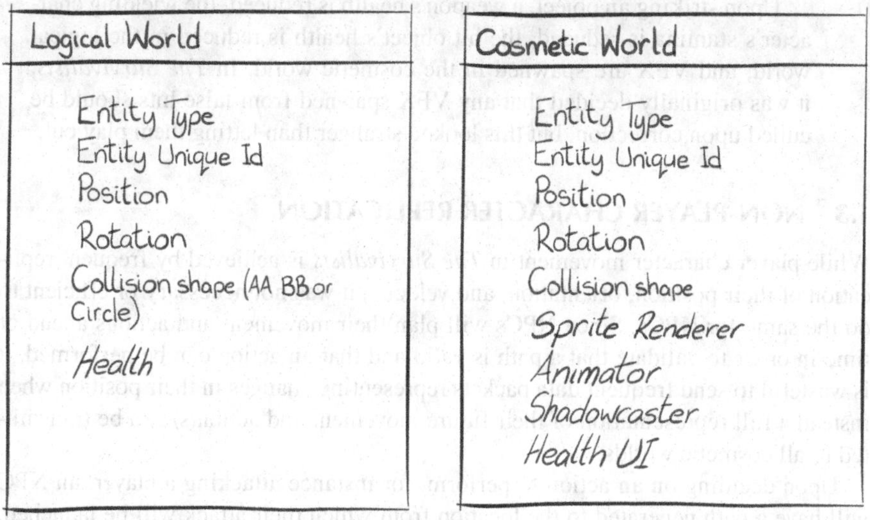

Logical World	Cosmetic World
Entity Type	Entity Type
Entity Unique Id	Entity Unique Id
Position	Position
Rotation	Rotation
Collision shape (AA BB or Circle)	Collision shape
Health	*Sprite Renderer*
	Animator
	Shadowcaster
	Health UI

IMAGE 1.2 A simplified representation of the components required to represent a simple entity in their logical and cosmetic worlds. The italicised components show components unique to a world.

Since the logical world is the sole authority over movement and collision, it is excusable to question the requirement to have the cosmetic entity outlined in Image 1.2 feature a collision shape. When a player is moving towards an obstacle that they can collide with, it is required that they perform their own collision detection within the cosmetic world. This is due to the round-trip time of data being sent to and received from the server. Relying on the server's logical world to detect, and then correct a position, will result in several frames of the player being within collision as the time taken for the new position to be sent to the server; the collision detection to be performed and the resulting correction to be sent back to the client is not instantaneous. Rather than constantly walking into and being corrected out of collision, it is more robust for collision detection to be performed in the cosmetic world. This means the only correction required would be an edge case, such as a cosmetic world stopping their player character upon detecting collision with an object which has just been destroyed on the server and the de-spawn message not yet being received by the client. In this case, the server will send a correction with an updated position and velocity at around the same time that the de-spawn message is received for the object that was falsely collided with. Similar cases exist for interactions with objects, with the visual effects (VFX) of the interaction being spawned immediately and only corrected if the object can no longer be interacted with. Examples of these interactions are, but are not limited to:

- **Collecting an item and adding it to your inventory**.

    If the item was subsequently destroyed or picked up by another player, then the correction will see it removed from the inventory.

- **Striking an object with a weapon**.

    Upon striking an object, a weapon's health is reduced, the wielding character's stamina is reduced, the hit object's health is reduced in the logical world, and VFX are spawned in the cosmetic world. In *The Survivalists*, it was originally decided that any VFX spawned from false hits should be culled upon correction, but this looked stranger than letting them play out.

1.3   NON-PLAYER CHARACTER REPLICATION

While player character movement in *The Survivalists* is achieved by frequent replication of their position, orientation, and velocity, it was not necessary or efficient to do the same for NPCs. Since NPCs will plan their movement and actions ahead of time in order to validate that a path is valid and that an action can be performed, it is wasteful to send frequent data packets representing changes in their position when instead a full representation of their future movement and action(s) can be transmitted to all cosmetic worlds.

Upon deciding on an action to perform, for instance attacking a player, an NPC will have a path generated to the location from which their attack will be launched. Since this path must be generated to confirm that the action can be completed and will be followed, this path data can be optimised and leveraged by sending it to every cosmetic world attached to this logical world. When a path is generated, it goes through a post-process in which any inline points are removed as displayed in Image 1.3 to provide the smallest amount of data to be replicated to the cosmetic world.

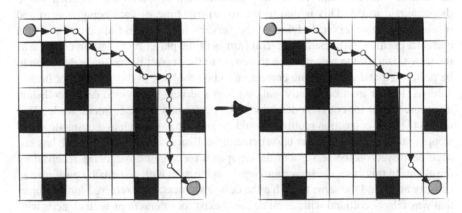

IMAGE 1.3   Left, a raw generated path. Right, a path pruned of all inline points.

Once the path data has been slimmed down to the fewest points required, it goes through another process to provide all information required by the cosmetic world. The resulting data is known as a *Path Chunk*.

1.3.1　Path Chunks

A path chunk is a representation of a path that will be followed by an NPC and contains a list of multiple *Path Points*. A *path point* contains three key pieces of information, as shown in Code Listing 1.1, that allow the cosmetic NPC puppet to perfectly follow the path, exactly as their logical-only counterpart will. These include the following:

- **Position**: The global position of this point within the world.
- **Arrival Time**: The time at which the path follower will arrive at the path point.
- **Speed**: The speed at which the character will be moving upon reaching the path point.

Code Listing 1.1: The information required to represent both spatial and temporal points on a path allowing a cosmetic puppet to follow the path in unity with their logical counterpart.

```
struct PathPoint
{
        Vector2 position;
        float arrivalTime;
        float speed;
}
```

1.3.2　Creating Path Chunks

After generating and pruning a path, and before packaging it up to be sent to the connected cosmetic world(s), a further step must be completed in order to set up the arrival times and speeds at each *path point*.

First, the velocity of each point must be calculated. Each character has a predetermined walking speed, running speed, acceleration, and deceleration to be used when beginning and ending their movement. When turning corners, no deceleration and subsequent acceleration are applied. Using simple linear acceleration, it is possible to determine the distance required to accelerate to and decelerate from the desired speed when following a path. This allows an additional two *path points* to be added to the path, one at which acceleration completes and a top speed is reached, and one at which deceleration begins, with the final *path point* being the point at which speed reaches 0. Image 1.4 shows a path with all of this representative information at each *path point*, including the points injected into the path to show where acceleration ends (B) and deceleration begins (E).

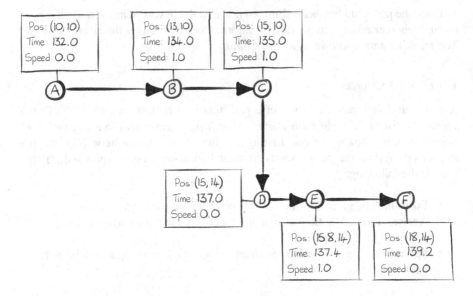

IMAGE 1.4   A series of path points ready for cosmetic world consumption.

1.3.3   Consuming Path Chunks

Upon receiving a path chunk, the cosmetic worlds' entity will queue it until the arrival time on the first *path point* is reached and will then commence with interpolation along the path. Since the *path points* contain all the data required to interpolate the entity between each *path point,* the amount of work required of the cosmetic entity is small. An inverse of the linear acceleration formula can be used to determine the position between points when interpolating between two *path points* with different speeds, whereas a much simpler interpolation can be performed between two points with matching speeds. The same solution is performed on the logical entity meaning both entities, logical and cosmetic, will be fully synchronised. In addition to the interpolation along the path in both worlds, corner smoothing is applied to make navigation of the path less angular. Upon approaching a corner when following a path, an NPC (logical and cosmetic) will use a quadratic function to create a curve between two points equidistant from the actual path point, one before and one after. Images 1.5 and 1.6 show the resulting path that NPCs will precisely follow in both the logical and cosmetic worlds.

IMAGE 1.5 Monkeys following their smoothed paths when following the player. The *path points* can be seen as the sequence of larger X's and O's along the path.

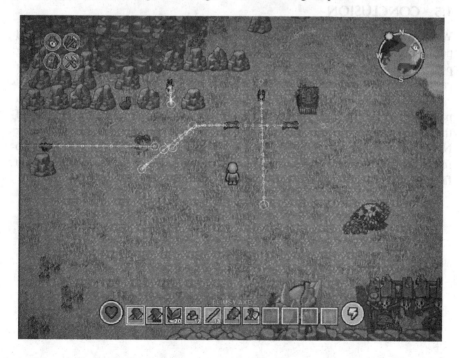

IMAGE 1.6 The paths of the more erratic rabbits escaping the player.

1.4   HANDLING PATH INTERRUPTIONS

An NPC receiving a new path when stationary requires no additional work, but it receiving a new path when already following another requires some correction. Upon a client receiving a new path when part-way along another means that some divergence will be evident, as during the time taken to receive the new path, the NPC will have continued along the old path. This is masked by blending from the old path onto the new path within a maximum of a fifth of a second. This is the only time that desynchronisation between client(s) and server occurs. Image 1.7 gives an idea of how much a path could diverge under these circumstances.

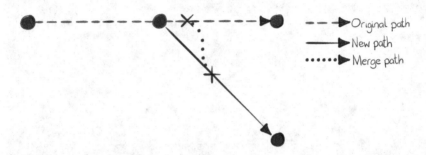

IMAGE 1.7   The diverged path taken when merging from an expired path to a new path.

1.5   CONCLUSION

While in no way a perfect solution, the decision to share an entire path to be followed per NPC proved to be a much more bandwidth-efficient solution than the streaming positional data for many NPCs in perpetuity. It also gave the guarantee that, in most cases, NPC positions were synchronised between server and client.

The solution adopted required a little extra work to build and consume a data packet per path, per NPC that fully represented their positions for the entirety of their movement but saved on the work required to offer client-side prediction for NPC movement. This hopefully saved a lot of frustration from players attempting to interact with NPCs with locations not quite synchronised with the server, resulting in false positive player hits only to be corrected to a no-hit after a few frames.

2 Going Stateless
An Evolution of Behaviour Trees in Team17's The Survivalists and Beyond

Steven Dalton

2.1 INTRODUCTION

During the late stages of development on Team17's *The Survivalists* it was decided that mobile devices be added as a launch platform alongside PC and consoles. Among the many challenges that this lofty goal unearthed was a significantly stricter runtime memory limitation, memory that was taken up by a variety of AI systems, but none more so than the behaviour tree framework.

2.2 PRUNING THE BEHAVIOUR TREES

After plenty of profiling and deliberation about what could be saved, where, why and how, it was proposed that the existing one instance per non-player character (NPC) behaviour tree implementation be investigated first. This was intended to allow a single behaviour trees' instance to be shared between many NPCs, with the runtime behaviour tree state moved elsewhere, to be owned by each executor of the single behaviour tree instance.

The reason that behaviour trees were an initial focus was because of the sheer amount of memory they consumed during busy gameplay scenes. A typically frantic scene in *The Survivalists* would see a single player, up to twenty companion NPC monkeys, a maximum of forty hostile NPCs and several ambient NPCs, such as the island's wildlife, all interacting with each other and their surroundings. This eighty-plus strong NPC assembly would see the memory taken by behaviour trees alone balloon to a peak of just under 300 MB, a huge chunk of the total 1.8 GB capacity on some of the more restricted target devices.

Another reason to select behaviour trees as one of the first areas to look at stemmed from the shared data approach taken, which is described in Chapter 4, Dynamic Behaviour Trees: Building for Scalability. This was the approach taken to create many of the small behaviour trees used by the majority of NPCs. This meant that the above-described scene would see eighty instances of many of the same behaviour trees sitting in memory all at once. If it did indeed prove simple to reduce this from eighty instances of each behaviour tree to one, then immediate improvements would

DOI: 10.1201/9781003323549-2

be realised in the region of hundreds of megabytes; a huge contribution to the run-time memory curtailment effort.

After a little prototyping, a solution was arrived at that not only elegantly transferred the entire ownership of a behaviour trees' state to each of the NPCs executing it but also proved rather surprising in its simplicity.

2.2.1 EXAMPLE BEHAVIOUR TREE

Image 2.1 shows a significantly simplified approximation of the root and combat behaviour tree shared between all melee NPC archetypes in *The Survivalists* and will be used as an example from which comparisons between stateless and stateful implementations can be made.

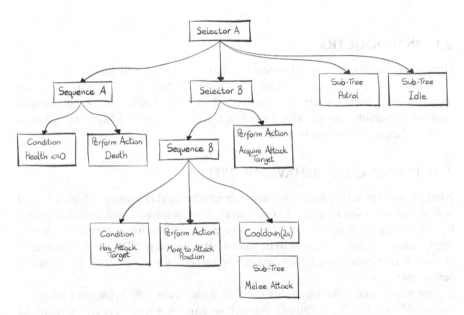

IMAGE 2.1 A simplified behaviour tree demonstrating the basic root and combat behaviour used by all melee NPCs in *The Survivalists*.

2.3 PREPARING FOR STATELESSNESS

The first consideration for moving to a stateless implementation was that of the run-time mutable and immutable states in each of the most common nodes in the existing behaviour trees. Each of these node types are described below, along with their immutable/mutable states.

2.3.1 SEQUENCE

A sequence node features one or more child nodes executed in order until either all
children return Success, in which case it returns Success, or a single child returns
Failure, in which case it returns Failure.

Immutable state:

- List of references to child nodes. In the implementation employed in *The
  Survivalists*, this is a list of indices into a parent list containing every node
  owned by the containing behaviour tree shown in Image 2.2.

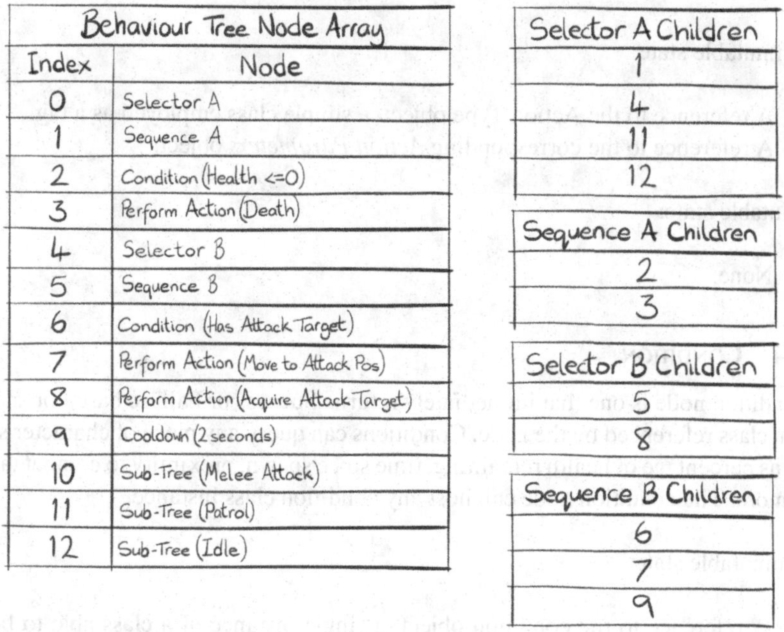

Behaviour Tree Node Array	
Index	Node
0	Selector A
1	Sequence A
2	Condition (Health <=0)
3	Perform Action (Death)
4	Selector B
5	Sequence B
6	Condition (Has Attack Target)
7	Perform Action (Move to Attack Pos)
8	Perform Action (Acquire Attack Target)
9	Cooldown (2 seconds)
10	Sub-Tree (Melee Attack)
11	Sub-Tree (Patrol)
12	Sub-Tree (Idle)

Selector A Children
1
4
11
12

Sequence A Children
2
3

Selector B Children
5
8

Sequence B Children
6
7
9

IMAGE 2.2 A representation of how nodes are referenced by their owning behaviour tree
and by sibling nodes.

Mutable state:

- The index of the current child being executed.
- The execution state of the current child being executed (Running, Success
  or Failure).

2.3.2 SELECTOR

A selector node features one or more child nodes executed in order until either all
children return Failure, in which case it returns Failure, or a single child returns
Success, in which case it returns Success.

The only difference between a selector node and a sequence node is the termination state; the mutable and immutable states are identical.

2.3.3 PERFORM ACTION

The Perform Action node is used to request that the NPC in question performs a bespoke action using the game's *actor* and *action* system. *Actions* include Attack, Interact, Pick-up item, Drop item and the like with a specific *action parameters* data object specified on the node and passed to the *actor* to drive the requested *action*. The perform action node can request any type of *action* and host any type of *action parameters* data.

Immutable state:

- A reference to the Action Type object, a simple class employed as a tag.
- A reference to the corresponding *Action Parameters* object.

Mutable state:

- None.

2.3.4 CONDITION

A condition node is one that immediately returns Success or Failure based on a condition class referenced by the node. Conditions can query any piece of character state such as percentage of health remaining, time since spawn, proximity to combat target and more. The condition node can host any condition class instance.

Immutable state:

- A reference to the condition object, a single instance of a class able to be shared.

Mutable state:

- None.

2.3.5 DELAY

Upon starting, the Delay node will retain focus until a specified duration has elapsed, and then return Success.

Immutable state:

- A float representing the duration for which the delay will be active.

Mutable state:

- A float representing the time elapsed while this node is active.

2.3.6 COOLDOWN

A cooldown node is used to modify a child node, blocking the child after execution until a specified time has elapsed. For example, a 10-second cooldown node modifying a *perform attack* node will immediately return Failure every time the node is attempted to be executed for 10 seconds since the last time the *perform action* node completed successfully, meaning it can only be executed at most once every 10 seconds.

The cooldown node is similar to the delay node in that it hosts a duration that is immutable at runtime and an elapsed time value that changes when the node is active. The only difference is that a cooldown node counts down while other parts of the tree are active, whereas the delay counts down only when active itself. It is therefore much more likely for multiple cooldown nodes to be counting down at the same time than it is for multiple delays to be active.

It should be noted that it is only *less* likely for multiple delay nodes to be active at once, not impossible. Upon introducing the *parallel* node, a node that allows multiple children to be executed at once, it was made possible for multiple delay nodes to be active at once, at most one for each child of a parent *parallel* node. This became a major factor when discussing where the mutable state for the delay and cooldown nodes should be moved to, a consideration that will be discussed in detail later in this chapter.

2.3.7 SUBTREE

A subtree node is used to reference and pass control to another behaviour tree, often used to promote the reuse of smaller, encapsulated behaviour trees with a single purpose that can be reused in multiple places, and to make working with and editing trees more manageable.

Immutable state:

- The behaviour tree to execute.

Mutable state:

- None

As can be seen above, some of the most used nodes were implicitly dealt with as they had no state to modify at runtime, these nodes being the *perform action, condition* and subtree nodes. Not a bad position to start in, but not an outright win as where to move the mutable state of the other nodes was still in question.

2.4   MOVING THE MUTABLE STATE

Since the behaviour tree framework was already making use of a blackboard per NPC to store various pieces of NPC and world state to be accessed by behaviour trees, it was initially thought that all states could simply be pushed to the blackboard. This only proved to be unworkable once it was realised how many bespoke blackboard keys would have to be generated, either automatically or by those working with the behaviour trees, to handle all mutable states. For example, if you assume that a single NPC would make use of ten behaviour trees in total, each with an average of ten composite nodes (sequence, selector, etc.). It would require 100 unique blackboard keys to be generated to track the 100 composite nodes' mutable states that determine their current child to be executed. While by no means impossible, this created an additional task in which unique blackboard keys must either be generated automatically or must be vetted for duplication after being created manually. The act of manually creating and managing this number of unique blackboard keys would have added a layer of complexity and concern to the creation and editing of behaviour trees that could likely be avoided.

2.4.1   REMOVING THE MUTABLE STATE

Rather than automatically generating a lot of the blackboard keys and pushing a swathe of additional data to the blackboard, it was investigated whether this step could be removed entirely. Instead, a single structure containing a reference to the current executing behaviour tree, the index of the current executing node and the executing node's execution status (Running, Failed or Succeeded) was created and maintained, as a behaviour tree was executed. The composite nodes that once relied upon an index into their list of children to be maintained could instead infer what to do next upon a child node terminating by querying this execution state metadata object, as defined in Code Listing 2.1.

```
Code Listing 2.1: A very simple data structure containing
all data required to represent the current state and
infer how to progress a behaviour tree.

public enum ExecutionStatus
{
        Running, Succeeded, Failed
}

public struct ExecutionState
{
        public BehaviourTree _tree;
        public int _nodeIndex;
        public ExecutionStatus _executionStatus;
}
```

Images 2.3–2.6 show how this simple data structure representing a behaviour tree's state changes when moving between nodes. Rather than relying upon mutable states within the composite nodes, it can simply be inferred what to do next. If the child of a sequence node completes successfully, then it should simply move to the next child, the index of which can be found by finding the failed nodes' index in the list of children, and selecting the next. If the child fails, then the parent sequence node also fails.

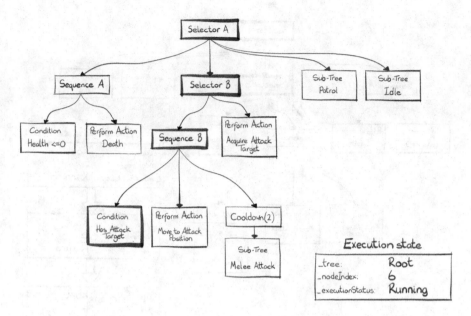

IMAGE 2.3 A behaviour tree and the execution state representing a condition node in progress.

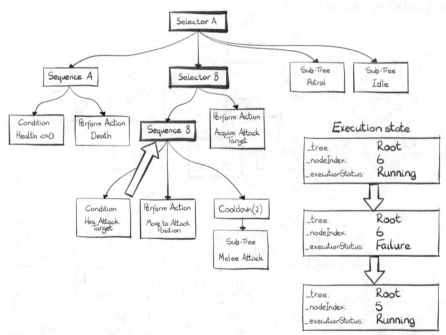

IMAGE 2.4 A behaviour tree and the representative execution states of an active sequence node and a failed child node.

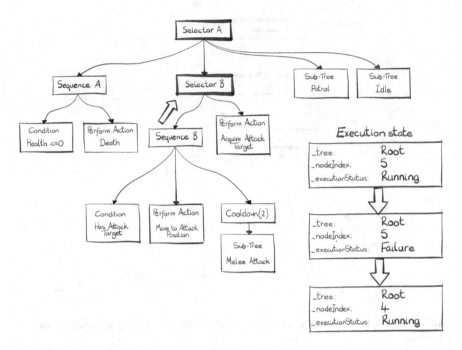

IMAGE 2.5 A behaviour tree and the representative execution states of an active selector node and a failed child node.

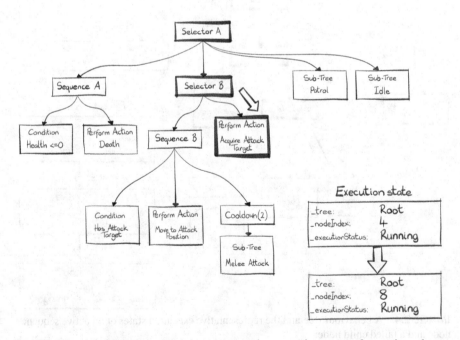

IMAGE 2.6 A behaviour tree and the representative execution states of an active selector node moving to its next child.

2.4.2 Problem Nodes

2.4.2.1 Delays and Cooldowns

As mentioned earlier, the delay and cooldown nodes required some consideration. With the possibility of multiple cooldown or delay nodes being active at the same time, it was not possible to store their mutable *time remaining* state in the blackboard under a single key. Multiple active nodes would fight each other, continuously updating this value and invalidating it for all but the last node to post an updated value. Instead, it was required that each of these nodes have a user-specified and unique key against which their state was pushed to the blackboard. This not only adds some responsibility to those creating and editing trees to pay attention to duplicated blackboard keys but also allows some freedom with it. If a designer could guarantee that two cooldown or delay nodes would not be active at the same time, then they were fine to share the same space in the blackboard to store their mutable state. While this saved a few bytes of memory here and there, it was totally overshadowed by the potential for bugs to be introduced by these particular nodes overwriting each other's data. The additional overhead of keeping an eye on this would have been incentive enough to automate the blackboard key generation for these nodes if only time was not such a limited resource.

2.4.2.2 Subtrees

The subtree node's mutable state proved to be a far less stressful issue to resolve. Each NPC has only one behaviour tree active at any one time, with subtrees taking the focus from their parent behaviour tree upon execution starting and handing back focus upon completion. For each executing behaviour tree, an *ExecutionState* object is required to represent its state, so the solution to allow for tracking multiple behaviour tree states was to replace the single *ExecutionState* object with a stack of *ExecutionState* objects. Upon a subtree taking focus, a new *ExecutionState* was pushed onto the stack representing this behaviour tree. Upon this tree finishing execution, its *ExecutionState* was then popped from the stack and the parent tree, upon becoming active once again, would have its *ExecutionState* on the top of the stack in the exact state it was left in when control was originally handed over to the subtree.

2.5 CONCLUSION

While the decision to investigate such an invasive change late in the development of *The Survivalists* at first caused significant concern, confidence was quickly gained when the relatively elegant solution was suggested and prototyped. A lot of this concern stemmed from the sheer amount of data that needed to be moved, how it would be stored and the likelihood of unchecked or unnoticed blackboard key clashes. Once the solution was implemented though, it was quickly realised that a lot of the data used to track a behaviour tree's state was in fact superfluous. Instead, the relevant data being inferred at the cost of a few more clock cycles, clock cycles that became easier to justify using the frantic attempts to find more memory became more time-sensitive.

3 Monkey Business
NPC Player Imitation in Team17's The Survivalists

Steven Dalton

3.1 INTRODUCTION

A key gameplay component of *The Survivalists* is the crafting mechanic allowing players to construct, strengthen and protect their settlements, forge tools and weapons to aid in exploration and concoct and create recipes for health and statistic-boosting meals among many other commodities. Those who have played games with an emphasis on resource gathering and crafting will be aware of the amount of time that must be committed to farming and harvesting these resources and to the potentially lengthy process of construction, especially when creating more valuable items on offer.

In *The Survivalists*, the player is encouraged to focus more on exploration than on the grind of crafting items and building bases. To reduce the amount of time, a player must commit to the farming and crafting processes, side-quests exist that see the player rescuing and befriending a maximum of twenty monkey companions from the clutches of the evil inhabitants of the game's numerous islands. These new friends can be commanded to mimic any of the actions that the player can perform, automating tasks that would have otherwise taken up a significant amount of the player's time, time that can instead be spent exploring the game's world and even used to further bolster the number of helpful monkey companions.

3.2 WORK SMART, NOT HARD

The intention of adding the companion non-player characters (NPCs) was to empower the player to offload the time-consuming tasks in order to use their time for other activities. To achieve this, the player must be able to issue commands to their simian assistants, preferably without having to trudge through numerous menus, after all the goal is to save the player time. This is achieved by giving the monkeys the ability to observe the player when performing a task to interpret the individual steps into a sequence of bespoke actions that they can then perform to repeat the process. To achieve this, a banana is thrown to the monkey(s) to be given a task, putting them into an observation state in which they will record everything the observed party is doing. They will continue to observe the actions performed by the player for a brief period until they either lose interest (a 30-second timer expires) or until they fully observe a task that they are capable of performing. They will then perform this task

DOI: 10.1201/9781003323549-3

until it is no longer possible due to resources being exhausted, a required equipped item expires or the player instructs them to stop or to observe a new action.

The actions that the player and monkeys can perform include, but are by no means limited to:

- Chop down trees and shrubbery (requires a cutting tool such as an axe or a sword).
- Destroy rocks (requires a clobbering tool such as a pickaxe and the like).
- Gather resources from the ground, such as wood from felled trees and stone from destroyed rocks.
- Deliver gathered resources to designated locations such as storage chests, placed constructable blueprints or crafting benches.
- Craft items from player-generated blueprints at crafting benches.

Given this list of actions, it is possible to take your primate accomplices to an area rich in resources, such as trees and rocks, and set up a production line resulting in the creation of the most basic of items through to rather complex items, crafting a plethora of required ingredients along the way. The process might look something like this, given a troop of four monkey companions, each instructed to perform a different task, and the most basic of resources:

- Monkey #1, wielding an axe, will cut down trees, producing timber.
- Monkey #2, wielding a pickaxe, will break rocks, producing stone shards.
- Monkey #3, crafting tool in hand, will attend to any player-generated blueprints on three nearby crafting benches and will craft:
  - Tool handles out of wood from fallen trees,
  - Axe blades out of stone from destroyed rocks and
  - Axes, from the tool handles and axe blades created at the other crafting benches.
- Monkey #4, will collect and deliver any resources required by the three crafting benches.

This is shown in Image 3.1, which is a screenshot from *The Survivalists* and shows the monkey companions working on their tasks. This process could be expanded to craft more complex tools and items at crafting benches, to creating static structures, or to even building additional crafting benches. This results in a process that takes the simplest of materials and eventually, given a large enough workforce and sufficient resources, crafts the most complex and time-consuming objects available. All of this is achievable by having a troop of monkey buddies each watch the player perform a different task only once and then copying it ad infinitum.

IMAGE 3.1 A simple monkey troop engaged in four different mimic behaviours: chopping trees, mining rock, crafting at and delivering to a crafting bench.

3.3 INTERPRETING PLAYER ACTIVITY

To mimic the player's behaviour, companion monkeys have a system to interpret an action, or sequence of actions, into *something* that they can perform. This is done by binding *Action* tags to any of the atomic actions that they can perform and *Subject* tags to any object that an action can be performed on. These tags are then combined to define *Mimic Signatures*, used by the observing NPC to look up a behaviour tree to activate, which results in them performing the same task. These *Mimic Signatures* can consist of one or more *Action* and *Subject* pairings that must be observed in order. Using the simple axe factory outlined earlier as an example and a few related behaviours, Images 3.2–3.4 depict the definitions of the required signatures.

Signature: Chop Tree	Signature: Mine Ore
Action: Attack	Action: Attack
Subject: Tree	Subject: Rock

IMAGE 3.2 Harvesting signature.

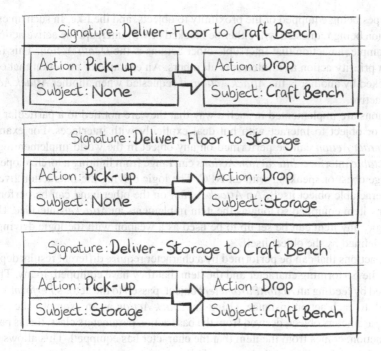

IMAGE 3.3 Delivering signature.

Signature: Create	Signature: Create	Signature: Repair
Action: Craft	Action: Craft	Action: Repair
Subject: Craft Bench	Subject: Blueprint	Subject: Repairable

IMAGE 3.4 Crafting signature.

The concept of *None*, with regard to the subject on which an *Action* is performed, can be interpreted in different ways depending on the task in question. For example, repairing *None* subjects is interpreted as repairing *everything* that is damaged, whereas delivering to a *None* subject is interpreted as delivering to a specific single location on the ground. This will be discussed further when elaborating more on how behaviours are defined a little later in this chapter.

3.4 ACTING

The Survivalists features an Actor and Actions framework in which every character, player-controlled or NPC, has an actor component, providing an interface through which actions are requested. Actions define the atomic activities that a character can perform, such as pick up an item, drop an item, perform an attack, interact with an object or craft an item, each with prerequisites for whether they can be performed. These prerequisites include checks for other actions being currently active, particular item types being equipped or the proximity to objects, and the like. In such an event, the action being requested will either be blocked or will interrupt the active action(s). For example, an action that interrupts other actions is the *Death Action*. This is the highest priority action as it interrupts all others. An example of an action that could be blocked by another is the *Attack Action*, if requested when another *Attack Action* is still active.

Actions are implemented in such a way that they are not tied to a particular item to use or object to interact with but deal explicitly with interfaces. For example, the *Interact Action* can be performed on any object in the world implementing the *Interactable* interface. *Interaction Actions* can range from lighting a torch to opening a storage chest or speaking with an NPC. The logic driving the interaction lives on the interactable object itself. An *Attack Action* on the other hand can be performed with any item equipped so long as the item implements an *Attacker* interface. Using this logic, any item can be set up to be used as a weapon with the logic driving the attack defined by the object itself.

The actions that can be performed by a character require different results depending on the performing character and the item that they have equipped, if any. This is achieved by feeding an *ActionParameters* object, passed to the actor's *PerformAction* method, to each action instance. Using an *Attack Action* as an example, the *Attack* action parameters object, derived from the base action parameters class, that is passed to the action, comes from the item that the character has equipped. This allows each item to define the effect of their use and allows any item to be used as a weapon by simply adding to it the component that hosts this attack data.

3.5   MIMIC BEHAVIOUR

Mimic Signatures and a monkey's actions are tied together using behaviour trees. For each mimic signature that a companion can interpret, there is a corresponding behaviour tree. These trees, as with the actions, are kept relatively general purpose to allow reuse. For example, most of the many gather and deliver behaviours share the same behaviour tree with simple branches that deal with different gather locations and delivery destinations, such as the ground versus a storage container. The items that are to be used, the subjects they are to be used on and the local area of the task being mimicked does not need to be known at the time of creating the behaviour tree but is passed in every time a new *Mimic Behaviour* begins. Image 3.5 shows a simplified version of the behaviour tree used for gathering and delivering any item to any receiver or location.

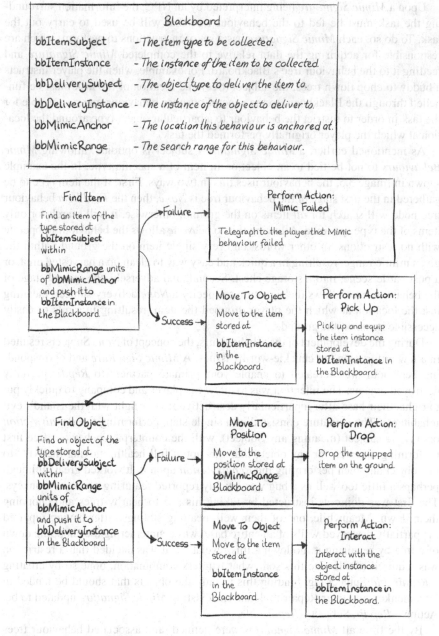

IMAGE 3.5 A simplified version of the behaviour tree responsible for all variants of the gather and deliver *Mimic Behaviour*.

Upon a *Mimic Signature* being interpreted by an NPC, the information surrounding the task must be fed to the behaviour tree that will be used to carry out the task. To do so, each *Mimic Signature* has a set of instructions to perform, which are responsible for acquiring the data relative to the completed *Mimic Signature* and feeding it to the behaviour tree's Blackboard. For example, when the player instructs a buddy to chop down trees, the subject (tree) and location of the task must be funnelled through the Blackboard to the general-purpose behaviour tree responsible for the task in order to restrict the behaviour to a particular object type around the location at which the player originally performed the task.

As mentioned earlier, a *Mimic Signature's* subject is optional, allowing *Mimic Behaviours* to not be tied to an object or an item of a specific type. In the example shown in Image 3.5, the behaviour uses this in two ways. First, if the item type to be gathered in the first stage of the behaviour tree is *None*, then the *Find Item* behaviour tree node will search for *all* items on the ground; otherwise, it will search for only items of the type specified. Allowing this to be *None* allows the behaviour to operate with no restrictions; in other words, on every single item on the ground within the given mimic range, resulting in a quick and easy way to clean up a harvested area, or a post-battle scene, into a storage chest. Second, and adversely, the second stage of the behaviour tree allows the signature to specify a *None* delivery subject, meaning just the location at which the player dropped the item, resulting in a pile of easily accessible items on the ground.

During the development of these behaviours, the concept of *None* Subjects resulted in a few unforeseen but chuckle-worthy issues. A *Mimic Signature* and corresponding behaviour were created to enable your primate partners to *Repair* partially destroyed objects. The intention was to allow the player and company to quickly put to rights their base after a particularly destructive raid or fight with the island's evil inhabitants. The signature consisted of a single step, performing the *Repair Action* on a *None* subject (meaning any Subject), with the counterpart behaviour tree first performing a search for any object that was not at full health, moving the NPC to this object and then performing the *Repair Action* upon it. It worked great, although perhaps a little too well as a bug was quickly reported featuring a pair of monkeys. The first was doing as instructed by taking his axe to nearby trees and chopping them down. Meanwhile, one of their well-meaning siblings, after having repaired the partially destroyed walls of an entire base, was counteracting the chopping down of a tree by repairing it. Following this revelation, it was decided that a restriction was required to alleviate this somewhat fruitless combination, done so by creating a *Repairable* Subject tag, binding this to only the objects that should be tended to by a monkey and their Repair tool, and the existing *Mimic Signature* updated to be: Action – *Repair*, Subject – *Repairable*.

By the time all *Mimic Signatures* were defined, and associated behaviour trees implemented, there were in excess of thirty signatures defining bespoke tasks but only six different behaviour trees to define the steps required due to the way data was fed to them, allowing the behaviour trees to be implemented in a generic way. Decisions on which tools could be used to complete these tasks were also left open to the player to decide. A monkey could be instructed to break rocks with little restriction on the tool equipped, and it might not be wise to use a delicate yet expensive sword or a bow and arrow with limited ammunition, to get the job done, but if it is what the player wants, then it is what the player gets!

In order to further reward the player for delegating the time-consuming tasks to their helpful gang, a simple system exists that rewards the player for giving their monkeys tasks. Upon performing a task, a monkey will acquire experience for that type of task, contributing to the level of competency they have for it. Each of the five competency levels sees the monkey perform the task both quicker and more efficiently. For example, a monkey well versed in breaking resources such as trees or rocks will have the damage inflicted upon each strike buffed, the delay between strikes reduced and the wear on the item being used lessened. A monkey with significant experience of delivering items will be able to store more items in their personal inventory and will move faster to items and delivery targets. Upon reaching the maximum level, a monkey will be able to perform a task multiple times more efficiently than the player.

3.6 ADVANCED MIMICRY

Given the complexity, or lack thereof, of the mimic system, it was discussed frequently how much further it could be taken. The first and most logical suggestion was to enable monkeys to perform multiple tasks in sequence rather than limiting them to a single task. For example, a monkey chopping down a tree, then mining rock, then gathering the resulting wood and stone and taking it to a crafting bench to craft a selection of items. Unfortunately, this did not make it into the shipped game but is something that would be easy to implement with just a couple of small changes. Rather than a monkey exiting their observation state upon observing the *first* task that they can perform, they would stay in observation mode and record *every* task in sequence until the player instructs them to stop observing. They would then attempt to perform each of the recorded tasks in the order that they were observed, building a sequence of behaviours to be carried out.

Another wish list feature that did not make it into the shipped game was monkeys teaching other monkeys. Again, an easy feature to implement as all that was required was the ability for the player to set an observation target rather than it implicitly being the player. The actions performed by the monkeys are the same actions as those performed by the player, so all emit the same action tags, meaning an observer will observe the same actions and subjects no matter which character they are observing. Given this general-purpose implementation, it would be possible for the player to instruct a monkey to observe another monkey in order to get them to perform the same task rather than requiring the player to perform the task themselves. This could even be extended to have monkeys observe hostile NPCs in order to learn and mimic combat tasks, or to observe ambient, foraging NPCs in order to learn and mimic gathering behaviours.

3.7 CONCLUSION

During the design stages of the mimic feature in *The Survivalists*, there were concerns about how complex the *learning* logic may be and how difficult it could be to define the bespoke steps required to mimic a task. Upon work beginning on the technical design and prototyping, it was quickly discovered that the very simple pattern-matching solution discussed in this chapter would not only allow the NPCs to perform every task desired of them but would even empower designers to quickly and easily experiment with and test new mimic behaviours, not in the original design. If ever proof was needed to back up the keep it simple, stupid (KISS) design principle, this is it.

4 Dynamic Behaviour Trees
Building for Scalability

Jonathan Keslake

4.1 INTRODUCTION

Behaviour trees are one of, if not, the most used behaviour architectures for AI within the industry since their first major breakout role in the *Halo* franchise (Isla, 2005). They are such a constant that any move to use any other system such as a Goal-Oriented Action Planner or a Hierarchical Task Network can be difficult to justify. This popularity stems from familiarity with many designers already comfortable with the systems. Making a move away from using behaviour trees can be the wrong call for a game, given their inherent ease of use.

At their best, the simplicity of behaviour trees allows a designer to take one look at a tree, and work out what an AI does and in what order it will do it. At their worst, they are a large jumble of complex interactions that require following a series of spaghetti strands around a far too large graph to work out why an AI has suddenly decided to investigate a rabbit warren in the middle of combat. They are prone to small errors that fail quietly and, due to the simplicity of their construction, often lack ways to share trees between different non-player characters (NPCs) easily. This leads to one of their greatest failings and large amounts of duplication, compounding the chance for small errors to seep in.

This chapter explores the different methodologies that were used in the development of *The Survivalists* to encourage behaviour tree reuse and different ways to *hack* your trees to improve their reusability. This chapter promotes the construction of smaller reusable behaviour trees to allow the builder to focus on what is important in a tree without having to concern themselves with the myriad of systems present in a single game.

4.2 BEHAVIOUR TREES

Behaviour trees are considered simple, but only if they are viewed as a black box. The actual underlying system can become quite complex. Fortunately, there are many good resources about how to best write your own implementation in significant depth (Champandard and Dunstan, 2013). Alternatively, you can always just grab an existing implementation. Commercial engines tend to have good implementations lying around their asset stores, and Unreal Engine has one built into the core engine itself (Epic Games, 2022). Whether you build it yourself or use a third-party implementation, the overall layout of the system should be consistent with the brief explanation covered below:

DOI: 10.1201/9781003323549-4

The basic structure of a behaviour tree consists of a *root* node, *composite* nodes and *leaf* nodes and is depicted in Image 4.1. The elements depicted are as follows:

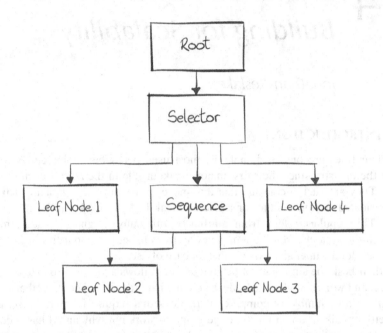

IMAGE 4.1 Basic layout of a behaviour tree.

- The *root* node is the entry point for the graph, and leaf nodes comprise all actions that can be taken by the AI.
- A *leaf* node, once executed, can opt to either stay within itself for a certain amount of time or return success or failure, which is only relevant to the operation of their parents and principally by the composite nodes.
- *Composite* nodes define how leaf nodes should lead into one another. While other types exist, such as *parallel* nodes, the two main flavours of composite nodes are *selectors* and *sequencers*. Selector nodes run all their child nodes in a sequence (leaf nodes or other composites), until the first node that returns success prompts, the selector itself to return success. If it gets through all its child nodes without any success, it returns failure. Sequence nodes run all their child nodes in sequence until a node returns failure, and then the Sequence node itself returns failure. If it gets through all its child nodes without any failures, it returns success.

That is all there is to behaviour trees really, a very simple tree structure with basic flow control. The tree is run from the root downwards, from left to right, evaluating nodes according to the rules of the composite nodes until it arrives at the end of the tree. Once there, it just restarts the tree and does it all again. Connect this up to an AI character and you can watch them navigate the tree, making decisions and running behaviours.

4.2.1 INTERRUPTS

One additional element of behaviour trees that we will be discussing is the concept of an *interrupt*, also known as a *monitor* (Champandard and Dunstan, 2013).

As a behaviour tree is run left to right, sometimes a higher priority node that was originally evaluated as false might suddenly become true. A simple example of this is shown in Image 4.2.

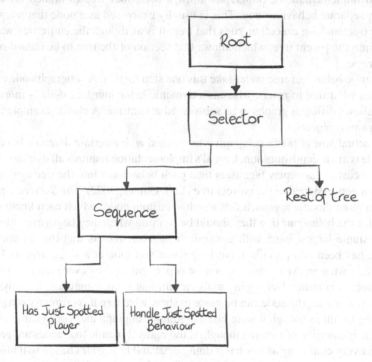

IMAGE 4.2   Simple implementation of handling spotted players.

The issue is the selector on this branch will only be re-evaluated once the tree is re-evaluated. Leaving the NPC to finish their current behaviour, for example, an NPC completing a full patrol before responding to the player. This can be solved using the concept of an interrupt. An interrupt will take control away from the patrol behaviour when the player is spotted and restart the tree. This allows the NPC to respond immediately.

The interrupt introduces a new problem for behaviour trees. No longer can we consider a branch of the tree in isolation. All other branches could now be waiting to rip control away from the current leaf behaviour. For behaviour trees to still function as described, interrupt nodes work on a prioritisation level with only interrupt nodes of a higher priority being checked, ensuring that once the world state changes, the NPC will know it needs to re-evaluate its tree.

This is a good and logical trade off. The behaviour control is maintained within the tree instead of relying on an external system. It is good practice to visually highlight the interrupt nodes, so they do not need to be inspected to determine that they are in fact interrupt nodes. For the behaviour tree system built for *The Survivalists*, this was done with an in-your-face bright red exclamation mark.

4.2.2 DYNAMIC BEHAVIOUR TREE NODES

The ability to use subgraphs is ubiquitous in behaviour trees and is available in all good implementations. Subgraphs allow a behaviour tree to branch off to run another, separate behaviour tree. This is usually expressed as a node that references another tree, and, on execution, runs that tree. It is as though the entire tree was just pasted into the parent tree, which allows that section of the tree to be reused by different trees.

Dynamic behaviour tree nodes take this one step further. A subgraph node explicitly states what tree to insert, whereas a dynamic behaviour tree node is more flexible. It allows different graphs to be substituted at runtime. A classic example of this is using smart objects.

The actual *how* of how a subgraph is associated with a certain dynamic behaviour tree node is an in-depth question. Unreal's implementation requires all dynamic nodes to have a custom gameplay tag; users then push behaviours into the tree against that tag and it gets assigned to the correct tree (Epic Games, 2022). *The Survivalists* supported a more flexible approach that also had custom nodes which each knew where to poll for the behaviour tree they should be running when they begin execution.

The single largest issue with dynamic behaviour trees is that the simplicity of the tree has been compromised. No longer can you look at a single tree and work out exactly what an AI is doing. It is now dependent on whatever scenario an NPC encounters at runtime. Debugging tools can mitigate this somewhat, if analysing a live behaviour tree, the node can be made to show what tree it is currently running or intending to run as though it were just a common subgraph and not dynamic. When editing a tree outside of runtime though, if too many dynamic tree nodes are present, it can get very confusing as to what is doing what and how your change will affect all the different possible trees that will be substituted.

Dynamic behaviour trees are at their best when they comprise small bits of self-contained behaviour. They are then substituted into a node which itself is very explanatory about what the extension data is expected to do. Essentially you should be able to treat that dynamic behaviour tree node as though it is a concrete subgraph, so nothing too wacky or controversial can occur, but small changes in behaviour are accepted.

4.2.3 EVALUATING GOOD CHANGES TO TREES

Adding functionality to behaviour trees can serve to complicate the run of the tree and create new problems. Therefore, it is a good idea to establish a few important metrics for how to make sure your change goes off without a hitch:

- **Visualisation**: Always ensure the change you made is immediately obvious on looking at the tree. For example, drawing a big red exclamation mark for interrupts helps drive home the point that this is not a normal node.

- **Integrate into Debugging**: Good behaviour trees can be visualised at run-time, allowing the builder to follow the run of the tree as it goes. Great behaviour trees allow nodes to present runtime information about what is going on within them, such as which dynamic tree node they intend to run.
- **Maintain Prioritisation**: Behaviour trees rely on their left-right prioritisation, do not mess with that.
- **Keep It within the Tree**: Changes which rely on external systems just add another point of failure to your system. Keeping everything within the tree allows the builder to see everything relevant to the AI from a glance.

4.3 PARENT–CHILD TREES

Have you ever had two trees be almost identical save for a few nodes? You are try-ing to reuse the organisation of sequences and selectors and contain data in shared behaviour trees, but it just seems impossible. Essentially, you just end up recreating the same structure repeatedly, whenever you are creating a new tree for an NPC. As an example, take a look at Image 4.3, which is based on an actual behaviour tree from *The Survivalists*.

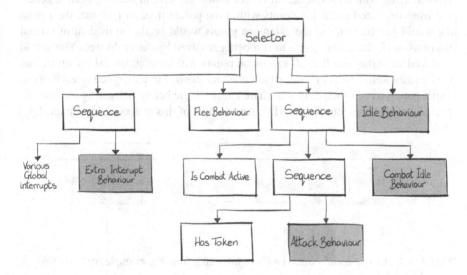

IMAGE 4.3   Example parent behaviour tree.

In this example, the highlighted nodes in the tree are the actual points of varia-tion. When you make a new tree for a new NPC, you copy everything else in the tree and then just change each of those points to the NPC's specific behaviours. In *The Survivalists*, we had groups of NPCs with just slightly different attacks, yet we were still having to create the whole graph for each individual NPC.

The issue here is one of composition versus inheritance. Behaviour trees are per-fectly happy to make use of composition to build their behaviours out of subgraphs, but no equivalent methodology exists for inheritance. If this were a class, you could make the highlighted nodes into virtual functions, and each class that comes along would fill in the little bit of data when prompted, but would not have to know anything about how the parent class functions.

Instead of duplicating each of these trees, you could make a new shared tree, dubbed a parent tree, for all NPCs of this type. Then, change each of the highlighted nodes instead to dynamic behaviour tree nodes. Each NPC then needs a child of this parent tree, with the ability to fill in these nodes with their own custom per-NPC logic. The child tree automatically inherits the layout of the parent tree.

The true beauty of this solution comes from how simple this proves to be on a per-NPC basis. When creating a new NPC, you can select a parent tree, and then a lot of the extension points can be filled in with generic subtrees. In the example from *The Survivalists*, the behaviours for the new NPC are already constructed for us; the only new trees required are the actual NPC-specific ones relating to managing how they attack.

But what do our child trees look like? They need to be able to specify what tree they inherit from, but then also identify what needs to be overridden. If you were building this into a behaviour tree system from the start, you could consider this from the ground up. Only graphs with no parent would get the traditional behaviour tree layout starting with a root node, all others would get several starting points, generated from the listed extension points within the parent tree. At runtime, the parent tree would just be run, but the extension points would be the equivalent of virtual functions, with the actual graph to run being resolved by the child tree. You would also need to make sure that all extension points within subgraphs show up in that child tree as well. *The Survivalists* had an attack control tree assigned to each of the hostile parent trees which did some shared attack logic before delegating out into the specific *Attack* behaviour for an NPC. An example of this is depicted in Image 4.4.

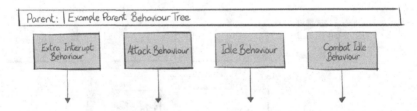

IMAGE 4.4 Example child behaviour tree inheriting from the example parent behaviour tree in Image 4.3.

This approach, however, would take a lot of work and time, time that was not available when developing *The Survivalists*. Besides, most of the time, these extension points will be pointing to a subtree, as they will be shared behaviours. Additionally, if you do fill in each node with custom nodes, the layout will quickly become a mess. It is therefore advisable instead to just require each node to be a subgraph.

For the implementation used in *The Survivalists*, a separate data asset was created to wrap this information. Instead of an NPC referencing what behaviour tree it used, it would instead reference the asset, dubbed Behaviour Tree Data (BTData). This data contained which parent tree to use along with all relevant data for an NPC's behaviour. This is shown in Image 4.5.

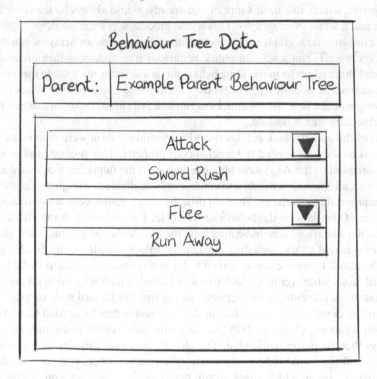

Behaviour Tree Data

Parent: Example Parent Behaviour Tree

Attack ▼
Sword Rush

Flee ▼
Run Away

IMAGE 4.5 Example Behaviour Tree Data (BTData) asset.

Each NPC was guaranteed to have a unique BTData asset, and therefore the parent tree dynamic behaviour tree nodes were written to look up the asset associated with the NPC they were operating on and pull out the graph they were supposed to run for each override. On startup, instead of running whatever behaviour tree was selected, the AI would instead consult the BTData and start whichever parent tree was set.

The behaviour tree data becomes a central hub for data related to an NPCs' behaviour and is the first step for any designer trying to work out what an NPC is up to. *The Survivalists* implementation ended up with four different parent trees, one for hostile moving enemies, one for pacifist moving enemies, one for hostile plants and one for monkeys. This meant that adding NPCs to the game was faster, and it was also far easier to maintain. It also prevented a lot of the inevitable small mistakes that would have occurred due to copying behaviour tree data around.

4.4 SHARING ATTACK TREES

The Survivalists had NPCs that shared everything apart from which *Attack* behaviour to perform. A custom attack graph was therefore required for each NPC. As most

NPCs had multiple possible attacks, small trees were favoured as it often required making a tree for each attack. The small tree was then combined into the custom attack graph, which, due to this mix of constraints, would always be the same i.e., a selector and a series of subgraphs. This whole process was automated.

The custom attack graph was presented to a designer as an array of prioritised attacks on the BTData asset. An attack behaviour tree node was then created that could read this and perform the same behaviour as a selector node using that array of behaviour trees as its children. This node is then slotted into a generic attack control tree. Designers can now list out attacks to run in a prioritised order on that asset, and no intermediary tree is needed.

Each of the actual attack actions the NPCs would perform were created as separate assets as they all needed to be networked properly. This process was an external requirement to the AI system but ended up with the duplication of entire attack graphs with all their movements and conditionals duplicated, with just a substitution in the appropriate asset to run. To avoid this, the attack action asset was removed and made part of the data on the behaviour tree data. Each element of the attack array then listed a behaviour tree indicating how the attack should be controlled and the data for the actual attack, including the damage values and all that modifiable goodness. The attack tree node was modified to fill in a specific blackboard variable with the attack asset whenever that attack tree was loaded, which resulted in all the attack behaviour trees launching whatever asset was in that blackboard node instead.

A further complication arose late in development – attacks needed to be varied based on weapons. Only one NPC in the game could carry items that being the monkeys that the player befriended. The player could give these monkeys weapons and the monkeys would fight by their side. The monkey's behaviour tree needed to appropriately choose which attack to run based on the active weapon. To facilitate this change, the same list of attacks from the behaviour tree data was added to each item and then read out in a node to run. This allowed the monkeys to take advantage of all the attack behaviours previously set up for each enemy character. Additionally, this provided item-specific behaviours for how to, say, mine with each weapon or chop trees with each weapon, all using a behaviour tree and a node which knew to grab what it needed from each item.

All this made adding new similar attacks very easy, you just opened an NPCs behaviour tree data asset, selected the parent tree and selected what attack pattern you wanted to copy from the several generic attack trees available to us. Anytime new behaviour was required, it would be built in the same generic way, allowing us to then reuse that data down the line just as easily.

By taking a flexible approach to your behaviour trees, you can make changes which speed up development and reduce the amount of maintenance that must be done around the behaviour trees themselves. *The Survivalists* ended up with designers creating different variations of attacks, such as just attack once in range, or check if a cooldown is complete before attacking, or maintain distance from the enemy and attack. They were then able to select the most appropriate attack for a new NPC or create a new attack for that specific NPC.

4.5 SHARING INTERRUPT LISTS

An element of the behaviour tree approach that appeared as though it should be automated but proved the most difficult to get automated was the global interrupt system. In *The Survivalists*, the list of interrupts at the start of the behaviour trees grew and grew. These were to perform quick actions, such as being knocked back, or to block behaviour entirely, such as when the character dies.

Interrupts have always been problematic in behaviour trees. Often, the addition of features to your game will require a custom response from an NPC, and that generally involves interrupting the current behaviour to play some unique behaviour. This distinctive set of nodes are usually located at the start of a behaviour tree and consist of a list of checks and responses for scenarios. For example, "Am I dying?", "did I get hit?", "was a grenade just thrown at me?" or "is a player currently talking to me?".

Using sensible behaviour tree logic, you can make a subgraph to house all of these interrupts. The subgraph can then be assigned to the behaviour trees of every NPC in the game. Whenever a new interrupt is required, it can be added to the graph and be propagated through to all NPCs in the game.

This approach works well, until a stalwart NPC comes along that wants to react to the whole *knockback* interrupt with just a grunt. You could split this off into a whole new group, but the NPC is the same in every other way. To handle this scenario, it is advisable to turn each response to an interrupt into a dynamic behaviour tree. Now every NPC can provide a custom override for a certain interrupt and, if your system supports it, a default tree can be assigned as well, requiring NPCs to define only how they differ from the norm.

This solves your problem, until later, a whole new interrupt is required for a single NPC. Monkeys in *The Survivalists* entered this situation all the time, with players able to interact with them in multiple different ways. The simplest solution was to add an interrupt to the global interrupts and hope it would only be activated for the one NPC. The issue with this approach is that it not only bloats the global interrupts but also causes all other NPCs to constantly check for an interrupt that will never happen, or worse, it happens and interrupts a behaviour it should not. To address this, you can split the interrupts graph into two, a global interrupt subgraph referenced by all NPCs and NPC-specific interrupts that can draw the extra interrupts out of somewhere on the NPC itself. These interrupts are themselves trees and so can be combined and shared easily. Any new interrupts can be added to only trees that care about them and trees can be split, added to, or combined into the required custom interrupts for each type of NPC.

This approach proved to be sufficient for *The Survivalists*; however, a more complex game could take a similar approach to the attack graphs. Interrupts are basically a prioritised list of responses, so can be boiled down to a condition, a priority and a response. This can easily be represented as an ordered array of conditions and responses, or generated from multiple arrays, with one being a global array for all NPCs.

4.6   BLACKBOARDS

Flexible approaches to behaviour trees always struggle when it comes to the blackboard. The blackboard, for anyone unaware, is a map of data that the behaviour tree can read from and write to. This map allows the behaviour tree to maintain data in the tree, writing it in one part and using it in another or allows external systems to write in data that will then be considered during the processing of the tree.

The issue is that behaviour trees expect certain entries to be in the blackboard. If you know the exact details of what is going to be in your tree at startup, you can pre-allocate it, but this would have to be the per-NPC type, rather than per-tree, as each will construct unique trees. If we took this approach in *The Survivalists*, there would be a need to ensure every behaviour tree on all weapons in the game were included in the monkey's pre-allocation.

The approach taken was for all NPCs to make use of the same blackboard structure. In other words, they each have their own instance, but the blackboard layout was identical across all NPCs. This can cause the blackboard to be bloated for some NPCs who use it but also allows easy caching of blackboards for use by the next spawned NPC, saving valuable construction time. Additionally, the data is always laid out the same, allowing incredibly fast lookups of data. This relies on all NPCs sharing similar enough data, which was mostly true for *The Survivalists*, except for monkeys who had several specific ones. We could have spent the time to make a monkey blackboard that was a child of the general blackboard and tried to save some memory that way, but we managed to ship with a maximum of 200 simultaneous NPCs on mobile phones with 2 GB of RAM without the size of blackboards even coming into question as an issue.

If this approach is not possible, there are several approaches you can take. The first would be to make a general blackboard to encapsulate any variables which will be shared among all trees and then have a unique blackboard per-behaviour tree. This may still cause the general blackboard to encapsulate NPC-specific behaviour though, so this general tree could be further subdivided depending on the active NPC, which then needs to ensure that it is never assigned to an NPC whose blackboard does not support its type.

A final suggestion is questioning why blackboards need to be pre-allocated in the first place. Just make the blackboard an empty hash map with a getter which checks whether the entry exists and creates it if it does not. This can often be non-performant as all your data lookups would need to go through a hash map, but if the too-large general blackboard is an issue, hash maps are an option.

4.7   CONCLUSION

Embracing different methodologies for reusing behaviour trees not only speeds up development but also makes the remaining trees easier to maintain. Using shared parent trees for different types of AI and then building behaviour trees to represent each unique response to each extendable part of the tree produced a very flexible system while keeping true to the ideas of behaviour trees.

Finally, building new mechanisms into behaviour trees do not always yield results or may lead to the system being seen as overly confusing. Care should be taken to not make changes too radically different from standard behaviour trees. Additionally, extra care needs to be taken with any shared trees as making any changes in one tree for just one NPC will affect all users. The behaviour asset suggested in this chapter which is ensured to be generated for each NPC independently can help to mitigate this.

REFERENCES

Champandard, A. J., and Dunstan, P. (2013) The behaviour tree starter kit. In *Game AI Pro*. Edited by Steve Rabin. CRC Press, Boca Raton, FL, Pp. 73–91.
Epic Games. (2022) *Unreal Engine*. Epic Games.
Isla, D. (2005) Handling complexity in the Halo 2 AI. *Game Developers Conference*, Moscone Centre West, San Francisco, CA, 2005.

5 Building a Buddy
Choosing the Right Brain

Dale Green

5.1 INTRODUCTION

As video game artificial intelligence (AI) goes, buddies arguably have the greatest scope for complexity. They are typically highly visible by design, meaning their actions often have a direct consequence on the player's experience. This impact presents many challenges. No matter how great the story, music, or atmosphere of a game, a single rogue decision from a buddy can undermine it in an instant. Picture a buddy making a bad positioning decision and walking casually into a boss encounter. Buddies also, however, present many opportunities. From Elizabeth's relationship with Booker in *BioShock Infinite* to Ellie's combat support in *The Last of Us*, well-crafted buddy AI gives us the opportunity to develop meaningful and robust companions that help to define an experience.

The systems that underpin such AI have the potential to be complex and vast. What appears to be a self-contained expression of intelligence is, in reality, the product of multiple systems collaborating to put on a convincing puppet show. Understanding what is required of your buddy AI, along with the different technologies and tools available, is crucial in being able to build an efficient, purposeful system capable of bringing your character to life in the way you envisioned.

In this chapter, we will look at the key components of a buddy AI, highlighting the differences between a buddy and non-buddy AI. We will also highlight some of the challenges and considerations that buddies bring, along with scoping their desired intelligence and choosing suitable technologies.

5.2 DEFINING BUDDY AI

5.2.1 WHAT IS BUDDY AI?

Buddy AI is a collective term for the systems that result in a specific type of AI agent – a buddy. A buddy, or companion, if you will, is an agent whose behaviours are designed to aid and accompany the player in their journey. The earlier examples of Elizabeth and Ellie are examples of very competent buddies, but the scale is vast. Sparx the Dragonfly, Spyro the Dragon's long-serving companion, has much simpler behaviours, but is nonetheless a valued companion.

Whether the buddy joins the player on their whole journey, or for a single encounter, any AI that has behaviours to accompany and/or aid the player in their journey, to some extent, can be described by the term.

 DOI: 10.1201/9781003323549-5

5.2.2 BUDDY AI VS NON-BUDDY AI

The goal of any AI agent is to act acutely within an evolving game world. From this perspective, a buddy agent and a non-buddy agent have a lot of overlap. The key behaviours for both can be broken down broadly into the three phases depicted in Image 5.1.

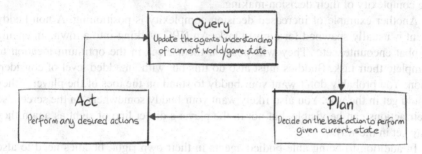

IMAGE 5.1 Three key phases of AI processing.

All AI agents must be able to query the world state and perform actions as a result. While there are certainly some differences within these phases, such as a buddy character perhaps needing to query more information than a standard agent, it is the Plan phase where some key differences lie. A buddy is an active participant along with the player, and this needs to be reflected in the decisions they make and how they interact with the world. They need to be able to aid the player without knowing ahead of time what they might do. This, however, needs to be balanced, so they are not too smart or over-eager, solving puzzles or killing enemies before the player has a chance to do so. Buddies must consider how their actions impact the player's experience of the game in a way that non-buddies do not.

One of the greatest challenges of creating a competent buddy is a result of their time in focus. This has a direct impact on their perceived intelligence, the scope of their decision-making, and how much room for error they have. Picture a standard enemy agent that is spawned in to take part in a firefight. This agent's lifespan is scoped to a single encounter, meaning they are not likely to be in the direct focus of the player for very long, if at all. If at any point the player does have them in focus, so long as they are either – in-cover, moving, or shooting at the player, they will be perceived as intelligent; unless they do something outrageously stupid, there is simply not enough time for them not to be. A buddy, however, will be with the player throughout their journey, meaning they are in focus much more frequently. There is a greater opportunity for any simple, repetitive, or flawed behaviours to be spotted by the player. This means buddies must work harder, and more reliably, than their non-buddy counterparts to reach the same level of perceived intelligence.

This difference in lifetime between a buddy and a non-buddy also creates a difference in how much their respective behaviours need to be considered. Following on with the example of a firefight, consider both agents shooting a weapon. If they are only to take part in a single, small battle, a non-buddy agent likely doesn't need to consider how much ammo they are using. They are likely cheating with unlimited ammo anyway! If you can't get away with unlimited ammo for your buddy, their decision-making surrounding shooting needs to be much more considered. You do not want them running out of ammo at the start of a battle and then being useless. This same logic applies to any usable resource, such as health. A buddy's actions, to avoid making them look myopic, must consider the future to some degree, increasing the complexity of their decision-making.

Another example of increased decision complexity is positioning. A non-buddy agent is usually spawned for a given task. An NPC walking into a town, an enemy combat encounter, etc. They will position themselves in the optimum location to complete their task. Buddies must also do this but with an added level of consideration. You probably don't want your buddy to stand on the toes of the player – they would get in the way. You also likely want your buddy somewhere on the screen, so their actions can be visible, but not in the player's direct line of sight as again they may get in the way.

In addition to being able-bodied agents in their own right, buddies need to also facilitate the player in their actions. To do this, they need a suitable system underpinning their decision-making.

5.2.3 Determining Needs

To choose the correct system(s) to bring a buddy to life, it is crucial to first outline the desired behaviours, level of desired autonomy, and resulting challenges. Questions such as the following should be answered:

- What kind of behaviours will they exhibit?
- How much free will should they have?
- How much should they contribute to gameplay?
- Do they share the same abilities as the player?
- How will they navigate the world?

The answers to these types of questions will determine the scope of your buddy's abilities. From that, the challenges of your design can be inferred and, in turn, what technologies would be most suitable. Naturally, the more restricted a buddy's abilities, the fewer unknowns and therefore potential for issues there are. The less they can do, the less can go wrong. The downside of this is their potential for contribution is reduced. A buddy with many abilities and complex decision-making, however, has a much greater scope to make an impact, but also a greater scope for challenges to overcome.

When identifying desired buddy behaviours, their ability to contribute and impact the game needs to be balanced such that the desired game experience can still be reliably presented. For example, if you were making a highly story-driven, cinematic game, a buddy with lots of free will has the potential to disrupt the desired experience. In this case, a more restricted, tightly controlled buddy would likely be more appropriate. It is important to identify this early so the most suitable technologies can be identified early.

The most suitable technology is the one that provides just what you need, efficiently, with minimal technical debt. While Goal-Oriented Action Planning (GOAP) is a great technique, it is almost certainly the wrong choice for a small, linear, on-rails game. Determining buddy needs and scope for your game will help determine their required intelligence and level of autonomy. These are key metrics to identify early as it will heavily inform the system(s) that would be best used to bring your buddy to life.

5.3 CHOOSING A BRAIN

Once the requirements of a buddy are clearly outlined, appropriate systems can. be chosen. We identified intelligence and level of desired autonomy as key metrics in choosing a technology, so those presented in this chapter have been roughly grouped by those criteria. Each of the following systems has different balances of control and authoring versus resulting autonomy. Generally, the less autonomy they have, the more their behaviours are going to need authoring, and vice versa. Though presented individually, these systems are not mutually exclusive, you just need to be aware of your performance budget when mixing and matching.

5.3.1 LOW AUTONOMY: SCRIPTED CONTROL

Scripted control gives full control over a buddy's behaviour at the expense of practically any autonomy. When driving an agent via scripting, instead of actions being determined by some behavioural system, they are authored manually. Any other competing behavioural systems (if present) would get paused and the agent instead runs a fixed sequence of actions.

The main benefit of scripted control is that you know exactly where your agents will be, when they will be there, and what actions they will perform. When directly authoring every action, you have full control, and with that comes full confidence in your agent's behaviour. To be able to do this, however, you need to know what the game state will be, so when your buddy plays their action sequence, the world is in the state they were authored against.

Practically, this mostly limits full scripted control to situations such as on-rail sections or real-time cutscenes, where the game state can be assured. There is also authoring overhead to consider. Every action you want your buddy to perform needs authoring against a set game state or environment, and if either of those changes, your script may need re-authoring too.

For these reasons, scripted control is usually used in conjunction with more advanced behavioural systems, reverting to scripted control only when you need to directly control the buddy to ensure the correct experience is presented to the player.

5.3.2 MEDIUM AUTONOMY: BEHAVIOUR MODELS

While scripted control certainly has its place, most agent behaviours will be the result of more advanced systems, such as a finite state machine (FSM) or a behaviour tree. These systems present behaviours via topological models, reducing authoring from an entire sequence of fixed actions to individual behaviours and transitions. How these models are executed is then determined at run time, typically based on factors such as the current game state.

5.3.3 FINITE STATE MACHINES

FSMs are one of the simplest ways of modelling behaviour. You need to only define discrete states and the transitions between them. All nodes are connected at the same level, there is no hierarchy, so execution moves from node to node as transition criteria are met. Image 5.2 shows an example FSM.

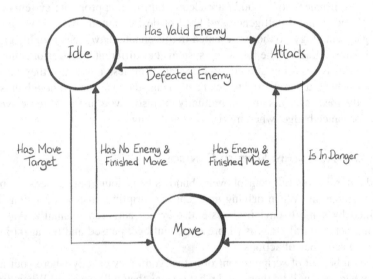

IMAGE 5.2 FSM example.

Transitions between states here are simple and well-defined which results in a rigid behavioural flow. This may be suitable for an agent with simple behaviours, but it can become difficult and cumbersome to model more complex and nuanced behaviours in this way. Hierarchical FSMs offer a potential solution to this problem, whereby states themselves can be entire FSMs; however, a more common solution is the behaviour tree.

5.3.4 BEHAVIOUR TREES

Much like a FSM, a behaviour tree is a method of modelling and executing behaviours. Behaviour trees, however, are hierarchical structures and contain more elements, making it possible to build complex, branching structures as opposed to the more rigid structures of a FSM. This makes behaviour trees better suited to the complex needs of a buddy AI, and they are one of the most common AI systems as a result.

The base elements in a behaviour tree are tasks. These are the leaf nodes in the model and encapsulate some functionality that, when called, will result in an action. Whenever a node of this type is executed, the associated logic will be run, and a return value passed from the node to its calling parent stating if the node was successful or not. The 'parent' node here would be a composite node. These nodes have one or more children and determine how your individual tasks will be run, for example in sequence, or trying one at a time to see which one passes first.

With just leaf nodes and composites, AI behaviours can be put together as in Image 5.3 where a buddy agent would move to an item, try to pick it up and then use it.

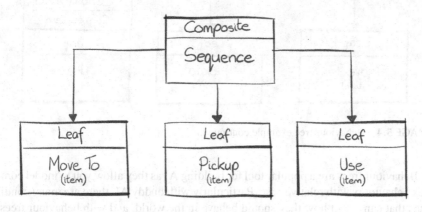

IMAGE 5.3 Behaviour tree example.

Other critical elements of a behaviour tree are Conditionals and Decorators, both of which sit atop leaf nodes. Conditionals allow us to define conditions that must be met before a leaf node is executed. Decorators are instructional nodes that allow us to do two things. First, they let us change the return value of a node, for example forcing it to always return true, which can be useful. They also let us change how the node itself runs, for example ensuring it runs indefinitely. This type of decorator is commonly used on base tree elements to keep the tree running indefinitely.

To build on the previous example, suitable conditions might check that there is an item to pick up and that it can be used. A suitable decorator might ensure this whole sequence runs indefinitely so the agent is always evaluating if there are items to pick up. The updated behaviour tree is depicted in Image 5.4.

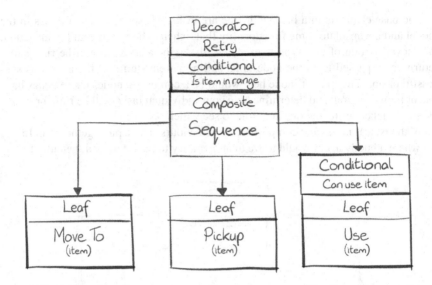

IMAGE 5.4   Behaviour tree example continued.

Behaviour trees are a popular tool for building AI as they allow you to model complex behaviours with relative ease. Particularly with buddy AI, there are many conditions that can affect how they should behave in the world, and with behaviour trees, you can account for that via conditions and modelling of appropriate behaviours.

Earlier in the chapter, an example of choosing a position to stand at was given to demonstrate the considerations that buddies must make when executing seemingly simple behaviours. Using behaviour trees, we could account for the factors that were called out via conditions and different behaviour paths, something a simpler implementation might not have given us. This is a simple, but real-world, example of how determining a buddy's needs upfront helps to inform which technologies are suitable.

Behaviour trees are not without their drawbacks, however. Since they are typically fixed, their topology as standard does not change at runtime, meaning they can only execute a path that has been authored ahead of time. They can branch at different levels of hierarchy, creating some variation, but every potential path must be manually authored. Buddy agents can be some of the most complex agents in a game, so expressing all their behaviours is not a light task, and the resulting behaviour trees can become vast, consisting of thousands of nodes spread throughout multiple sub-trees. This size becomes cumbersome to manage and can be difficult to pinpoint specific behaviours amongst the many branches. Debugging behaviour trees is entirely possible, though can be difficult without proper tooling. Having the ability to step through execution, add breakpoints to certain nodes, etc., will make erroneous behaviours much easier to track down, though it introduces tool costs if you are implementing the system yourself.

Behaviour trees are very powerful and highly authorable and thus are common place in game AI. Their flexibility and balance of authored content versus autonomy make them suitable for a wide range of agent types and abilities. Described here briefly is a standard behaviour tree, but there are many variations that can be made to tailor it to your needs specifically.

5.3.5 HIGH AUTONOMY: PROCEDURAL BEHAVIOURS

An alternate approach to modelling behaviours hierarchically is an approach known as GOAP. With FSMs and Behaviour Trees, we are defining states or actions and then transitioning between them. With GOAP, however, we uncouple our states and actions from authored transitions, instead letting a planning system determine the best set of actions that will allow us to reach a set goal. This results in procedural behaviours constructed at runtime, giving our agents the possibility of maximum autonomy.

Goals in GOAP define the resulting state(s) that we want the agent, and/or the world, to be in. For example, having a buddy revive the player. We might consider this goal complete if the player is not currently downed. But how does the buddy complete this task? Through actions. Much like a leaf node in a Behaviour Tree, an action is an encapsulation of some functionality. Actions in GOAP, however, have both pre-conditions that determine if they can be executed and the resulting effects that determine how they change the state of the world and/or agent. They also come with an associated cost set by their author that is used in the planning stage.

With our goals defined, and sub-actions capable of putting the world/agent into a state to satisfy those conditions, we pass over to our planner. This is the stage where a plan of action is generated for our agent. For a given goal, the planner will perform a search, such as A*, over the available actions to find all possible routes from the current state to the goal state. Image 5.5 shows an example of how a goal of 'Eat' might look.

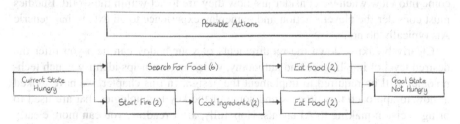

IMAGE 5.5 GOAP example.

There are two possible paths identified. Overall, it is cheaper for the agent to start a fire and cook ingredients, however, if they do not have any ingredients to cook that branch would not be possible, so they would fall back to the more expensive approach of searching for food. Since the availability of actions differs based on the current game state, the same goal can be achieved in multiple different ways, bringing variability to decision-making that would be difficult to replicate with a fully authored model such as a behaviour tree. The process of determining action sequences at run time allows agents to react dynamically within their world. It also provides a time save for production. With GOAP, there is no need to implement defined behaviours into a complex behaviour tree. Once the new behaviour is implemented, it is simply added to the pool and the planner will do its magic at runtime.

The benefits of GOAP do not come without drawbacks. Depending on how many actions you have, the planning stage can be processor-intensive. For each goal to be evaluated, it will search over all actions available at the time, until the goal is met, within the set action limit. There is also re-validation of the current goal that needs to be done periodically to ensure that the initial game state has not changed, such that the current goal no longer makes sense.

Another consideration, particularly applicable to buddies, is the lack of control over the resulting behaviours. Given they will be generated at runtime based on transient data, the current game state, it might be difficult to reproduce a given set of actions at a particular point in time. The procedural nature of the system means that without tightly controlling the game state, you could not be certain of what behaviours would be executed. This variability will also increase the need for stringent testing of the agent, ensuring that all behaviours can lead into/from one another without issue and that no bad sequences are generated.

GOAP is a great system for bringing plenty of autonomy to an agent, allowing them to determine what to do at runtime without the need for explicit authoring. There are performance considerations to be made, however, if your design permits a highly autonomous agent, this is worth digging deeper into.

5.4   CONCLUSION

Any intelligent AI is the result of multiple systems and technologies working together. Buddy and non-buddy agents have a lot of overlap as they share a common goal of acting acutely in an evolving world in a realistic way. Differences between the two come into view when we consider just how they are to act within the world. Buddies must consider the player's action and gameplay experience to an extent that generic AIs typically do not.

Clearly breaking down the requirements of your buddy can help you infer the desired level of intelligence and autonomy, which in turn helps identify which technologies will be required to implement the design. In this chapter, we have looked at how to approach this process and some of the key technologies that are used to bring decision-making to AI agents. Hopefully, after reading, you can more clearly identify your own buddy needs, and have an idea of which type of system(s) will be most suitable.

6 Making Up Your AI's Mind

Decision-Making Architectures

Tobias Karlsson

6.1 INTRODUCTION

One of the first and most fundamental decisions you must make when you are creating an AI to control a creature in a game is what decision-making architecture to use. The decision-making architecture is the framework within which your AI decides what behaviour to execute and then executes that behaviour at any given moment. This chapter explores the more popular options available, their respective strengths and weaknesses, and under what circumstances you would choose one over the other.

For this chapter, a behaviour is defined as a set of actions an AI can take to achieve a specific goal or to react to a specific situation. The granularity of each behaviour is up to the implementer, for instance, you could choose to have a behaviour for combat or to have many behaviours for different aspects of combat, such as a behaviour for reloading the AI's weapon and one for throwing grenades. The granularity you choose depends on what makes sense for the AI in your game. The AI for an individual creature is created by giving it a set of behaviours and the information needed to select the appropriate behaviour at runtime.

6.2 IMPORTANT CHARACTERISTICS

There are many different characteristics of decision-making architectures, and which are more important in a given situation depends on the exact nature of the problem you are trying to solve; however, for most projects, many of the following characteristics will have some relevance.

6.2.1 PREDICTING BEHAVIOUR SELECTION

Every agent will have a set of behaviours. Some of these behaviours may be quick reactions to a surprising event, whereas others might be a fallback behaviour that is only active if no other good behaviour can be found. It is important to be able to reason about when and under what circumstances a particular behaviour will become

DOI: 10.1201/9781003323549-6

active and the priority of one behaviour when compared to another. This might seem like a simple requirement, but as the complexity of your AI grows, keeping track of all the conditions for when behaviours can activate or not and how they interact becomes more and more difficult. Even the simplest of agents tend to acquire an impressive array of tests and conditions for behaviour selection as you get closer to ship, to cover all the possible edge cases. A good decision-making architecture will make it easy for both the author(s) of the AI and anyone who will subsequently have to maintain it, to get a picture of the conditions for when an agent's various behaviours will be selected for execution by looking at the data.

6.2.2 Understanding the State of a Decision-Making Process at Runtime

Even under the best of circumstances, you will find that your AI is going to choose the wrong behaviour as you test it; hence, it is critical to be able to inspect the state of the decision-making process at runtime so that you can determine why an agent decided to do what it did. You need to be able to understand what behaviour your agent is running, why a specific behaviour was selected, and why a specific behaviour was not selected. Ideally, you will also have access to not just the current state of your agent but also to a history of how it got there. Depending on how your architecture selects behaviours, the problem of describing a specific decision can range from trivial to requiring tracking a significant amount of extra data that may also be difficult to display. It is worth noting that having external applications, most commonly the editor pulling double duty, that can connect to an instance of the game and display that agent's state, is becoming more and more popular. This is a great capability that is something you should seriously consider, but even with an external app, you will want to be able to display at least some of the AI's state in game for quick debugging. This will allow for better information gathering, which can be used by your QA partners who may not have access to the editor. Something related and very beneficial is the ability to dump the current state of the AI to a file to be inspected later. This allows someone testing the game to easily provide you with a large amount of data about an agent that behaved unexpectedly.

6.2.3 Modularisation

Being able to create a behaviour from simpler, reusable parts is extremely powerful. Even if your game only has one agent, you will find that there are many functions and tests that recur in most behaviours. Being able to reuse the building blocks is going to save you development time, as you only need to write and test them once. More importantly, you can add metadata to your building blocks to improve your ability to debug your AI. Building blocks are frequently used to assemble the AI's behaviour in a visual editor, but there are, of course, other options that create the same effect. Another benefit of using building blocks is that it becomes easier to learn and understand the AI system. A new developer only needs to learn how the building blocks work, rather than having to understand the details of each and every behaviour.

6.2.4 HIERARCHICAL DECISION-MAKING

Modelling decision-making as a hierarchy of decisions can be very helpful. It matches well with how humans think about decisions. You make the big picture decision first, and then add more and more detailed decisions until you eventually reach the point where no more decisions need to be made and actions can be taken. An additional advantage of hierarchical decision-making is that it allows multiple behaviours to share decisions, meaning that you do not have to make the same calculations twice. For instance, if you have several behaviours that depend on there being a valid path to the targeted enemy, then collecting them all under one instance of that test in a hierarchy, allows you to make the test once and reject all of the behaviours together if the test fails. This also helps by making it easier to understand how an agent is going to behave, as decisions are split up into multiple, simpler decisions, and by runtime debugging becoming correspondingly simplified as it is easy to see where in a hierarchy a decision node failed.

6.2.5 EASE OF ADDING NEW BEHAVIOURS

Whenever you add a new behaviour to a character, you must ensure that it interacts well with all existing behaviours. This is always going to require some work, but some architectures make it easier to localise the changes, while others inherently have more dependencies between behaviours that need to be explicitly dealt with.

6.2.6 ABILITY TO MODEL STATES AND STATE TRANSITIONS

Often, AIs have distinct states that they can be in, with procedures for how to transition between them. An example of states that commonly occur in games is an agent being in either an *Idle*, *Alert*, or *Combat* state. Each of these states will come with a particular selection of valid behaviours, and the transitions between these states often require a specific process, for example, playing a surprised reaction when transitioning from *Idle* directly to *Combat*. In games, you will most often find clear instances of states at the very highest level of an AI as in the case of the idle-alerted-combat scenario, and at the very lowest levels, such as how a melee grapple attack works.

6.2.7 SEQUENCING BEHAVIOUR

The ability to sequence behaviour, i.e., first do A, then B, then C in that order is often very useful if the AI is to execute some more complex behaviour. Sequencing is a sub-problem of states and state transitions but can be implemented without states. Sequencing is normally relatively easy within an individual behaviour building block but becomes more difficult when creating sequences of separate behaviours, something that is usually desirable for modularisation.

6.2.8 NON-STATIC BEHAVIOUR PRIORITIES

For some agents, the relative importance of performing an action compared to another one is dependent on the circumstances of its runtime environment. For example, imagine a bot in a classic first-person shooter arena deathmatch that has a behaviour for collecting health and one for ammo. If the bot's health is critically low, getting health becomes much more important than if its health is nearly full. Similarly, getting more ammo becomes more important the less ammo the bot has. If the bot is close to dying, getting more health becomes more important than getting more ammo, even if it could do with more ammo, though if it does need more ammo, and if it is just a small detour to get some ammo when going to get health, making that detour might still be worth it. To properly solve this problem, the AI cannot rely on fixed priorities between behaviours and needs to be able to calculate relative priorities at runtime.

6.2.9 ACTIVE BEHAVIOUR STICKINESS

An important sub-problem of dynamic priorities is a desire to increase the priority of the currently active behaviour. Many times, the AI has several behaviours of similar, if not equal, priority, and under those circumstances, you may want to increase the priority of the active behaviour to prevent the AI from switching back and forth between behaviours. For instance, in the example above with the health and ammo pickup, if the need for both health and ammo is very similar, there is a risk that the AI will be ping-ponging between the two behaviours due to small changes to its perceived situation. Making the AI stick with a particular decision, even if that decision is not the optimal one, as long as it is good enough, generally leads to a better-behaving AI.

6.3 IMPLEMENTATION-DEPENDENT CHARACTERISTICS

In addition to the above characteristics of the different architectures, there are some characteristics of your implementation that are going to have a significant impact on how easy it is to work with it and how effective it is going to be at solving your problems. It is easy to ignore these, but there will be a cost down the line.

6.3.1 OVERHEAD

The quality of your AI will be highly dependent on your ability to create valid behaviours for most, if not all, scenarios an agent is likely to experience, closely followed by your ability to create behaviours that are observably distinct from each other. Consequently, as an AI developer, you are going to spend a large portion of your time adding and modifying AI behaviour. Minimising the amount of overhead that is required to add a new behaviour, a new behaviour building block or other capability for the AI is crucial. Any system that requires significant amounts of boilerplate work to create simple additions is going to result in a poorer product, as that time could have been spent on making better AI. If you start to notice that your behaviour building blocks are becoming more and more complex while the number of building blocks remains more or less the same, then that is a good sign that adding a new building block is too complicated and requires too much work.

6.3.2 DATA FLOW

Your AI will be calculating data ranging from the success or failure of a specific task to a path found between two points as it performs validity tests and executes behaviours. Frequently, that data is of interest to other parts of the decision-making process as well as the behaviour execution, and how this data is communicated is very important. Success or failure is often communicated as a direct return value, and it is popular to use blackboards for more complicated data. While blackboards offer a lot of flexibility, they also act like global variables with many of the same drawbacks. These include data being globally visible and devoid of local context, which means that if your AI is considering different targets for potential melee and ranged attacks, you will need both a melee and a ranged target in your blackboard, even though in the local context, they would just be working on a target. Code reuse will be complicated as you need to know which target the code is meant to access, potentially making code less generic. Passing data directly between the building blocks of your behaviours, or in other ways scoping the data to the local context, avoids this problem and makes it easier to break up tasks into parts that produce and parts that consume data.

6.4 COMPARING DIFFERENT ARCHITECTURES

Different decision-making architectures have different strengths and weaknesses, and selecting the right one for your AI will make your development experience a lot easier. These strengths and weaknesses are described in the following section and summarised in Table 6.1.

TABLE 6.1

Strengths and Weaknesses of Different Decision-Making Architectures

Architecture	Predictability	Debuggability	Modularisation	Hierarchical	Adding Behaviour	Sequencing	States & Transitions	Non-static Priorities	CPU
Prioritised list	++	++	-	-	+	--	--	--	++
Hierarchical prioritised list	++	+	=	+	+	--	--	--	++
Behaviour tree	++	+	++	++	=	=	--	--	+
FSM	++	++	=	=	--	++	++	--	+
hFSM	++	+	+	+	- -	++	++	- -	+
				+					
Utility-based	--	-	+	=	--	--	--	++	=
Hierarchical utility-based	--	--	+	+	--	--	--	++	=
Planners	--	--	+	=	++	++	=	=	--
Hierarchical planners	--	--	+	+	++	++	=	=	--

++ Means Very Strong, + Strong, = Neither Strong nor Weak, - Weak, and -- Very Weak

6.4.1 PRIORITISED BEHAVIOUR LIST

A prioritised behaviour list is one of the simplest architectures available, yet it is surprisingly effective for a wide range of scenarios. It lists all the agent's available behaviours in priority order. When a new behaviour needs to be picked, the AI will start from the top of the list and test each behaviour for validity until it finds the first valid behaviour which it will select for execution.

It is very easy to understand which behaviour has priority over others as that is just the order of the behaviours in the list. Adding a new behaviour is also straightforward. You only need to decide where in the list it goes. Understanding which behaviour is currently selected is also easy. However, prioritised lists do not encourage modularisation and can easily be implemented with monolithic validity tests and behaviour execution. As modularisation helps with more detailed debugging, as well as with reuse, there is a risk of a lack of both. Finally, prioritised lists are flat by nature, meaning that there is no hierarchical decision-making, and they also lack any mechanism for state transitions or sequencing.

6.4.2 HIERARCHICAL PRIORITISED BEHAVIOUR LISTS

As noted, prioritised behaviour lists are not hierarchical, but there is no reason why you cannot make them so. The hierarchical version only differs from the flat one in that validity tests can either lead to another prioritised list or to a behaviour to execute.

The hierarchical prioritised behaviour list gains hierarchical decision-making for the cost of a small increase in complexity, but otherwise shares the same strengths and weaknesses as the prioritised behaviour list.

6.4.3 BEHAVIOUR TREES

Behaviour trees are the perfect embodiment of hierarchical decision-making. They are also very strong when it comes to modularisation given that most implementations are built with a heavy emphasis on reusable building blocks, even though technically that is not a requirement. Behaviour trees allow the author good reasoning about which behaviour is going to execute, as their execution order is the depth-first search order of the tree until the first valid leaf is located. Understanding the current state of a behaviour tree and why a specific behaviour has been selected is straightforward. Just looking at the current active branch will give you most of the information, and by saving a little more data, you can easily display exactly which tests failed and which succeeded. Displaying the current state of a behaviour tree in game can be a little tricky since fitting trees on a screen quickly becomes difficult as they scale, but many systems have solved this problem by connecting their tree editor to the run-time, which allows for good visualisation. Where behaviour trees fall short is when you are dealing with states and state transitions. For instance, a node, like one playing an animation, that cannot be immediately exited requires some awkward compromises.

6.4.4 FINITE-STATE MACHINES

FSMs excel when it comes to describing states and transitions between them. They make it easy to understand under what circumstances a behaviour is going to be active, and they are straightforward to visualise, yet FSMs' real weakness is in those same transitions. The problem is that each state needs to have one transition per state that it is possible to transition to from that state. Often, most states are available from a given state, which leads to n^2 transitions. This results in a maintenance nightmare to keep track of all the transitions as the number of states grow. This creates a lot of work to add all the needed connections when adding a new state and makes it difficult to visualise a large number of states and transitions. Another related issue is that in many cases, there is no need for states with elaborate transitions in the first place. For instance, in combat, an agent may switch freely between most actions available to it assuming that they are valid. It might want to switch from attacking to moving closer to its target as soon as the target moves out of range, and back to attacking when it gets within range again. The AI does not need a complex transition from attacking to moving, it just needs to start moving, and when it is close enough, it will switch back to attacking again. Implementing this in an FSM just adds unnecessary overhead.

6.4.5   HIERARCHICAL FINITE-STATE MACHINES

Hierarchical Finite-State Machines (hFSMs) are FSMs where each state can contain a nested state machine that forms a hierarchy. hFSMs are like FSMs in their strengths and weaknesses, with the difference that they gain the advantage of hierarchical decision-making.

6.4.6   UTILITY-BASED DECISION-MAKING

Sometimes, it is not possible to assign static priorities to behaviours, and instead, each behaviour's relative priority needs to be decided at run time. Utility-based solutions were designed to solve this problem. In utility-based solutions, a utility score, i.e., a measure of how useful a particular behaviour would be for the AI to execute, is calculated for each behaviour, every update. The behaviour with the highest score is then selected to be executed. In many ways, utility-based decision-making is very similar to the prioritised behaviour list, except that instead of having static priorities, the behaviours are re-prioritised each update. This flexibility to be able to reprioritise the behaviours for a given situation is utility-based decision-making's biggest strength, but the complexity of making it work is also its biggest weakness. Usually, when utility-based decision-making is described in literature, there will be a 2D graph showing how the utility of two different behaviours changes based on a single variable. It is easy to look at the graph and see where one behaviour becomes more important than the other, and the AI's behaviour can be both easily understood and modified using this graph. Unfortunately, in order to create an interesting agent, your utility calculations will depend on a large number of variables, not just one, used to calculate the utility of a significant number of behaviours, often using non-linear functions. To illustrate how the different behaviours interact, you would need a graph with one additional dimension for each additional variable, something that quickly becomes impossible to illustrate. Keeping track of all these interactions is very challenging for any interesting AI system, which is why in practice you will see most utility systems divide their behaviours into classes that occupy distinct utility bands. This results in sets of a few behaviours in each band (often as few as just two or three), needing to have their utility calculations tuned against each other as the utility scores of all other behaviours are guaranteed to be outside their band.

6.4.7   HIERARCHICAL UTILITY-BASED DECISION-MAKING

As with most of the other solutions, it is easy to create a hierarchical version. Utility-based decision-making is no different and allows this approach to gain the strength of hierarchical decision-making.

6.4.8   PLANNERS

Planners allow the AI to construct plans at run time that match the current situation the AI finds itself in. These plans are constructed by assembling individual actions from a selection of actions that the AI has available to it. The actions come with pre- and post-conditions and the planner uses these conditions to create a string of actions that allows the AI to transform the world in such a way that by the end of the plan, the current world state is transformed into the goal state. The most popular planner in games is Goal-Oriented Action Planning, but it should be noted that there are many other planners out there with different pros and cons.

The big strength of the planners is that they allow the AI to solve situations that its creator has not thought of in advance. Assuming that there is a way to solve a situation with the actions available, the AI will be able to generate a plan to do so. This allows the programmer to focus on what actions an agent can take, which is a smaller problem, than on all the ways in which those actions can be combined. Another strength of planners is the ease of how they can be extended. Adding an action to the list of available actions immediately allows the AI to use that action in all situations that apply.

Planners also have significant weaknesses. The most important one is that it is by far the most CPU-intensive way to come up with a plan. The architectures discussed previously offload this work to the programmer who creates all the plans available to the AI offline, and at run time, the AI only needs to decide which plan is the best option at any given time. Of course, that puts the onus on the programmer to come up with a plan for all possible scenarios to ensure that an agent always has a reasonable response, and if there are scenarios that the programmer has not considered, then there might be exploits or just bad reactions of the AI in the shipped product. It might sound like a tall task, but as it turns out, for many games, it is not that difficult. In most games, particularly action games, the AI's life expectancy is very short, and they are engaged in a very constrained activity (usually combat). Commonly, the majority of development time is spent on finding and fixing edge cases, something you would have to do when using a planner too. To compound the issue of the overhead for planning, plans in these kinds of environments usually do not last very long, often mere seconds, or even just fractions thereof, after which a new plan needs to be generated, exasperating the performance problems.

Where planners do shine is in situations where the AI can create long-term, complex, and stable plans where optimising its actions is important.

6.4.9 HIERARCHICAL PLANNERS

As with many of the other solutions, planners can be hierarchical. Hierarchical Task Networks is the most well-known version of a hierarchical planner. Such an approach has a significant benefit compared to non-hierarchical planners in that it is easy to create a system that is only creating a partial plan. This gets filled in as needed and can result in significant CPU savings.

6.5 CONCLUSION

At this point, you might be wondering which architecture is the best as all of them seem to have strengths and weaknesses. The short answer is that none of them is the best. They are all good at different things. Understanding these strengths and weaknesses allows you to correctly analyse how a particular solution fits the needs of your project.

You may also have heard of a successful game that used an architecture that this chapter suggests would not be the most suitable for that type of game and AI. For instance, there are several high-profile action games that use planners as the basis for their AI. Does that mean this chapter is wrong? No. Just because an architecture is not as well-suited to or is overkill for a specific problem does not mean that it cannot be used to solve that problem. Additionally, the decision of what architecture to use is not made in a vacuum. A company may have existing code, tooling, and expertise that may make using a certain type of architecture easier for them; however, as such things go, most decision-making architectures are just a small fraction of the AI code written for a project, and an initial investment in a well-chosen architecture can go a long way in making the development more pleasant.

Another important point is that there is nothing preventing you from mixing and matching solutions. If the top level of your AI is best described by an FSM, but behaviour trees are more suitable for the rest, then you can use both, and if there is a need for deciding between those health and ammo pickups, you can have a utility-driven node in your behaviour tree. Of course, implementing multiple solutions comes with some significant additional work, and perhaps you can only pick one, in which case pick the one that is best suited to the problem you are trying to solve.

7 High-Speed Vehicle Driving in *Wheelman*

Dr Allan Bruce

7.1 INTRODUCTION

One of the core gameplay features of *Wheelman* is being involved in high-speed pursuits against AI-controlled enemy vehicles through the busy city of Barcelona. The game has two types of AI vehicles. The first is a richly populated traffic system consisting of vehicle AI that moves around the world slowly and in a predictable manner. The second type is a high-speed and unpredictable vehicle AI that behaves more akin to those seen in movie car chases. Players and AI need to navigate around the traffic and other obstacles whilst involved in high-speed pursuits with each other. This chapter describes the methods used to ensure the high-speed AI-controlled vehicles navigated around these obstacles and avoided collisions whilst maintaining the high speeds required to keep the player engaged in the gameplay.

The approaches detailed throughout this chapter are termed 'High Speed Vehicle Driving' or HSVD for short. These include converting the navigable 3D world into a linear path-space that the AI can more easily reason with, where all obstacles are simulated and represented, the methods used to make the AI drive more organically and like a player, calculating an optimal solution to navigating the path-space, and the method by which this is then transformed back into the playable world. HSVD is what allows the AI to drive around the world of *Wheelman* in a fast-paced believable way.

7.2 BUILDING PATH-SPACE

Making AI reason in three dimensions is a daunting task. Thankfully, the playable world in *Wheelman* is essentially flat and can be easily represented as a 2D plane. Pathfinding is achieved using traditional nav-meshes which follow the streets for high-speed pursuits. To further simplify the problem-space for the AI, a transformation is performed from the top-down 2D world-space to a linear path-space. This representation removes all cornering from the problem space and ideally the AI vehicles just drive along this transformed space, and therefore only need to reason about their offset from the centre of the road. Image 7.1 shows the result of converting from world-space to path-space.

The method used to do this conversion is to iterate over each segment of the road and use the length of the centre of the road segment to depict the length of the segment in path-space. To convert a point in world-space, calculate the perpendicular distance of that point from the centre line in addition to the perpendicular distance of

DOI: 10.1201/9781003323549-7

each side of the road at each end of the segment. The fraction of the point's distance from the centre to the side of the road is used as the y coordinate in your path-space, where the centre of the road has a value of 0, negative numbers denote points to the left of the centre and positive values to the right. If the value of this y coordinate is −1, then the point would be at the very left-hand edge of the road, whereas +1 would be on the very right-hand edge of the road.

To calculate the x coordinate for the path-space, perform a similar calculation as above but instead find the distance along the segment parallel to the centre of the road. This fraction along the segment would be 0 at the start of the segment and 1 at the end of the segment. Each segment is also indexed sequentially with 0 being the current segment the AI is located on. Negative values are also used to represent segments behind the AI's current segment.

In Image 7.1, two example points are shown in world-space and path-space. Point A is on segment 2 and is approximately half the way down the segment so the x coordinate would be approximately 0.5. The point is a small amount to the left of the centre line so the y coordinate would be approximately −0.1. This would then be referenced as a 3-parameter vector as $(2, 0.5, -0.1)$. Using the same techniques, it should be easy to see that point B would be represented in path-space approximately by $(5, 0.9, 0.8)$.

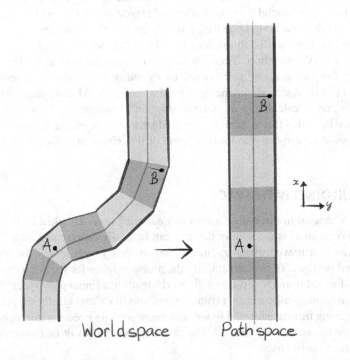

World space   Path space

IMAGE 7.1   Converting from world-space to path-space.

It is worth noting that these path-space *y* coordinates are not restricted from −1 to 1 as the nav-mesh is usually wider than the roads. Sometimes, the pursuits can wander off-road if the player guides them that way. The AI is allowed to follow off-road, but it does try to remain on the road as much as possible. The *x* coordinate, however, is bound from 0 to 1, and if it goes beyond, this then the point would be on the previous or next segment.

7.3   OBSTACLES

With a simple representation for AI vehicles to reason with, obstacles can be added to the problem space for the AI to avoid. The simplest type of obstacle is a static one and these come in two varieties: unbreakable and breakable. Since static obstacles do not move, you simply need to get the bounding box of the obstacles and transform each corner into the path-space. Since the vehicle being driven also has a finite size, expand each transformed point of the obstacle by half the width and length of the vehicle being driven. This then means you can reason about any point outside of an obstacle that the vehicle can occupy without overlapping the obstacle. Image 7.2 shows how an obstacle would be transformed from world-space into path-space. The road segment in the left image shows an obstacle with a bounding box labelled A, and a vehicle being driven with a bounding box labelled B. The road segment in the right image is the same road segment but represented in path-space. This shows how the obstacle's bounding box is transformed into path-space. The dashed boxes are the half-extents of the AI vehicle which are expanded to the obstacle's resultant bounds.

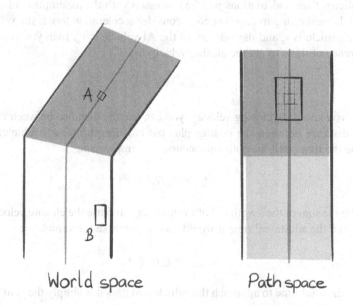

IMAGE 7.2   Transforming obstacles from world-space to path-space.

When adding these obstacles to the path-space, a weight is included that discourages the AI from choosing to drive through them. If the obstacle is unbreakable, simply add a very large weight but if the obstacle is breakable, apply a weight proportional to the mass of the obstacle. For example, if one obstacle were a traffic cone, it would have a very small weight, whereas if it were a bus stand, it would have a much higher weight. These weights are discussed in more detail later.

7.4   SIMULATING VEHICLES AS OBSTACLES

To avoid other vehicles, a method to map the vehicle's bounds into path-space as obstacles is required. Since these vehicles are dynamic, you will need to simulate where they will be relative to your own vehicle at each location on the path-space. Split this into two categories: deterministic and non-deterministic. As the name implies, deterministic vehicles are those whose location can be accurately predicted over time. You can use this for the traffic within the game as you know what speed the traffic vehicles are driving at and their chosen route through the traffic system. For simplicity, traffic in *Wheelman* did not generally react to pursuits happening in its proximity and drove as if there was no pursuit. The only time the traffic reacted was when a head-on collision was imminent, in which case they would choose to swerve out of the way.

Since the speed that the traffic vehicle will be travelling at is known and you control your own vehicle speed, you can predict the time it would take to collide with the vehicle. You can also calculate the time it would take to completely pass the vehicle. For simplicity, these calculations will be discussed with the assumption of constant velocities; however, in-game, you need to consider acceleration too. If the velocity of the traffic vehicle is v_t and the velocity of the AI vehicle is v_a, then you simply find the difference of these to get the closing velocity v_c:

$$v_c = v_a - v_t$$

Now that you know the closing velocity, you can use the distance between the vehicles (the distance between the centres plus the half-length of each vehicle), d_{ta}, to determine the time until the collision occurs, t_{col}, simply using:

$$t_{col} = d_{ta}/v_c$$

If you take the sum of the length of both vehicles, l_{ta}, and use the closing velocity, you can then find the additional time it would take to overtake the vehicle as:

$$t_{overtake} = l_{ta}/v_c;$$

therefore, the total time to approach the vehicle and pass it is simply the sum of these times:

$$t_{pass} = t_{col} + t_{overtake}$$

If you now convert these times to distances, you can find the distance to collision as the product of your speed and the time to collide as follows:

$$d_{col} = t_{col} \cdot v_a,$$

and the distance to completely pass the vehicle as the product of your speed and the time to pass completely:

$$d_{pass} = t_{pass} \cdot v_a$$

For example, consider an AI vehicle that is travelling at 35 m/s and a traffic vehicle travelling in the same direction at 15 m/s with a 50-m gap between them. Using the equations above, you can calculate that the distance to collision in this case would be 87.5 m (assuming constant velocities). If the total length of both cars is 4 m, you can calculate the distance to totally pass the traffic vehicle as 94.5 m. If, however, you have the same scenario but with the traffic vehicle now travelling in the opposite direction i.e., oncoming, then its velocity would be −15 m/s resulting in a collision distance of 35 m and a total pass distance of 37.8 m. Image 7.3 shows the current location of the AI vehicle and the two example traffic vehicles above in world-space and transformed into path-space.

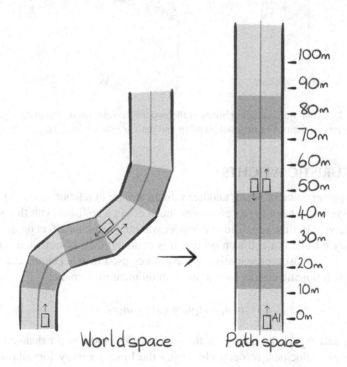

IMAGE 7.3 Current location and direction of travel of an HSVD AI vehicle and two traffic vehicles.

Image 7.4 then shows the simulated positions of the traffic vehicles in path-space including the additional AI vehicle bounds to guarantee no overlapping. It also shows these collision bounds are transformed back into world-space, although it is worth noting that this is not used for any purpose other than debugging.

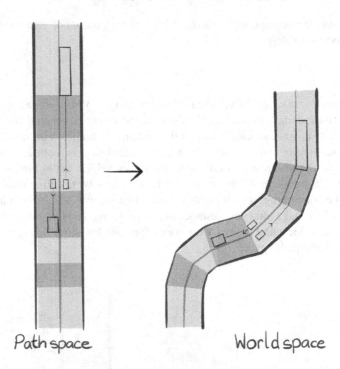

Path space   World space

IMAGE 7.4   Simulated bounding boxes of the two traffic vehicles shown in dark grey as the AI vehicle passes them. The original location and path are shown in light grey.

7.5   HEURISTIC WEIGHTS

With a representation of where another vehicle will be in relation to the AI vehicle's progress, you also need to represent how much effect a collision with that vehicle is going to have. For this, you need to consider what the resultant effect on the AI vehicle velocity will be if a collision occurs. It is assumed that the collisions are elastic since those are most representative of the physics used in *Wheelman*, and therefore can use the following elastic, conservation of momentum formula:

$$m_1 u_1 + m_2 u_2 = m_1 v_1 + m_2 v_2, \tag{7.1}$$

where m_1 and m_2 are the masses of the two vehicles, and u and v denote the initial and resultant velocities, respectively. Using the kinetic energy formula for elastic collisions, which is:

$$m_1 u_1^2 / 2 + m_2 u_2^2 / 2 = m_1 v_1^2 / 2 + m_2 v_2^2 / 2 \tag{7.2}$$

You can rearrange the first equation, and represent it in the following way:

$$m_1(u_1 - v_1) = m_2(v_2 - u_2) \tag{7.3}$$

And if you rearrange the kinetic energy equation (7.2), you get:

$$m_1 u_1^2 + m_2 u_2^2 = m_1 v_1^2 + m_2 v_2^2 \tag{7.4}$$

$$m_1(u_1^2 - v_1^2) = m_2(v_2^2 - u_2^2) \tag{7.5}$$

$$m_1(u_1 + v_1)(u_1 - v_1) = m_2(v_2 + u_2)(v_2 - u_2) \tag{7.6}$$

Dividing (7.6) by (7.3) gives the following:

$$u_1 + v_1 = v_2 + u_2 \tag{7.7}$$

and rearranging that you get:

$$v_2 = u_1 + v_1 - u_2 \tag{7.8}$$

If you now substitute this equation for (7.8) back into (7.1) you get:

$$m_1 u_1 + m_2 u_2 = m_1 v_1 + m_2(u_1 + v_1 - u_2) \tag{7.9}$$

Finally, rearranging this, you can get an equation to calculate the resultant velocity of your AI vehicle, v_1, knowing only the initial velocities and masses as shown:

$$m_1 u_1 + m_2 u_2 = m_1 v_1 + m_2 u_1 + m_2 v_1 - m_2 u_2 \tag{7.10}$$

$$m_1 u_1 - m_2 u_1 + 2 m_2 u_2 = v_1(m_1 + m_2) \tag{7.11}$$

$$v_1 = (m_1 u_1 - m_2 u_1 + 2 m_2 u_2)/(m_1 + m_2) \tag{7.12}$$

Knowing the initial and resultant velocities, you just use this loss in velocity and multiply it by a tuneable parameter as shown:

$$w = k(u - v)/u,$$

where w is the weight to add for your obstacle, k is the tuneable parameter, u is the initial velocity of the AI vehicle, and v is the resultant velocity.

7.6 NON-DETERMINISTIC SIMULATION

The steps above detail how you simulate the traffic in a deterministic manner. Players and other HSVD AI are non-deterministic, so you must take a slightly different approach to simulate them. Since these vehicles are likely to deviate over the time, it would take to collide with them, their simulation does not need to be as accurate. The same collision weight calculations are used based on the resultant speeds after the collision, but since the vehicles are travelling at similar velocities, the weights are generally much smaller. The path of non-deterministic vehicles is not well known; therefore, it is simply assumed they are travelling in a straight line at their current velocity. As this simulation is less accurate, you do not place a full obstacle into the path-space as with deterministic obstacles. Instead, you add a repulsor which will be discussed later.

7.7 SUB-DIVIDING OBSTACLES INTO CELLS

Once you have the obstacles mapped into path-space, you need to determine a method to analyse the problem space and calculate a preferred position to drive towards. To do this, you need to break the problem space down into quadrilaterals using the boundaries of all obstacles, and taking the current AI vehicle location as the source, project straight lines through each vertex of each obstacle.You also need to break down the space by projecting vertical and horizontal lines through each edge of the obstacle. Each of these quadrilaterals is referred to as a cell. Image 7.5 shows an example of how the cells are generated around a single obstacle.

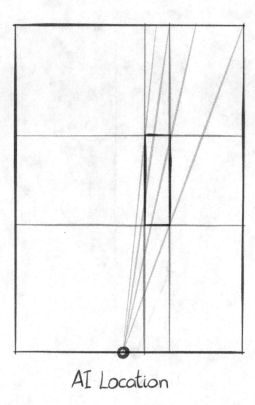

AI Location

IMAGE 7.5 Basic problem space showing one obstacle and how the world is subdivided around the obstacle into cells.

The goal is to find a location in this 2D path-space which minimises the cost of a set of heuristics. The only heuristic discussed so far is the obstacle weight. Additional heuristics that were applied to achieve smooth, organic driving are discussed later.

The approximation for the path the AI will choose to take is to drive in path-space from the current location to a given single point and then continue to drive parallel with the road from there on. Image 7.6 shows such a goal path and shows how you start to score the cells.

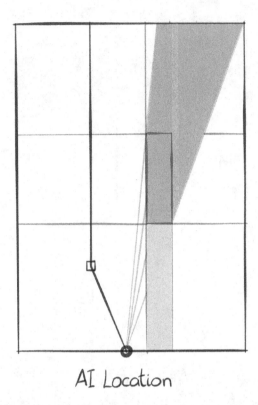

AI Location

IMAGE 7.6   An example goal path for the AI is shown in dark-grey and heuristic scores are in varying shades of grey.

The mid-grey cells show a constant high cost since choosing the goal point within these cells would guarantee colliding with the obstacle. The light-grey cells are weighted less since driving to the goal location does not guarantee a collision. The follow-on parallel path might find a better goal in the next few frames to avoid collision. The weight in these light-grey cells varies depending on the distance from the obstacle, with the highest weight being at the obstacle boundary.

7.8   CELL DECOMPOSITION

The method used to determine the optimal goal location is to calculate the minimum cost (the sum of all the heuristics) for all the cells and adding them to a list. Then use a guided search, similar to A*, to determine which cells are most relevant to decompose. The cell with the lowest cost is removed from the set and sub-divided into two smaller cells. Those two new cells are then analysed to find their new minimum cost and placed into the set of all cells. This subdivision is continued until the area of the best cell is sufficiently small which results in its centre being your chosen goal location.

The cells are subdivided by taking their longest dimension and dividing it, ensuring you always make two new quadrilateral cells (or triangles). If you consider the light-grey area in Image 7.6, then again in Image 7.7, it shows how that cell is subdivided twice. The light-grey cell is first subdivided into a smaller light-grey cell and a mid-grey cell. If you then subdivide the mid-grey cell, you get the smaller mid-grey cell and a dark-grey cell. When you evaluate the cost of a given cell, you find the minimum value of each heuristic individually for that cell and sum them to obtain the total minimum cost. When a cell is subdivided, the two new cells are not guaranteed to have the same minimum cost as their parent; however, they are guaranteed to never have a lower cost than their parent.

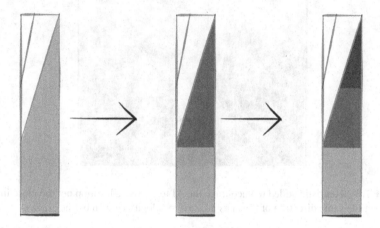

IMAGE 7.7 Sub-dividing cells to generate smaller cells.

7.9 ADDITIONAL HEURISTICS

Avoiding collisions is one part of believable driving through the busy streets. Another is making the vehicle move smoothly and drive like a playert. To ensure this behaviour is achieved, you need to add some weight heuristics to the path-space to guide the vehicle. Two such important heuristics are used to ensure that the AI chooses flowing paths rather than ones that steer wildly from side to side. The first of these is to ensure the AI tries to steer further down the path rather than very close to the current location. This is done by adding a gradient starting with a high weight at $y = 0$ and fades to zero at a given distance along the y-axis. This distance varies depending on speed, i.e., the distance is shorter for lower speeds as opposed to being longer at higher speeds. The second heuristic to apply is to prefer steering in the current direction. Points along the direction of current velocity are weighted 0 but as the angle increases away from the velocity, the points are weighted higher. These combined heuristics are shown in Image 7.8 and you can see a 'sweet spot' with the minimum cost (lightest shade of grey) that would be chosen if no other heuristics were considered.

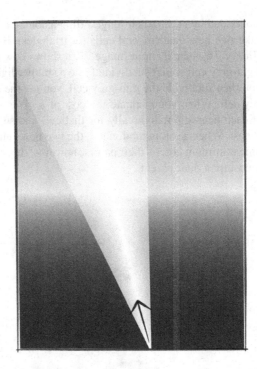

IMAGE 7.8 Heuristic added to encourage the AI to choose a location not too close in front and along the same direction of travel as its current velocity (shown by the arrow).

Several other heuristics can be used to ensure the AI drives organically. These will not be discussed in detail, but they include:

- A heuristic to try to encourage the AI to travel within lanes of traffic going in the same direction and to discourage the use of lanes in the opposite direction. This heuristic is also weighted such that if the AI is going to travel in a lane, it prefers the centre of the lane.
- Another heuristic is used to discourage the AI from choosing to drive on the medial strip or pavements, and a further weight to discourage travelling beyond the pavement.
- A heuristic to discourage driving very close to another vehicle.
- A further heuristic that prefers choosing a goal location for a short time. Add the previous frame's chosen location as a negative weight which gets stronger for a short time if rechosen before fading to zero.

The final heuristic added to the path-space is to aid formation driving. At certain points during gameplay, you may want the AI to drive in a formation and use the vehicle to ram into the side of the player or remain in a location relative to the player so that the player can easily predict their position and ram them back. To do this, you apply a negative weight to these areas which the AI will choose to go to if there are no obstacles in the way. These are termed repulsors as first discussed in the non-deterministic simulation. Repulsors are used to dissuade the AI from choosing a given location if the weight is positive and to persuade them to choose a given location if the weight is negative. These repulsors are very small in size, approximately $0.5\,m^2$, but have a fade over a further distance should the exact point not be suitable.

Putting all these heuristics together, you have a process resulting in AI vehicle driving that looks organic and realistic, avoids collisions well, and can be used to encourage formation positions. The final part of the puzzle is to determine the speed for the vehicle. This is relatively simple as you often merely want to match the player's speed. Therefore, using the player's speed as a base, you set a target speed to be slightly slower than the player if the AI is ahead or slightly faster than the player if the AI is behind. In some scenarios, you may want the AI to drive as fast as possible, so you can merely set the target speed to be the vehicle's top speed. The only time the AI should override the speed to slow down from these target speeds in path-space is when the goal location that is chosen is inside any potential collision cells (as shown by the light-grey cells in Image 7.6). When this scenario arises, simply set the target speed to match the vehicle it would collide with and, once there is a collision-free goal, you can increase its target speed again.

7.10 TRANSFORMATION BACK TO WORLD-SPACE

With a method for finding a collision-free path in path-space, you need to transform it back to world-space so that the AI can steer correctly in the game world. To do this, find each intersection of the goal path, and segment edges in path-space, and transform those locations back to world-space. Image 7.9 shows an example of a typical scenario that an AI would encounter in *Wheelman*. Image 7.10 then shows the simulated outcome and chosen goal path transformed back into world-space.

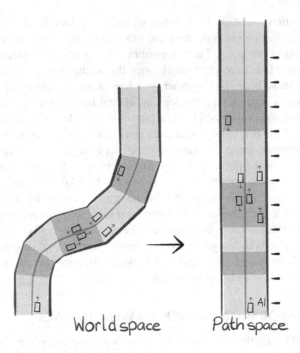

IMAGE 7.9   A typical in-game scenario showing several traffic vehicles to avoid.

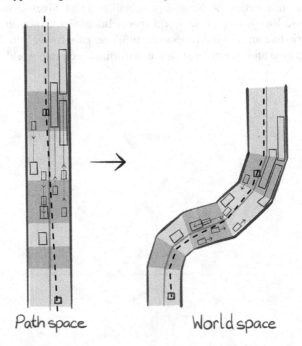

IMAGE 7.10   The typical in-game scenario simulated and showing the goal path through the traffic in dashed dark grey. This is shown in path-space and transformed back into world-space.

You now have a path to follow in world-space that the AI can steer along and avoid any collisions, but one final part of the problem remains. No consideration has been given to the curvature of the goal path in world-space. Since the AI is driving physics-simulated vehicles and not cheating, you need to look along this world-space path and limit your chosen speed by the curvature of it. This ensures that the AI remains on the path and does not under-steer and collide with the obstacles you have worked hard to avoid. To achieve this, you need to build speed tables for the vehicle in a test level made up of one giant flat plane. For each AI vehicle type, set them to drive at constant speeds with regular intervals, e.g., 5, 10, 15 m/s, etc. Then, steer the vehicle fully in one direction at each of these speeds and record the radius of the arc they can achieve. As part of this test, also record how quickly the car can decelerate so you can accurately gauge braking distances. Once you know the curvature of your path in world-space, you can look up the speed tables and determine if you need to slow down to achieve the path with no under-steering.

7.11 CONCLUSION

In this chapter, the method used for driving through the busy traffic environment in *Wheelman* at high speed avoiding any collisions has been outlined. How to transform world-space roads to a linear path-space and also how to represent obstacles in that path-space were shown. It was also shown how you can simulate moving vehicles in this space and how to use a set of heuristics to guide the AI in choosing a smooth-flowing, organic path similar to how players might drive. How to dissect the path-space and find a goal location to drive towards was detailed and how also this is translated back into the 3D world.

The results of this approach worked very well. The AI would drive around with very few collisions and look natural whilst doing so. There were up to six AI vehicles driving at any given time during the game, and each of these executed this cell decomposition method every frame on PC, Xbox 360, and PlayStation 3 hardware, so it was also very efficient.

ACKNOWLEDGEMENTS AND PERMISSIONS

A special thanks goes out to Ben Marsh who developed some of these ideas and was part of many lengthy discussions, and to Shaun Himmerick for allowing us to share these ideas and methods in this book.

8 AI Awareness in Sports Games

Paul Roberts

8.1 INTRODUCTION

In any sports game, there is a lot for a non-player character (NPC) to assess. This chapter will focus on the game of American Football. When on Offence, NPCs need to be aware of their teammates as well as their opponents, they need to position themselves such that they can receive the ball without an interception occurring, and they need to assess threats and react accordingly. When on Defence, analysing threats posed by opposing players is a challenge. As plays are secretly selected, there is no way for the Defence to know what an opposing player will do and where they will go. This is a core component of the game and reacting appropriately is what stops the Offence from gaining those precious ten yards.

However, the human player needs to feel like they are the ones making an impact. If the AI shuts down every play, or alternatively fails to shut down any plays, the human player feels cheated, or as though the game is playing itself. Then the AI team is in a constant cycle of "the Offence is too good", so improvements are made to the defensive AI. Then, "the Defence is too good", and additional changes are made to improve the Offence. The cycle goes on. It would be easy to simply modify stats, such as speed, to allow one team to perform better, but this can be a blunt tool.

This chapter details a couple of the approaches that were taken to allow for different players who have the same role (i.e., two Cornerbacks), and process the same code, to act differently. This approach allowed for the correct decisions to be made by the AI, but as those decisions were based upon what was deemed as a threat, via their awareness of the opposition; at that time, different and more believable responses were able to be chosen.

8.2 POSITIONAL AWARENESS

Take the role of a Wide Receiver. It is their job to get into a position where the quarterback can safely pass the ball to them. This could mean getting as far downfield as possible and creating separation between themselves and the cornerback whose job it is to mark them, or it could mean cutting in or zigzagging to send the Cornerback going in the wrong direction to create that separation. If the chosen approach is to simply run downfield, then the speed difference between the Wide Receiver and the Cornerback is all that is required. This does not show intelligence from the Wide Receiver though. What about a Wide Receiver who has the same speed as the player marking them or who is slower. Such a player should never be selected for the team

DOI: 10.1201/9781003323549-8

and will always be a bad option for a pass. It is in these situations where AI awareness becomes invaluable.

Awareness of opposing players is achieved by allowing each player to retain their own local information about their opponents. This local information is what they *think* about the opponent and not actual information. By refreshing this data periodically, you ensure players have a degree of awareness but also allow players to react more slowly to developments on the field.

To achieve this, a list of structs is required per player, where each struct in the list refers to an opponent. The struct contains the following details:

- Player ID
- Last known position
- Estimated position
- Direction
- Velocity
- Current refresh time
- Refresh duration

The idea is that each player will keep track of where they *think* the opponents are on the field. So, at the start of the game, each struct will be populated with the exact details of the opponent in question. As a play progresses, the player will refresh the struct with accurate positional data when they look at that player or when the refresh time has expired. At all other times, the data in each struct will be updated with a guess as to where the player thinks the opponent will be. This is achieved by taking their direction and velocity and calculating what position on the field they would be if they had continued with that trajectory.

Take a look at Image 8.1. The player in black is a Cornerback and is looking to defend any throws to the Wide Receiver behind them. The Cornerback looks to position themselves between the Quarterback and the Wide Receiver, usually a yard or two away from the Wide Receiver. The image also shows the route the Wide Receiver is planning to take. The Cornerback does not have this information and should react to developments as they play out on the field. At this stage, the Cornerback stores the position of the Wide Receiver, the direction he is running and his speed and then sets the refresh counter ticking.

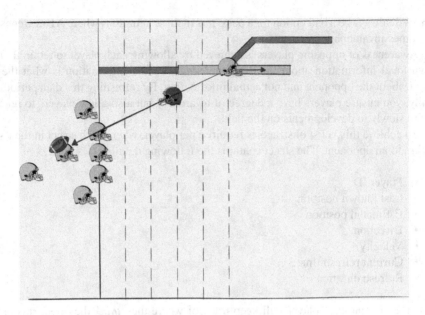

IMAGE 8.1   Awareness based on the exact data at the start of a play.

When the play starts, the Wide Receiver takes off running and the Cornerback needs to react. If their awareness refresh rate is too long, the location where they *think* the Wide Receiver is may be correct, but they could also be wrong. The example shown in Image 8.2 has the opponent zigzagging behind, which means the Cornerback is now defending the wrong position. The Wide Receiver has created the separation required to allow the Quarterback to make the pass, and this had little to do with the speed of either player.

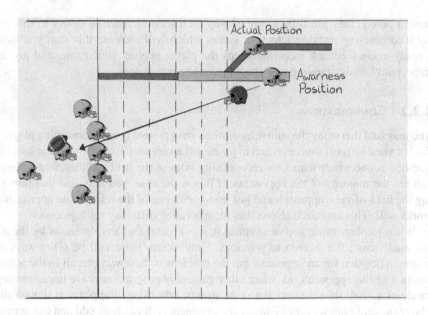

IMAGE 8.2 Awareness resulting in the player defending the wrong position.

8.2.1 REFRESH RATE

The refresh rate has a big impact on the perceived intelligence of a player. There are three forms of refresh rate awareness. The first approach is to refresh each opponent's struct based on the timer. The second approach is to use an overall refresh rate, which resets all opponent data to be accurate when the refresh occurs. Both approaches can be enhanced by incorporating an awareness stat for that particular player (the observing player). An awareness stat is a value between 0 and –1, with 0 indicating a player with great awareness and a 1 indicating a player with a low awareness span. The refresh time for the observing player is then set as the maximum refresh time multiplied by this stat. Therefore, a player with an awareness stat of 0 will have a refresh rate of 0.0 seconds, meaning they get the most up-to-date information every frame. A player with a stat of 1 will have a refresh rate set to whatever the maximum refresh time is. Around 0.6 seconds worked for us.

The third approach to refreshing the data is the field of view approach. If a player can see an opponent, then that opponent's data gets refreshed immediately and they have the most up-to-date information on that opponent. Other opponents that are not within the field of view are only updated when the refresh time has passed (approach one or two). This approach emulates when a player would cast a glance around the field to ensure they know where an opponent is. Adding an animation to do this would also help to sell the illusion.

By combining these approaches, you get the desired result of seeing players running behind or out of sight and getting away from their predicted route and creating separation. Players look reactive and as though they are attempting to handle the threat in the correct manner, and no player has an opponent or teammate that is so far out of date that they appear to be stupid. If you expose the awareness stat to the human player, they are fully aware of why their team is reacting slower to threats. By incorporating training into your game, which will increase this stat, you have a ready-made feedback loop that keeps the player playing your game, and just as importantly, understanding why the AI plays the way it does.

8.2.2 Considerations

You may find that using the auto refresh when an opponent is in the observing player's field of view kills off this approach to positional awareness. Especially, if the sport in question is one where teams are on opposing sides of the field and therefore a player can see the majority of the opponents. If this is the case, you may find that removing the field-of-view approach and just going with one of the refresh rate approaches works well. This approach also makes incorporating difficulty settings easier.

When implementing such an approach, it is crucial that any decisions by the AI are made using the awareness positions. Quite often, there will be other ways of getting a position for an opponent, but the problem is these ways result in the actual position of the opponent. So, when other gameplay programmers are implementing mechanics, they should query the same structs; otherwise, it appears as though the player suddenly knows exactly where the opponent is. It can look odd and can appear as though the AI is cheating.

8.3 THREAT AWARENESS

Another area of player awareness that impacts AI sports people is how to determine which opponents are deemed as threats. Whether on Offence or Defence, the opposing players pose a threat to the goal of the team. How these threats are assessed is an important aspect of the awareness of each player on the field.

When looking at the AI for a Cornerback, if the player they are marking crosses paths with another player, it is for them to decide which one to mark. Do they stay with the Wide Receiver they started with, but who has now headed into the centre of the field where a teammate could cover them, or do they stop marking their target and pursue the opponent that is now heading to the edge of the field. Different players will do different things depending upon the scenario, but in video games, the AI needs to look like they are at least making smart decisions.

8.3.1 Threat Filters

To ensure code is reusable and compartmentalised, the concept of a threat filter was developed. Different AI behaviours use as many or as few filters as required, and these are detailed in the next section. When assessing threats, the observing player stores an array of values (one for each opposing player on the field) which indicates the weighting of the threat. At each update, the weighting is set to a value of zero before the available filters are processed. Each individual filter will modify this weight based on the criteria of the threat. Each threat can return a maximum value of one, but in most cases will return a weighting for that filter. The weighting is a tweakable value that can be set by design but can never exceed one. When all filters have been processed, the accumulated weight is divided by the number of filters to give a threat value between 0 and 1. The observing player will now understand which opposing players are the greatest threat to their team.

There are a wide variety of different threat filters that can be applied, and only a subset of those used is described below. What is important is that each filter handles one assessment, and more complex assessments are made by layering up filters.

8.3.1.1 Distance of the Opponent to the Ball Carrier Filter

If the observing player is on the Offence, it is their job to protect their teammate who is running with the ball. To identify if an opponent is a threat to the ball carrier, the distance between the ball carrier and the opposing player being analysed is divided by a maximum distance to give a 0 to 1 value.

8.3.1.2 Distance of the Opponent to the Observing Player Filter

At times, the distance of an opposing player to the agent assessing the threat is an important factor. Those closer are deemed a higher threat than those further away. For example, the observing player could be the ball carrier who wants to make as many yards upfield as they can before they are brought down. If this threat is available to the behaviour, then the distance between the observing player and the opposing player being analysed is divided by a maximum distance to give a 0 to 1 value.

8.3.1.3 Distance of the Opponent to the Endzone Filter

If the opposing team has the ball, the distance of the ball carrier to the end zone is a huge consideration. The closer they are to the end zone, the greater the threat. When incorporating this filter into the threat analysis, the distance between the ball carrier and the endzone is divided by a maximum distance to give a 0 to 1 value.

8.3.1.4 Positioning upfield to the Ball Carrier Filter

When the observing player's team does not possess the ball, it is important for them to stop the ball carrier from making yards. If they are ahead of the ball carrier, they should treat the ball carrier as a threat, but if they are already behind the ball carrier, and there is little chance of them catching up, then there is little they can do. For this filter, the field position of the observing player is compared to that of the ball carrier's position. If they are upfield of the ball carrier (they are between the ball carrier and the end zone), the threat value is set to the weighting for this threat, otherwise it is scaled down to zero depending upon the distance away.

8.3.1.5 Opponent Positioning inside Zone Filter

For players that have a zone to protect, any opposing player within that zone is deemed a threat. Any opposing player inside the zone controlled by the observing player returns the weighting for this threat, and any opposing player not inside the zone returns a value of zero.

8.3.1.6   The Opponent Is the Ball Carrier Filter

The ball carrier on the opposing team is always a threat. So, this filter is simple. If the opposing player has the ball, then this results in a value of one, otherwise it returns a value of zero.

8.3.1.7   Opponent Positioning outside the Receiver Positioning Filter

When a defensive player is looking to defend against a receiver, it is important for them to see opposing players moving to the outer edges of the field as a threat. This is because the receiver can then run upfield with little obstruction and the Quarterback can throw ahead of them. To incorporate this into the AI, this filter is used to calculate a ratio of the opposing player's position to the field's half-width to give a threat value in the range of 0 to 1, 1 being the player farthest outside, and 0 when the player is in the centre of the field.

8.3.1.8   Opponent Is Currently Man-Marked Filter

Players will from time to time be marking opposing players. To ensure teammates don't all congregate around the same opponent, the concept of being man marked is used. Internally, this is a variable stored by a player that contains the player ID of the player marking them. This filter checks if there is already a valid player ID stored, and if so, returns a value of zero, otherwise the weighting for this threat is returned.

Multiple players deeming the same opponent as the highest threat is a valid outcome, and at times, there should be multiple players trying to handle this threat. This filter reduces the chances of this happening though and in-game at most two players at any one time (the marker and the observing player) try to handle a threat who has a teammate marking them.

8.3.1.9   The Opponent Is a Potential Receiver Filter

When on Defence, it is crucial that the AI can understand which opponents may have the ball thrown at them. Potential receivers are determined by their role on the team. These include the Wide Receiver, the Tight End, and the Running Back. This filter checks the role of the opposing player, and if it is a potential receiver, the weighting for this threat is returned, otherwise zero is returned.

8.3.2   THREAT FILTERS IN BEHAVIOURS

For American Football, threats are assessed differently depending upon a player's current role and the rules of the game. The approach that was taken was to analyse threats on a per-behaviour basis. A behaviour acts in the manner expected. A finite-state machine would be appropriate, or any other suitable approach. The important point is that the threat analysis is done external to the behaviour. The behaviours simply use the data to determine which opposing players are of the greatest concern and act appropriately. For example, the ball carrier will always look to work his way upfield but needs to avoid incoming threats. As threats change, the ball carrier will adjust to handle the next highest threat and manoeuvre in such a way as to avoid getting tackled.

Not all behaviours require a threat analysis, so to save CPU processing, threats are not assessed for behaviours that do not use the information.

The following behaviours required threats and are a subset of those required for the whole game. They do, however, show how different behaviours can use different combinations of the same filters to assess the threats in a way that suits the behaviour the player is currently enacting.

8.3.2.1 Zone Coverage Behaviour

When in zone coverage, a player is on the defensive side of the field and must keep track of opposing players looking to find a good position to catch the ball. They should also be aware of the ball carrier entering their zone, which would result in this behaviour being replaced with a simple behaviour that chases down the ball carrier and makes a tackle.

The threat filters assessed for this behaviour are:

- The opponent is the ball carrier filter.
- Opponent positioning inside zone filter.
- Distance of the opponent to the endzone filter.
- Opponent is currently man-marked filter.
- Distance of the opponent to the observing player filter.

8.3.2.2 Lead Blocker Behaviour

A Lead Blocker is a player on the offensive side of the field who runs ahead of the ball carrier and blocks off any incoming threats.

The threat filters assessed are:

- Distance of the opponent to the ball carrier filter.
- Distance of the opponent to the observing player filter.
- Opponent is currently man-marked filter.

8.3.2.3 Ball Carrier Behaviour

When any player on the field gets the ball, they have one job and that is to take it as many yards upfield as they can before an opposing player brings them down.

The filter required to assess threats for this behaviour is:

- Distance of the opponent to the observing player filter.

8.4 CONCLUSION

Awareness is a simple enough addition to any sports title and delivers great results. It does not remove the need for other stats such as sprint speed, it only enhances them. When it comes time to incorporate difficulty settings into your game, which always seems to be left late in development, modifying the awareness stat or the threat weightings is a subtle way of adjusting the difficulty of your game without any of the AI players doing anything wrong.

9 Crafting the Illusion
Difficulty Scenarios

Paul Roberts

9.1 INTRODUCTION

Difficulty is an aspect of games development that often gets left until the end of development. At which time there is panic because the game is too difficult, and some way is needed to make the AI play in such a way that it offers a challenge to the player, but is not so good that the player struggles to win. This chapter describes the approach taken to incorporate difficulty into the AI systems from an early stage, which was then expanded upon to create flexible difficulty and difficulty scenarios.

9.2 INCORPORATING DIFFICULTY

Difficulty should not be about the dumbing down of AI. Each agent in the game should make the best decision they can, given the information they have. If you do not give them enough information, they look stupid. Give them too much information and the AI is deemed to be cheating. The key here is for the AI to make the correct decision, so they do not look stupid, but their ability to enact their response is thwarted. In other words, they look incompetent rather than dumb. Imagine a stealth game where an AI guard is patrolling. The guard's field of view can simply be modified to allow the player to sneak past. The player will accept the agent not spotting them if the field of view is not too narrow, but what would be better is an agent that spots the player slightly late (narrowed field of view) and then responds by taking aim and firing, but the aim of the agent is not great, so they miss the target. Perhaps the agent also runs to trigger an alarm. The guard's run speed can also be reduced. This allows the AI to spot the player, make the correct response, miss when firing and be slow to trigger the alarm. In this scenario, the player is given the chance to avoid the guard, but if they fail, they have the opportunity to take out the threat, creating a more engaging encounter for the player, and one in which the AI does not look stupid.

One of the absolute worst ways of incorporating levels of difficulty into a game is to modify the AI on the player's side. For example, in a sports title, it is never fun for the ability of the player's team to be modified to make the opposition more difficult. The player will notice if their team is running slower or are now unable to make a catch that they were making in the previous match without any trouble. The player can see what is happening and the immersion is lost, along with it possibly the player. Instead, any modifications should be applied to the opposing AI. Even better, make any modifications to individual agents.

DOI: 10.1201/9781003323549-9

The example described highlights why it is important to consider AI difficulty early on. Imagine you have a maximum speed a player can run at and an agent on the player's team is set to this maximum, it then becomes difficult to have an opposing agent run faster without the physics looking broken. The game will have been continuously balanced throughout development and suddenly cutting down the speed of the player's agents will affect gameplay and possibly cause a whole host of unforeseen issues. Instead, by having a global maximum speed, one that looks and feels correct with the physics of the game, and then for agents to have a scale variable that is multiplied by this maximum, it is possible to modify the speed for all AI players on the team. It is also recommended to have a maximum scale that can be applied, which allows only the AI to go beyond. For example, if the maximum scale is set to 90%, then the remaining 10% can be used to scale for more difficult opponents. In the example of a sports title, the more difficult opponents can be faster because the highest range of speeds have been reserved, and the player's team do not feel like they have been unfairly modified.

This approach can be used for many player attributes beyond speed, and it is also possible to incorporate the same idea into all areas of information gathering for the AI. Areas such as AI awareness or threat analysis can incorporate a scaling factor and the field of view can be widened or shrunk based on a scale, as can a multitude of other areas. The AI still makes the best decision they can with the information they have, and they still react as quickly as they can, but you now have the ability to reduce their difficulty without them looking stupid. The difficulty of the AI, and thus the game, is now controllable through a collection of variables. If these are exposed to the design department, through onscreen UI or a spreadsheet, they can tweak those numbers and find the balance which works best for the game.

9.3   FLEXIBLE DIFFICULTY

Most games will have at least three levels of difficulty – Easy, Medium and Hard. This can be incorporated in a couple of ways. The first approach is to have a global scale for each difficulty level. When playing on a particular setting (Easy, Medium or Hard), simply multiply the maximum values by the scale for this difficulty setting. When individual agents require their own settings, they will multiply their scaler by the new (modified by difficulty scale) maximums. Alternatively, the second approach is to have a scaling factor for each area of the AI that has a maximum value. Then, multiply each one individually.

The second approach gives the most flexibility. Rather than the Easy difficulty dropping the scale of all areas by 50%, you can have different values per area. For example, modifying the speed of players by 50% can look ridiculous, but reducing the field of view by 50% looks fine. Table 9.1 gives an example of the AI areas and settings that could be applied in a sports title for a balanced game.

TABLE 9.1

Example AI Areas and Values for a Standard Game

Area Modifiable by the AI	Balanced Game
Attributes	75%
Positional awareness refresh rate (in seconds)	0.6
Field of view (in degrees)	90
Threat awareness weighting	80%
Pass accuracy	75%
Shot accuracy	70%
Time management	80%

The example values shown in Table 9.1 can be tweaked by designers until they get a good feel for the game and have it playing at a medium level of difficulty. With these settings, it is possible to then set the scaling values for each difficulty setting that will modify those for a standard game. Table 9.2 gives an example of how the settings in Table 9.1 could be modified for these different difficulty levels.

TABLE 9.2

Example Settings that Can Be Modified by Difficulty

	Easy	Medium	Hard
Attributes	−20%	−	+20%
Positional awareness	+60%	−	−100%
Field of view	−20%	−	+10%
Threat awareness	−10%	−	+10%
Pass accuracy	−30%	−	+20%
Shot accuracy	−40%	−	+30%
Time management	−20%	−	+10%

9.4 DIFFICULTY SCENARIOS

Adding some personality to a team (not to an individual player) is an interesting concept. In sports, teams can go on a winning streak where they play beyond what would be expected from the individual players, or maybe a good team has a slump and they lose their mojo, or maybe the coach gives the team a grilling at half time and in the second half the team responds. All of this can be done quite easily by expanding on the ideas already presented in this chapter.

Internally, there is no reason why there should only be three levels of difficulty. Exposing the player to the three levels is fine, but internally you could have more levels. Seven internal difficulty levels work well with the three (Easy, Medium and Hard) exposed levels. These internal levels could be called something like Very Easy, Easy, Moderately Easy, Medium, Moderately Hard, Hard and Very Hard. These internal settings should push the main setting to be slightly harder or easier.

It is not difficult to extrapolate the approach taken in the previous section to create seven levels of difficulty.

The reason for creating more levels of difficulty is to allow you to switch the levels at runtime without the player knowing. If the difficulty change is too great (i.e., Medium to Hard), the player will notice and feel cheated. Whereas changing from Medium to Moderately Hard is not such a large step. You can then switch from Moderately Hard to Hard and the player will accept the change. It just feels like the opposing team has got into a rhythm.

With these seven levels of difficulty, it is now possible to modify the difficulty before and during a game. The following scenarios all work well in a sports title.

9.4.1 Half Time Talk

At half time if the opponents are losing, or the score is even, the coach could give the team a pep talk that inspires them to play better. Whatever the external difficulty is set to, the difficulty setting is increased by one. For example, Easy (external) moves to Moderately Easy (internal), or Hard (external) changes to Very Hard (internal).

This should not guarantee the opponents a victory but should make them more difficult to play against in the second half. The human player should notice the change, and it helps if there is some gameplay indication that this has happened. For example, UI to inform the player or audio describing the coach's reaction.

9.4.2 Close Call

This scenario is a form of rubber banding. Whenever the human player's team takes the lead, the AI for the opposing team has its internal difficulty increased. When the scores become even again, the difficulty is dropped to its original (outward facing) difficulty setting.

This scenario keeps a match competitive without it being obvious that the opponents have suddenly got more difficult.

9.4.3 Momentum

If a team has momentum, possibly on a winning streak, this scenario will increase their difficulty. Stats are a big part of sports games, but so is psychology and game AI rarely brings this into the mix. This scenario allows the human player to look at the stats of the opposition, but then to see that they are on a winning streak, so to expect a fight.

9.4.4 Strong Defensive

Some teams are better at defending than they are at scoring, or vice versa. This scenario allows you to change the internal difficulty level when the human player's team has the ball. Simply increase the difficulty when on Defence and drop the difficulty when on Offence.

It would be possible to change the stats of the defensive players on a team and get the same effect, but using this approach is more flexible and allows for a straightforward way to get the same results. Changing the stats of multiple players takes a lot longer to do and balance than setting a scenario for a match.

9.5 CONCLUSION

Difficulty is something that often gets left until later in a project and then it is left to the AI team to find a way to make the AI easier to play against. By thinking about this early in the project, you can incorporate difficulty in such a way as to create interesting gameplay scenarios that improve the overall game and add some hidden depth. Although this chapter leaned on sports games for much of the discussion, there is no reason why these approaches cannot be incorporated into other genres. The approaches described in this chapter have all been implemented, worked as described and reduced the stress on the team when the spectre of difficulty raised its head.

10 Towards Controlled Design of Learning Agents for Automated Video Game Playing

Dominik Gotojuch

10.1 INTRODUCTION

Research into machine learning (ML)-driven game playing has led to several notable achievements with AI outperforming champion-level human players in complex video games, such as *Starcraft II* (Blizzard Entertainment, 2010), *Gran Turismo Sport* (Polyphony Digital, 2017) and *DOTA 2* (Valve Corporation, 2013) (Wurman et al., 2022). However, the impact of these milestones on commercial video game development has been limited thus far. Learning models have been effectively used in the agent AI of some select titles, including *Creatures* (Millennium Interactive, 1996), *Black & White* (Lionhead Studios, 2001), *Forza Motorsport* (Turn 10 Studios, 2005) and *Supreme Commander 2* (Gas Powered Games, 2010), but it is an uncommon practice (Miyake, 2017). While game industry research in the field is ongoing (Zhao et al., 2020; Sestini et al., 2022), reports from these studies are sparse, and their influence on published titles is yet to be seen. The complexity and risks of modern video game production make it difficult to justify using unreliable and expensive ML solutions (Zhang et al., 2016; Zhao et al., 2020), when approximations generated by *ad hoc* behaviour authoring methods deliver satisfactory results (Colledanchise & Ögren, 2018). Prior efforts to integrate learning models into agent AI workflows have not provided optimal solutions for professional game development, due to incompatibilities with industrial workflows (Politowski et al., 2022). A generalisable and non-disruptive approach to integrating learning into these workflows is required to address the requirements of game development and make it more accessible for application in future games. Context-guided agent design which potentially contributes towards this goal is presented in this chapter, along with its deployment procedure.

10.2 BACKGROUND

Because of their modularity, reactivity and scalability, behaviour trees (BTs) have become the de facto standard for implementing agent behaviours in video games (Yannakakis & Togelius, 2018). The transparent structure of BTs translates into a directed tree flow, updating the processing of a relevant traversal path through

DOI: 10.1201/9781003323549-10

the tree at a regular time interval by invoking logic implemented in tree nodes (Colledanchise & Ögren, 2018). To offset the limits and risks of manual behaviour authoring (Sagredo-Olivenza et al., 2019), dynamic restructuring and synthesis of BTs have been investigated (Colledanchise et al., 2018; Lim et al., 2010). This led to work on learning from demonstration by using recorded or live demonstrations to generate new or improved BT designs. While somewhat effective, these solutions suffer from limiting domain expert authoring control and obfuscating design transparency (Politowski et al., 2022).

Non-industry research into learning-driven game playing has been mostly focussed on General Game Playing, which uses screen scraping, rather than a game's internal representation, to learn a gameplay policy (Wurman et al., 2022). This approach incurs high training costs and is unlikely to be applicable in commercial game development within a reasonable time frame (Yannakakis & Togelius, 2018; Zhao et al., 2020). However, any black box learning model is unsuited for iterative development, as control over its design is limited (Zhang et al., 2016; Politowski et al., 2022). These constraints can be alleviated by integrating learning models into a BT (Colledanchise & Ögren, 2018; Zhang et al., 2016), thus allowing a partial transfer of robustness and modularity of a BT to learning models it contains (Colledanchise & Ögren, 2014). This was achieved by implementing a dedicated BT learning node, which embeds learning logic (Sagredo-Olivenza et al., 2017). While intuitive, the solution offers limited control over the learning node's execution and provides no controllable resolution, should the node fail to execute. Failure of execution may be defined as producing invalid output, such as undesired behaviour or violating execution safety, potentially compromising the execution flow of the entire agent's behaviour logic. Sprague and Ögren (2022) formally documented a safe, structural approach to tackle both these problems by embedding learning logic in a subtree, featuring *ad hoc* redundancy alongside learning logic.

10.3 CONTEXT-GUIDED AGENT DESIGN

10.3.1 OVERVIEW

To take advantage of the proliferation of the BT architecture in the game industry, context-guided agent design involves integrating learning with safety and performance guarantees into BT development workflows for agent AI. Human domain experts are expected to remain at the centre of the design process and retain as much control over the agent decision-making logic model as possible (Sagredo-Olivenza et al., 2017; Politowski et al., 2022). This could potentially decrease friction and the risks of using learning in runtime environments of commercial video games. Key concepts of the design are:

- **Context Guidance**: controlling behaviour flow through *ad hoc* authoring with a layered approach to separate the context of decision-making and action execution.

- **Safe Learning Integration**: directly integrating learning logic into a BT as subtrees, featuring a dedicated BT learning node, and ad hoc safety control logic.
- **Small-Scale Learning**: isolating the scope of learning for each learning model instance to its relevant, local context, to decrease training costs and increase output quality.

10.3.2 CONTEXT GUIDANCE

The hierarchical, subsumption architecture of a BT organically directs the flow of behaviour logic. By combining this inherent property of BTs with task decomposition similar to that of hierarchical reinforcement learning (RL), three context layers in a BT can be observed: *macro*, *proxy* and *micro* (Justesen et al., 2020). The *macro*layer represents strategic decision-making logic and occupies the top of the tree, while the *micro*layer contains low-level agent actions and is located at the bottom of the tree (Colledanchise et al., 2018; Colledanchise & Ögren, 2018). The optional *proxy* layer facilitates connections between the *macro*- and *micro*layers, if required. Such layering provides an organised structure for context-relevant positioning and flow control of learning subtrees. The context-guided structuring of the design is visualised in Image 10.1.

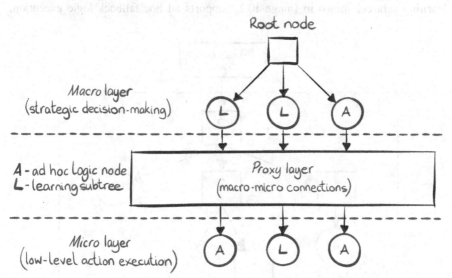

IMAGE 10.1 Context-guided architecture flow with a separation between *macro*–, *micro*- and *proxy* layers.

Macro- and *micro*layers can feature both ad hoc and learning logic, but if the *proxy* layer is present, it is expected to use ad hoc nodes exclusively to guarantee expert flow curation. The exact balancing of learning and ad hoc logic is left at the discretion of the designer, and the modularity of the outlined design allows for gradually scaling up the presence of learning subtrees.

Their development should begin with stub-like, ad hoc implementations. After the intended learning logic is put in place, the stub or its revised version becomes the worst-case, safety fallback execution path.

10.3.3 SAFE LEARNING INTEGRATION

Execution of learning logic is potentially unsafe and unreliable. Ad hoc safeguards and fallback logic are required to create performance and execution guarantees for integrated learning. In this case, reliability can be achieved by encapsulating learning models and ad hoc safety control logic in a single subtree, as discussed by Sprague and Ögren (2022). Before the learning node can run, the execution safety controller performs a series of designer-defined tests. In case of failure, the execution of the entire learning subtree is aborted. Otherwise, the performance safety controller logic conducts its own set of performance tests. Failure of performance testing results in triggering ad hoc fallback logic, followed by the conclusion of the subtree execution. If all tests are successful, the dedicated learning node (containing the actual learning logic) can be executed. Afterwards, the execution of the learning subtree is finalised.

The original proposal of Sprague and Ögren (2022) was modified to address two shortcomings of their design: lack of ad hoc fallback logic execution guarantees and limited scope of performance safety control. The revised composite flow of the learning subtree, shown in Image 10.2, supports ad hoc fallback logic execution,

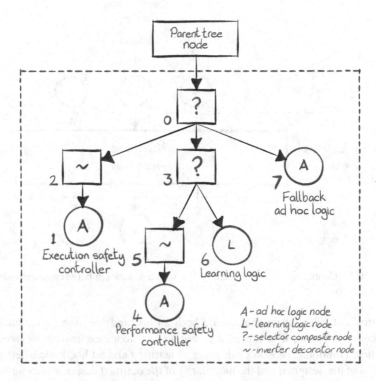

IMAGE 10.2   Learning subtree structure (node numbering indicates the order of execution).

following a failure of learning logic. Performance testing is structured to support multiple stability and safety tests, based on the concept of Lyapunov design methods for safety (Chow et al., 2018), instead of limiting it to a single-time response control test, as was the case in the original proposal. Any condition expected to invoke ad hoc fallback can be incorporated into the performance safety controller logic.

10.3.4 SMALL-SCALE LEARNING

Each learning subtree may operate independently, as an individual instance of learning logic, contained within its learning node. It is up to a human expert to assign the desired learning context to each subtree, in accordance with context-guided structuring of the BT. This procedure, inspired by automated task decomposition research (Justesen et al., 2020), should yield smaller and more specialised learning models, departing from monolithic model approaches. Benefits include increased modularity and design control, as well as a potential increase in flexibility of training and a decrease in its costs.

10.4 CONTEXT-GUIDED AGENT DEPLOYMENT

10.4.1 OVERVIEW

The deployment of a context-guided agent model instance is an iterative process of development-evaluation cycles, structured using the following steps, whose flow is depicted in Image 10.3:

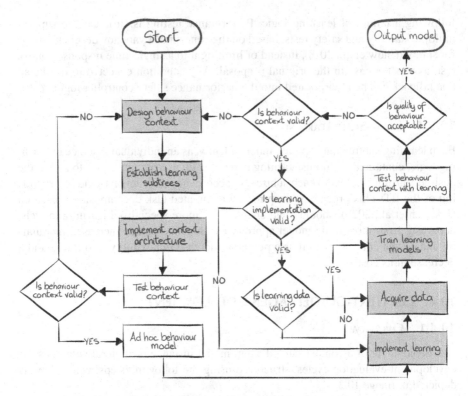

IMAGE 10.3   Context-guided design deployment workflow.

- Step 1: Design behaviour context
- Step 2: Establish learning subtrees
- Step 3: Implement context architecture
- Step 4: Implement learning
- Step 5: Acquire data
- Step 6: Train learning models

10.4.2   STEP 1: DESIGN BEHAVIOUR CONTEXT

First, the context of the intended behaviour flow must be identified, to inform the agent's AI design. By performing a requirements analysis of the target game environment with respect to the available action space and agent's goals, behaviour objectives can be mapped to the *macro*layer, selected actions to the *micro*layer and their connections to the *proxy* layer, if necessary. These assumptions can only be validated after the initial model is deployed. This may not be possible in the early stages of production, as complete knowledge of the game environment might not be available yet. In such a case, knowledge updates should be iteratively integrated into the design and expand the original scope of the behaviour context.

10.4.3 STEP 2: ESTABLISH LEARNING SUBTREES

Early design of the context guides ad hoc implementation of the behaviour flow but does not provide information about the inclusion of learning in the design. To incorporate learning into the agent's behaviour, designers need to identify flow segments that would benefit from being modelled with learning logic. Likely candidates include segments that fulfil any of the following conditions:

- Need to be highly adaptive
- Cannot be adequately represented using ad hoc structures, either due to the limitations of manually authored logic or the prohibitive complexity that arises when attempting to scale them up
- Are expected to produce imitative output, based on demonstration data

The decision to model a behaviour flow segment with learning should be supported by an informed selection of its learning policy generation method. Any individual technique compatible with context requirements is acceptable, but ensemble methods have been known to produce higher quality output if used effectively (Yannakakis & Togelius, 2018). The technique choice, in conjunction with context information, determines the data requirements for the target learning logic, and the scope of the follow-up technical work required.

10.4.4 STEP 3: IMPLEMENT CONTEXT ARCHITECTURE

Establishing a technical foundation of the behaviour context architecture involves BT flow structuring and implementing game environment-specific solutions to facilitate the flow of the behaviour context. These tasks may vary across different game environments and tools used, but the workflow remains the same:

- Implement functionality to interface with the game environment through BTs
- Implement ad hoc BT flow (*macro*-, *proxy*- and *micro*layers)
- Implement stubs of learning subtrees in the ad hoc BT flow
- Implement ad hoc fallback logic for each learning subtree stub

Once the implementation reaches a stage when evaluation becomes possible, an iterative cycle of testing and fine-tuning can begin. The implemented context architecture should be evaluated in the game's environment, with respect to the identified behaviour goals and functional considerations. If the produced behaviour is valid and representative of the intended behaviour context, an ad hoc agent model can be declared stable. Otherwise, the architecture needs to be revised by repeating one or all Steps 1–3, until the issues are resolved.

The output of this step is expected to be a BT-based implementation of the behaviour context outlined in Steps 1 and 2, including stub versions of learning subtrees. This ad hoc version of the behaviour flow will constitute the worst-case execution scenario, in terms of performance and quality.

10.4.5 STEP 4: IMPLEMENT LEARNING

At this point, the stable ad hoc agent model is already equipped with stub learning subtrees, which are still devoid of the actual learning logic. The learning logic, expressed within dedicated learning nodes, needs to be implemented and inserted into each learning subtree. The specifics of a dedicated learning node implementation will depend on a local set of technical factors, including the project architecture, tools used and the implementation of the game environment. In some cases, a single-node implementation will suffice, for instance, if the same learning technique is to be used across many learning subtrees. More complex scenarios would likely require a range of learning node specialisations, which could address local training and inference requirements.

10.4.6 STEP 5: ACQUIRE DATA

Different learning methods have varied data requirements. In some cases, such as with RL techniques, data will be derived from training-time observations of the agent, and as such would have already been covered by the learning implementation in Step 4. If that is the case, Step 5 can be skipped. Otherwise, appropriate data acquisition and transformation procedures will be necessary to prepare valid datasets for use in target learning models. It is beyond the scope of this workflow to explore this process, but it can be as simple, or as complex, as required. Input datasets must be usable in the target game environment and be compatible with the policy generation strategy of the relevant learning subtrees.

10.4.7 STEP 6: TRAIN LEARNING MODELS

The final step of the workflow focuses on iteratively training learning models. Each iteration of training produces an output agent model to be evaluated in the context of the game environment, to determine if its behaviours are valid and of satisfactory quality in terms of the outlined behaviour context. Multiple passes of training are likely since revisioning of the parameterisation and timing of training will impact the generated policy. It is recommended to conduct the agent model inference evaluation in the target game environment. Validation of behaviour context from Step 3 should be repeated in Step 6. If any issues with the underlying context are detected, Steps 1–3 might need to be repeated to resolve any problems identified. The evaluation of the quality of the behaviour is in many ways subjective and requires an assessment from a human expert. To complement that assessment, data-driven measures should be used to quantitatively compare different agent output model revisions. This enables automating of the iterative training-evaluation cycles and potentially driving their revisioning using evolutionary algorithms, to procedurally improve the output model. Quantitative comparison may focus solely on output fitness, but ultimately, a holistic perspective of the game context-derived measures is likely to be relevant for output quality. Quality concerns could lead to repeating all or some of Steps 4–6 to improve the learning implementation, its input datasets or policy training. After the trained gameplay policy reaches the desired quality level, the context-guided agent behaviour model is ready to be deployed in the target game environment.

10.5 CONCLUSION

The design described in this chapter demonstrates a game industry workflow-compatible approach to integrating learning logic into BT-based agent AI behaviour authoring. The concepts presented need to be applied and tested in commercial video game environments, to provide real, industry-viable scenarios of learning integrations. To that effect, the author is currently experimenting with the deployment of the proposed design in the game *60 Seconds!* (Robot Gentleman, 2015) to train game playing and automated playtesting agents based on skill and style player personas. Successful integration of learning into game agent AI and its incorporation into industry workflows has the potential to solve game playing and playtesting problems, where simpler or manual solutions would not suffice. However, it is not a replacement for ad hoc authoring and more importantly for human experts involved in creating AI.

REFERENCES

Chow, Y., Nachum, O., Duenez-Guzman, E., and Ghavamzadeh, M. (2018) A Lyapunov-based approach to safe reinforcement learning. *32nd Conference on Neural Information Processing Systems (NeurIPS 2018)*, Montreal.

Colledanchise, M., and Ögren, P. (2014) How Behavior Trees Modularize Robustness and Safety in Hybrid Systems. *Proceedings of IEEE/RSJ International Conference on Intelligent Robots and Systems*, Chicago, IL, June 2014, pp. 1482–1488.

Colledanchise, M., and Ögren, P. (2018) *Behavior Trees in Robotics and AI: An Introduction*. CRC Press, Boca Raton, FL.

Colledanchise, M., Parasuraman, R., and Ögren, P. (2018) Learning of behavior trees for autonomous agents. *IEEE Transactions on Computational Intelligence and AI in Games*, vol. 11, Issue 2, pp. 183–189.

Justesen, N., Bontrager, P., Togelius, J., and Risi, S. (2020) Deep Learning for video game playing. *IEEE Transactions on Games*, vol. 12, Issue 1, pp. 1–20.

Lim, C., Baumgarten, R., and Colton, S. (2010) Evolving behaviour trees for the commercial game DEFCON. *European Conference on the Applications of Evolutionary Computation*, Istanbul Technical University, Istanbul, 2010, pp. 100–110.

Miyake, Y. (2017) Current status of applying artificial intelligence in digital games, in Nakatsu, R., Rauterberg, M., and Ciancarini, P. (eds.) *Handbook of Digital Games and Entertainment Technologies*. Springer, Singapore, pp. 253–347.

Politowski, C., Guéhéneuc, Y-G., and Petrillo, F. (2022) Towards automated video game testing: still a long way to go. *IEEE ACM 6th International Workshop on Games and Software Engineering*, Pittsburgh, PA, May 2022.

Sagredo-Olivenza, I., Gómez-Martín, P.P., Gómez-Martín, M.A., and González-Calero, P.A. (2017) Combining neural networks for controlling non-player characters in games, in Rojas, I., Joya, G., Catala, A. (eds.) *Advances in Computational Intelligence*. Lecture Notes in Computer Science, Springer, pp. 695–705.

Sagredo-Olivenza, I., Gómez-Martín, P.P., Gómez-Martín, M.A., and González-Calero, P.A. (2019) Trained behaviour trees: programming by demonstration to support AI game designers. *IEEE Transactions on Games*, vol. 11, pp. 5–14.

Sestini, A., Bergdahl, J., Tollmar, K., Badganov, A.D., and Gisslén, L. (2022) Towards informed design and validation assistance in computer games using Imitation Learning. *Conference on Neural Information Processing Systems (NeurIPS)*, New Orleans Convention Center, New Orleans, LA, 2022.

Sprague, I.S., and Ögren, P. (2022) Adding neural network controllers to behavior trees without destroying performance guarantees. *IEEE 61st Conference on Decision and Control*, Cancun, Mexico, 2022.

Wurman, R.P., Barrett, S., Kawamoto, K., MacGlashan, J., Subramanian, K., Walsh, T.J., Capobianco, R., Devlic, A., Eckert, F., Fuchs, F., Gilpin, L., Khandelwal, P., Kompella, V., Lin, H., MacAlipine, P., Oller, D., Seno, T., Sherstan, C., Thomure, M.D., Aghabozorgi, H., Barret, L., Douglas, R., Whitehead, D., Dürr, P., Stone, P., Spranger, M., and Kitano, H. (2022) Outracing champion Gran Turismo drivers with deep reinforcement learning. *Nature*, vol. 602, pp. 223–228.

Yannakakis, G.N., and Togelius, J. (2018) *Artificial Intelligence and Games*. Springer, Switzerland.

Zhang, Q., Quanjun, Y., and Xu, K. (2016) Towards an integrated learning framework for behavior modeling of adaptive CGFs. *Proceedings of the IEEE 9th International Symposium on Computational Intelligence and Design*, Hangzhou, China, 10–11 December 2016, vol. 2, pp. 7–12.

Zhao, Y., Borovikov, I., Beirami, A., Rupert, J., Somers, C.S, Harder, J., de Mesentier Silva, F., Kolen, J., Pinto, J., Pourabolghasem, R., Chaput, H., Pestrak, J., Sardari, M., Lin, L., Aghdaie, N., and Zaman, K. (2020) Winning is not everything: enhancing game development with intelligent agents. *IEEE Transactions on Games*, vol. 12, Issue 2, June 2020, pp. 199–212.

11 Utility Systems for High-Level Group Management

Steve Bilton

11.1 INTRODUCTION

In the context of decision-making, utility refers to the *value* of a given action. As such, a utility system makes decisions by scoring all available actions and then executing the action with the greatest utility, producing what is essentially the *best* option available. This is a useful and well-documented technique that can be used to determine which action to perform at the individual level and can often result in emergent group behaviours (Graham, 2013).

The main advantage of this methodology is that it requires minimal authoring. Adding a new action does not usually require knowledge of other actions beyond the relative scores they produce, as the control flow between actions does not need to be specified. The trade-off is the loss of control that results by offloading the work from the developer to the system, it becomes more difficult to enforce an action order.

Instead of relying on the emergence of group behaviour, this chapter will explore using utility systems to manage groups of actors directly. This will allow us to determine the behaviour that individuals of a group should be exhibiting at any given point in time, allowing for more well-defined group behaviour in situations where cohesion is important. This high-level behavioural control can be applied to a variety of genres and has been proven in both management simulation and stealth action titles.

11.2 UTILITY SYSTEMS FOR GROUP MANAGEMENT

One clear use case for controlling a large group of individual actors that must act cohesively is in the management simulation genre. It is common for games of this type to involve many tasks that need performing in the world and many actors that could perform them, with a system that must allocate actors to tasks in an efficient manner.

In this scenario, the player typically takes a relatively hands-off approach when it comes to assigning actors to tasks, although they are likely to want to influence decision-making. Rather, they will request tasks to be performed (or construct objects that have associated tasks, such as a theme park shop that requires manning) and hire actors with varying skills that they wish to perform them. In addition to this, actors often have their own desires, such as adequate food and rest – things that are

DOI: 10.1201/9781003323549-11

not beneficial to the player but are required as part of the challenge of creating an environment that minimises this *wasted* time.

These problems lend themselves naturally to a utility system. You can continuously determine the utility between each actor and task pairing, and then assign out the pairings in order at the end of each evaluation cycle. This provides automated 'ant-farm'-type behaviour where the environment requires minimum player oversight, freeing them to make more high-level decisions within the game as they are relatively unburdened by micro-management.

11.3   UTILITY TASKS

A task is defined as a self-contained logical construct that is made up of two parts:

1. The utility function, which takes an actor state and produces a value that is a combination of the priority of the task for the current world state and the suitability of the actor.
2. The behaviour of any actor assigned to it, which specifies how an actor assigned to the task must complete it. The complexity of the behaviour can vary considerably, as it is highly context-dependent, but is typically a graph of atomic actions that need to be performed or a behaviour tree.

When determining a utility function, you must consider not only which tasks are preferable to perform over others, but also which individuals are best placed to perform them – and the relationship between the two.

This is highly context-dependent, but a starting point is often the distance between the actor and the task. For example, you may prefer Task A is completed over Task B all things being equal, but Task B may be very close to an actor and Task A very far away.

Similarly, it is often a good idea to encourage tasks whose conditions are more difficult to satisfy by giving them higher utility. This not only helps to produce a more even spread of executed tasks but also helps ensure that rare tasks are able to be executed at all.

Let us take what appears to be a relatively simple example, a fire that needs putting out. There are multiple considerations here: Do you prefer actors near a fire extinguisher or near the fire? If the latter, do you prefer fire extinguishers near the fire or near the actor? What if the agent already holds a fire extinguisher? Should you hold a task for every fire and assign them out, even if they are in proximity, or should you group them together into single tasks, or lower the priority if nearby tasks are already assigned to actors? Does the answer to that depend on how far the actors and extinguishers are from the fires, whether they are likely to spread, and how long an extinguisher can be used before it runs out?

As you can see, the complications can quickly spiral out of control, so it is often wise to start with the simplest implementation and see how that *feels*, rather than trying to create an optimal result – more complexity slows evaluation and makes understanding the system more difficult for both players and creators. In practice, simpler implementations are often sufficient and even preferred.

Care should also be taken to ensure it makes sense to create a task for a behaviour. While it can be very tempting to put as much logic under the same system as possible, using it to add a task that a single actor is required to perform immediately (with higher priority than any 'normal' task in the utility system) results in slower reactions and needless additional evaluation time. For example, tasks such as 'run away from grenade' or 'move immediately to a point requested by the player' should usually be handled separately, or, at least, the system should treat them differently for faster response times.

11.3.1 Multi-Actor Tasks

It is possible to expand tasks further, such as a task that requires multiple actors to complete, where each role available to an actor may be required or optional. A simple example of this would be unloading a truck: A required role could be the actual unloading, with an optional role for conversing with the unloader.

Despite the more expensive evaluation required due to increased combinations, the process is the same as with a single-actor task. You are simply testing every actor against every role within a task and scoring it accordingly. The main change to the assignment algorithm is when it comes to tasks that have multiple required roles, as you must ensure all can be filled before assigning out any individual actor. This is often a worthwhile addition for relatively little effort, as whether a task has multiple roles or not is entirely at the discretion of the task writer.

This added complexity allows us to use the system for further applications, such as enemy tactical behaviour in shooters. It can be used for both high-level core behavioural group management (such as which members of a group to advance on the player position and when they should do so) and short-lived gameplay *moments* like the Systemic Scripts created for *Splinter Cell: Blacklist* at Ubisoft Toronto (Walsh, 2014).

Creating tasks that involve communication and cohesion between groups of actors is nicely encapsulated in the system, as all the information necessary for managing such coordination is within the task. It allows for actor relationships to be clearly defined for the duration of the task, so group members can be aware of each other and what they are (or should be) doing, branching as required to handle player interaction, bringing in new members as required, and ejecting members as they become untenable.

Creating visible (and audible) group behaviours such as this is a highly effective way of making actors appear coordinated, as players who see cohesive behaviour are inclined to believe it happens more often than it actually does. Of course, that is not to say you cannot have tasks that only require a single actor in a tactical shooter, such as manning a searchlight or repairing a radio – but the addition of multiple actors allows for many more options, and to keep the various uses under a single umbrella system.

11.3.2   PLAYER-CENTRIC UTILITY FUNCTIONS

There is a lot of value in making utility functions take the player into account in addition to the world state. For example, using the earlier scenario, if a player observes a fire start in a room, then they typically expect to see an onscreen actor going to get a fire extinguisher, rather than an off-screen actor that is closer to the extinguisher doing so, even though the outcome for the player is better in the latter case. As such, prioritising visible responsiveness is often the best strategy.

Similarly, when tasks are used to create *interesting* rather than *required* behaviour, such as back-to-back searching, then it is usually worth prioritising tasks that the player is likely to see. This can be implemented by adjusting utility functions (or, indeed, dynamic creation and removal of tasks) based on the player's current or anticipated position, or whether relevant locations and involved actors are currently visible. For player-created tasks, such as construction requests in a management simulation, you can very simply adjust the utility function to prefer these over background tasks as well as increasing the utility if you believe the player is getting impatient waiting for it. The hard part, of course, is accurately determining what a player is *thinking* just by observing their actions.

11.3.3   ACTOR TASK SWITCHING

An actor will naturally change tasks whenever the utility function finds a more appropriate option for them, and another actor may steal their task at any point if their utility function scores higher. As such, it is usually valuable to add some stickiness to the utility function for a task that an actor is already assigned to.

It can be advantageous to consider *how* tasks are switched between actors, as there is usually some traversal involved from the actor to a task. As such, it can be useful to have the concept of *pending* actors for task roles, so swapping out only occurs when the new actor arrives and at a point in the task that is safe for the actor to exit. This can be useful when manning a piece of equipment, as it can be frustrating for a player if equipment such as a guard post is left needlessly unattended – even more so if other tasks rely on it being filled, such as a food counter with a required server and optional actors being served.

It is also important to take care to avoid cycling between tasks, which can easily occur if multiple competing tasks have a utility function that can change positively *and* negatively over time; a simple error case would be using Euclidean distance for calculating the distance to a task where the actor then ends up on a traversal path that takes them farther from the task position. This sort of problem can be difficult to eliminate entirely, so a temporary history of previously performed tasks and timestamps is valuable.

It is also generally preferable that a task is at least partially performed, if possible, as it can look foolish to begin something and then immediately stop. A time limit before willingly exiting is often helpful.

If an actor has no task available for them to perform, then they will fall back to their default behaviour outside of the utility system. This could be a simple wandering idle or a more complicated behaviour collection, but unless there are always open tasks around for every actor irrespective of state, then an actor having no task assigned will need to be handled.

11.4 PERFORMANCE CONSIDERATIONS

Performance of a system that effectively tests every actor against every role within every task naturally involves touching a lot of data and performing a lot of operations. Given the need for timely assignments, particularly when a task is no longer applicable, performance must be considered from an early stage. It is useful to break a task system into three distinct stages: data caching, evaluation, and assignment.

Data caching involves making expensive calculations that are likely to be required multiple times (such as a task priority based on the world state, independent of which actor is assigned), as well as determining which actors and tasks are to be evaluated. This is important because it is possible for tasks or actors to be added and removed mid-evaluation, but you do not want to handle these changes mid-evaluation. Typically, this can be performed threaded in a single frame but could be time-sliced if required.

Evaluation is the costliest process but can also be threaded and time-sliced. It can be difficult to find the most effective way to break up the evaluation such that it is spread evenly across multiple threads and frames, but doing so ensures consistency in the time taken within a frame and the total frame count.

Finally, the assignment takes the long list of task-actor pairs and assigns them out in order. This is easy to time-slice but cannot be easily threaded. Fortunately, it is not normally too onerous, as sorting even a large list is usually relatively quick, and assignment is typically inexpensive. At every stage, it is important to try and reduce the number of tests that need to be performed. It is critically important to perform cheap tests first and remove tasks or actors from lists wherever possible. This may not help the worst case, but it makes a dramatic difference to the average case, which is much more common. This includes sanity-checking the cached data every frame to ensure it is still valid to perform tests, removing tasks that have been assigned from the pairing list during the assignment, and excluding actors from jobs they could not possibly perform based on their current task as the priority will *never* be sufficiently high. Ultimately, it is more beneficial to fail to evaluate a task or an actor due to changing circumstances than it is to try and handle the change – everything will be re-evaluated next cycle anyway.

Continuous evaluation of every pairing in the system allows us to context switch, but if this is not required (such as a task being so sticky an actor may never leave it until completed), then it becomes possible to exclude actors from evaluation entirely if the task is still valid for that actor.

Similarly, there are trade-offs between speed and quality when it comes to expensive operations. Even if such operations are deferred, large numbers of line-of-sight tests (or worse, pathfinding queries) can result in the total frame count becoming far too large. As such, it is often necessary to avoid these tests, and unfortunately, this can sometimes be noticed (particularly when it involves taking a long route to a task when another, closer task would have been more appropriate). There are mitigations for this, such as performing a Breadth First Search from the task to estimate actors more accurately at short range, but as with most AI evaluation, you will often end up having to select sub-optimal, but faster, operations as the actor count increases.

11.5 COMMUNICATION OF TASK ASSIGNMENT

It is important to be able to communicate why a task has been assigned to an actor in any given processing cycle, as this is incredibly useful for debugging unexpected behaviour. This information can also be made player-facing, which is particularly useful in management titles as it allows players to better understand how to tailor their set-up in order to get their desired results.

The difficulty comes from logging the large amount of information that is processed. It is not difficult to show the calculated utility function results of the current cycle, as this must be stored anyway as part of processing. However, showing how that utility has been calculated requires a fair amount of data to be stored and, typically, custom code on a per-task basis.

As such, it is necessary to be strategic about the information presented. Of particular use is some information as to why an actor cannot be assigned to a task. A commonly identified problem is a failure to assign a task that the observer believes *should* be assigned. Showing this information, along with the calculated utilities of actor–task pairs, is generally enough to debug many problems at a relatively low cost.

It is useful to allow this information to be filtered by both actor and task, ideally by selection in the world, as it is rare that a visual dump of all the data is particularly valuable and this encourages those not involved in the system, particularly QA, to better understand what is happening and send through the pertinent information.

11.6 DESIGN AUTHORING

Designers are inevitably going to require some control of the values fed into a utility function, as well as some control over the creation and removal of tasks. For example, a level designer of a tactical shooter may want to create or remove 'patrol' tasks based on where the player is currently situated in order to encourage NPCs to patrol nearer to the player's position. Functionality can be provided for these requirements easily, and there is little reason not to include them.

Similarly, it is not unusual for a designer to want to directly assign a task to actors, particularly when loading the level, and this is not difficult to achieve. It is, however, often wiser to simply 'encourage' actors to take tasks by adding optional designer weighting to the utility function for both a task and an actor–task pair. By not enforcing the assignment, you are able to be more adaptive to circumstances, the designer may not have considered, such as enforcing task assignment when a player enters a trigger volume at the front of a building. For example, it does not make much sense for actors to be assigned a task if they have already travelled far away from the task's trigger volume. In such instances, a change of priority will encourage them to take it if they are still reasonably nearby, but not if there are more appropriate tasks to be performed.

Another useful addition for designers, albeit a more difficult one to implement, is the ability to create semi-scripted tasks, such as a generic 'patrol' task that takes a route around the environment that can be specified by a level designer. They are often necessary, however, as some degree of hand-authoring often produces better results than environmental analysis alone and it is not unusual for designers to want to carefully script moments of gameplay that are still triggered systemically.

One way to provide this functionality is to introduce the concept of task templates, which are used to construct tasks with optional custom data. Using the patrol example, the task template could take a patrol route per actor role within a task, enabling the creation of multiple tasks within the system which are functionally identical but involve using a different patrol route.

This injection of data into a template can also be generated on the fly, rather than being authored, which allows for highly dynamic behaviour. So, again using the patrol example, you could generate a patrol between the last known locations of a player in order to apply pressure in those areas, encouraging the player to try and advance from another direction.

11.7 CONCLUSION

Utility systems can be a valuable tool for managing large numbers of agents in a world with many activities that they could perform. This chapter has demonstrated the flexibility of such a system by detailing how it could be used to manage group behaviours in both management and tactical action games, which have very different behavioural requirements and would otherwise require complicated and inflexible hand-authored solutions.

The common thread for games that may benefit from the complexity of a utility system is how systemic they are – group control is relatively straightforward when it is highly authored but becomes more difficult to manage as the problem space expands.

This is a system that benefits most from being able to temporarily take control of individuals to perform interesting behaviour, then relinquishing them once this behaviour is performed. While it can be used for overall tactical control, it shines when performing relatively short-lived behaviour from a selection of possible options, creating visually interesting moments for the player to observe, and hopefully encouraging them to believe the AI are coordinating much more frequently than they are.

Conversely, this can be overly heavyweight in situations where you either have high levels of authoring such that systemic results are unnecessary or in situations where an optimal assignment of tasks is not necessary. In those instances, tasks do not necessarily need a coordinator, and it is almost certainly simpler to do more *ad hoc* assignment on an individual basis (or, for groups, by mutual agreement).

REFERENCES

Graham, D. (2013) An introduction to utility theory. In *Game AI Pro*. CRC Press, Edited by Steve Rabin, Boca Raton, FL, pp. 113–126.

Walsh, M. (2014) Modelling AI perception and awareness in splinter cell: Blacklist. *Game Developers Conference 2014*, San Francisco, CA.

12 Machine Learning-Based Automated Cinematography for Games

Phil Carlisle

12.1 INTRODUCTION

Games often want to be more *cinematic*, and the tools available for games' development are becoming more functionally capable of producing cinematic scenes. However, the creation of cinematic cut-scene content is still largely a hand-authored labour-intensive aspect of development. That, coupled with the relative lack of definition for what "cinematic" actually means, places a significant burden on smaller developers. The approach outlined in this chapter relies on an ensemble of machine learning (ML) models to develop procedural content generation tools for Unreal Engine for use in the sequencer interface.

12.2 WHAT IS A CUT-SCENE?

A cut-scene is defined as a series of edited camera sequences cut together to emulate the same overall effect as traditional cinematographic camera editing. Generally, it involves setting up a scene, actors, lighting, and camera movements to achieve a particular look. Most often, it disables player input during the playback of the scene so that the experience is mostly that of traditional cinema but played back within the game engine.

The aim is to replace a lot of the hand editing required currently with the Unreal Engine sequencer toolset when creating cinematic cut-scene content, with something that is more akin to a recommendation system. A ML approach is adopted where an initial scene set-up is outlined in brief, and then different compositions of the scene are automatically generated and offered to the user via a selection interface.

12.3 CINEMATOGRAPHY

There are a few conventions that have been adopted by film over the years. The aim of this chapter is to outline an approach taken to encoding the conventions of film within a ML model. The model learns the distribution of shot layout parameters with respect to the previous shot in a given scene, leading to an approach akin to a

DOI: 10.1201/9781003323549-12

recommender system. The model suggests the next n most likely shot configurations of a scene given the previous shot from which the user can select. Before this, it is important to declare some terminology used in cinematography.

12.3.1 MOVIE

A film/movie/video is defined as an ordered sequence of scenes, composed of shots, which are themselves composed of individual images (frames).

12.3.2 SCENE

A scene is a notional collection of shots across a specific aspect of the story. For example, a scene where two characters are drinking and talking in a bar, where the scene has multiple different viewpoints expressed in different shots, but the scene itself encompasses all the shots that make up this phase of the story.

12.3.3 SHOT

A shot is simply the sequence of images recorded via a given camera for a number of frames. Typically, this involves choices like camera lens, lighting, scene composition, and framing. You can think of the shot as the main unit of editing, with shot length in frames and shot timing and position in a scene being important attributes. An important feature of a shot is that the composition expressed within the sequence of frames can change over time. For the purposes of this discussion, everything will be discussed as though it is relative to the camera. For example, a character can enter the shot from the right (of the camera) and exit to the left (of the camera) over the duration of a shot.

12.3.4 THE PROSE CINEMATOGRAPHY LANGUAGE

A cinematography domain-specific language called PROSE (Ronfard et al., 2015) is used to define a given scene and set of shot transitions. PROSE defines a context-free grammar (CFG), which allows the definition of a given sequence of shots with respect to a given camera. Rather than give specifics like lens specifications and camera fields of view, PROSE suggests a limited set of shot types and transitions.

12.3.5 THE MOVIE NET DATASET

For a ML model to *learn* something, it typically must be given a lot of examples of the things it is trying to learn the distribution of. In this case, an existing dataset can be adopted and extended, which has collated information from 1,100 movies. The Movie Net dataset (Huang et al., 2020) and associated codebase can be accessed via the github (https://movienet.github.io/). The dataset itself consists of movies highly rated on IMDB with information on scene and shot start–end frame boundaries, bounding box detections for individual actors, subtitle and script information that is temporally aligned with the shot detection, and more.

12.4   MOVIE TIMELINES AS SPATIO-TEMPORAL GRAPHS

There have been previous examples of graph-based structures constructed from Movies. An example is the MovieGraphs dataset (Vicol et al., 2018), where a graph was constructed to describe key scenes in a variety of movies. A different approach is adopted here, by transforming the existing data of the MovieNet dataset into a series of spatio-temporal graphs. The general approach of the MovieNet dataset is to take each movie and perform a set of individual ML model feature extractions on it. So, for instance, applying a human object detector model on each shot to extract the bounding box of the actor. The MovieNet data is not supplied in graph form, so this must be constructed into a graph representation from the MovieNet annotated data. Additional ML models are applied to determine head and body poses from the frames supplied in the dataset. The bounding boxes and the body pose information are used to determine the PROSE values for things like facing directions and distance to the camera.

One important aspect of any understanding of film is that it has movement, both within the view of the camera (actors moving around relative to the camera) and the movement of the camera itself. This change needs to be captured in any system that seeks to understand the structure of a movie.

The approach here is to derive a series of graphs, connected in time via a timeline such that changes are stored in graph features over time. So, as properties of graph nodes (the position of an actor in the frame) change over time, it can be encoded to the node that represents the actor. The presence or absence of a node depicts that particular actor or object is not visually present in a scene.

This culminates in a series of graphs which depict the scene at any given frame, constructed by introducing a series of "key" graphs much like keyframes are used in animation or *keyframes* are included in video compression algorithms. The concept is to store at some regular interval a full graph and then represent changes in between keyframe graphs as simple changes in the timeline. This way you can reconstruct the graph for each frame by looking at the previous keyframe graph and then stepping through the changes since that frame and modifying the graph with any changes until the current frame. For example, adding and removing new nodes and edges, property updates on existing nodes, and the like. This way, a relatively sparse data structure is maintained but also allows for the capture of fine per-frame details as they are considered important.

The keyframe interval for graph construction is determined by constructing an initial full graph-per-frame and then adaptively removing unmodified graph nodes, whilst maintaining a maximum distance to a keyframe graph. You can control how far each edited graph is from a full keyframe graph, given the volume of graph edits in the given frame sequence in the overall timeline. The aim is to reduce the duplication inherent in graphs where there are unchanging elements. For example, a static object is unlikely to change unless given an impulse via another object.

The graph frames are stored in the OpenTimelineIO format (http://opentimeline. io/), where each shot is stored as a separate clip and each clip has each frame within it stored as metadata to the clip in NetworkX format, stored as a json object. A clip-per-shot is stored using the shot boundaries previously determined using the

Movienet pipeline tools. This relies on the PyShotDetect library to detect shot boundaries, but the essence is that a number of algorithms are used to determine changes in camera/lighting/scene composition. An OpenTimelineIO '.otio' file is constructed such that each clip in the timeline represents a shot detection boundary, this clip is then used to process the contents for the shot. The initial frame of each shot is determined to be a keyframe and a NetworkX graph is stored as metadata for the clip. This graph is stored as json format data within the metadata of the '.otio' file and can be parsed by the NetworkX python graph reading library.

Each frame, any changes to this graph structure are stored in NetworkX compatible json "frames" until a keyframe limit is reached, at which point another whole-graph NetworkX structure is stored. In order to make parsing for a series of shots more performant, all frames are analysed and stored as a dictionary of entities that appear in the series. In this manner, we're able to runtime cache all important features such as actors and simply enable/disable them in scenes where they are present.

Thus, we have a timeline which contains N clips, one per shot. Each shot has a keyframe graph as its first frame, then subsequent frames can have either partial change list-style graphs, or whole graphs depending on whether they are designated as keyframes or not. The graphs themselves can be of arbitrary complexity, which depends on the complexity of the cinematography and the purpose of the analysis.

12.4.1 What Is in a Graph?

An example graph for cinematography might contain elements such as:

- What actors are visible in the scene?
  - Where are they in the frame?
  - Where are the vertical centre lines of their bounding boxes?
  - How far away are they from the camera?
  - Which direction are they facing?
  - Are they looking towards the camera or at an angle?
  - Are they moving, if so, in which direction?
- Are there any props in the scene?
  - If so, where are they?
- Are the actors looking at or interacting with the props?
- Are the props moving?

These values can be presented as a graph encoded as an expansion of a CFG that is defined within the PROSE language. To generate the graph, you can use a ML model to learn the probabilities of a graph expansion for a given node when a set of criteria are presented to construct a scene. This is like the Meta-Sim2 architecture used for the generation of Unreal Engine driving scenes (Devaranjan et al., 2020).

The probability of any of the PROSE grammar rules being true is a function of the context (what is known about the scene, such as how many actors are required, or the subject of the scene) and the graph structure previously expanded. In essence, you treat the generation as a series of graph expansions, each one adding more information to the graph until you reach a terminal where no further expansions are possible.

To give a practical demonstration, consider the following scene. Two people are sitting at a bar, the camera is a medium shot of both characters who are equally in the frame. One of the actors (a female) is facing the camera. The other (a male, possibly a love interest) is attempting to appease the female, as in a prior scene, the female had seen the male with another woman.

If you have the partial graph as seen in Image 12.1, what would be considered for the next node expansion probability?

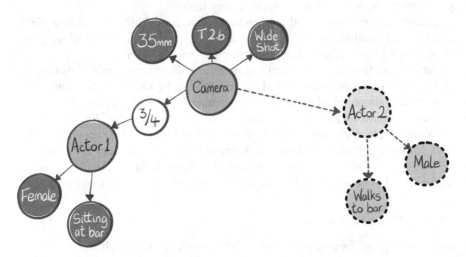

IMAGE 12.1 A simple graph representation of a scene where a woman sits at a bar facing the camera and a man approaches to enact dialogue – dashes represent potential node expansions.

From the scene context, we know that there are two characters in the scene, so the probability of expanding the graph with another actor would be high. Imagine that the graph expansion maximum probability is that another actor should be added to the scene, and then the proceeding graph expansion would be related to that actor's properties. In Image 12.1, it can be seen that multiple graph expansions are likely for properties of the second actor. Things like where they are in the scene, what direction they are facing, what age and sex they are, and the like.

Now with a mechanism for constructing probable graphs as a series of graph expansion probabilities, the discussion needs to turn to determining the probabilities in the first place.

A graph neural network (GNN) is used for this. GNNs are a flexible method of learning across graph representations. In this implementation, the Pytorch Geometric API (https://github.com/pyg-team/pytorch_geometric) was used to derive a graph attention network trained to learn the probabilities of graph expansions.

At model training time, you can simply load the OpenTimelineIO timeline for a given movie and parse the information for each shot in the movie. In essence, the GNN learns a matrix of probabilities given a set of input node values (the graph structure to this point) and the set of mask values. The mask allows you to invalidate the potential for expanding a node where it would break the grammar constraints. For example, the determination of the gender of an actor only makes sense in the context of having previously expanded that an actor node was placed. Similarly, expanding a prop in the graph should mask out the possibility of gender properties being returned. At the top level of the graph, the expansion probabilities are less constrained with this masked context. As the graph expands, the context becomes clearer, and fewer possibilities need to be considered. You can think of the masking process as a gating mechanism to maintain the structure of the grammar used to construct the graph. Once the probabilities are learnt, you have effectively learnt the distribution of movie properties and structure for a given input scenario; thus, allowing you to sample from that distribution to recreate a new graph.

One important feature of this graph expansion approach is that you must be able to expand multiple alternative graph proposals. You do this to supply the user of the system with valid options rather than a strict output. This means that you need to present the different output generations in a manner that allows the user to select between them. Whilst this is an ongoing area of research, our approach is to generate multiple matching outputs as top-K entries (K = 3 is a good default) and allow the user to select quickly between the matches before deciding on an edit. To facilitate this, you render the potentially selected outputs in a selection-overlay material colour to differentiate it from existing scene content. The final step once the model has produced output is that the user accepts one of the top-k choices and this is finally instantiated into the scene and the corresponding sequence. To do this is a simple matter of extending the existing Unreal Engine sequencer API based on some Python code present in the engine.

12.5 CONCLUSION

As mentioned, this matter of selection and adoption into an authored scene is an area of research, both from a usability and a generative modelling perspective. At the simplest level, the author of the scene can simply "swipe left" on scenes they do not like until they find one they do. However, it raises a bigger question of design intent and how such models adapt to user preferences. Ultimately, it is likely that because ML models can adopt new knowledge, we might end up allowing for user biassing of resulting generations based on how often they select a particular generated output. So, if they are authoring a given "style", perhaps the model will adopt more generations in the given style. For instance, opting to generate more Wes Anderson-style generations as part of a sequence.

Construction of a cut-scene therefore presents itself as a series of edits, recommendations, and shot selections and repeats this cycle until the scene is completed. From a user perspective, it might be perceived as a form of auto-completion, albeit of relatively complex scene construction data. One of the challenges with this approach is that it does still rely on the human using the system to select appropriate completions to form a narrative that is coherent. Individual shot choices are quite complex in traditional filmmaking. Often involving a whole new team in terms of editing the footage into a final film. It may eventually be possible to completely replace the human authorship of this approach entirely and simply infer an entire cut-scene timeline directly into a sequencer. Possibly by feeding it, some kind of script or other construction information. Given that language models are being used across a range of creative generations, it is envisioned that simply having a natural language description of the scene will eventually be enough for a model to construct the entire timeline. The aim is to eventually facilitate an authorial system where it acts very much like the Star Trek holodeck concept, allowing natural language to guide complex representations and behaviours for an immersive simulation.

REFERENCES

Devaranjan, J., Kar, A. and Fidler, S. (2020) Meta-Sim2: Unsupervised learning of scene structure for synthetic data generation. *European Conference on Computer Vision*, Glasgow, *2020*.

Huang, Q., Xiong, Y., Rao, A., Wang, J., and Lin, D. (2020) MovieNet: A Holistic Dataset for Movie Understanding. ArXiv, abs/2007.10937.

Ronfard, R., Gandhi, V. and Boiron, L. (2015) The Prose Storyboard Language: A Tool for Annotating and Directing Movies. WICED@Eurographics/EuroVis.

Vicol, P., Tapaswi, M., Castrejón, L., and Fidler, S. (2018) MovieGraphs: Towards understanding human-centric situations from videos. *IEEE Conference on Computer Vision and Pattern Recognition (CVPR)*.

13 Directed Acyclic Graphs for Fun and Profit

Ivan Mateev

13.1 INTRODUCTION

Directed acyclic graphs (DAGs) are a well-studied area of Computer Science and a strong candidate for a theoretical backbone for a wide variety of AI systems, which require solving the problems of scheduling, enumeration of choice and even pathfinding. DAGs are usually taught within the curriculum of graduate-level and advanced undergraduate-level Graph Theory classes and can sometimes end up ignored by a lot of students due to the threatening appearance of the wider study of graphs.

This chapter will summarise a semi-informal description of what DAGs are and present algorithmic solutions to standard graph problems but reframed and formulated to the framework of DAGs. It will also briefly cover some conceptual AI systems that run on top of DAG-like frameworks. Throughout, a hypothetical racing game framework will be used to motivate the set-up and the examples, but conceptually, the techniques can be used in any other conceptual environment. The techniques described in the chapter can be found and derived from publicly available sources, so this article should be thought of as a centralised point of reference on the subject.

13.2 HYPOTHETICAL RACING FRAMEWORK

The framework used throughout this chapter is that of a racing game with the following design requirements:

- Racetracks can have multiple splits in them, allowing for the flow of the race to diverge and converge as the level designer wishes. Some routes might be longer than others.
- Racetracks cannot have loops that back onto themselves and the flow of the race must always be from the starting line towards the finish line.
- The AI needs to make route choices, other than the shortest route so that the race does not turn into a procession.
- The AI needs to make route choices, such that the player always feels like they are in the race. Driving alone for miles behind or in front of the pack is no fun, so the designer wants the ability to motivate the AI to take longer or shorter routes throughout all possible choices to keep things interesting.

An example track is provided in Image 13.1, where the track splits into three and merges back into one again:

DOI: 10.1201/9781003323549-13

109

A track-building tool has already been built by the Tools department and each of the individual road segments (marked A, B, C, D and E on the image) have been stored somewhere internally as well as information about the next section of road. The Tools department has been very diligent, and they have added functionality, where the length of each road is baked into its internal representation – absolute legends!

The engineering requirement is to convert the above design requirements into a data structure, which can be modified and queried to answer questions as well as a technological unit, which motivates the AI to take and/or prefer a particular route at a given time.

13.3 ARCHITECTURE

A knee-jerk approach towards modelling the setup in Image 13.1 would be to track (pun not intended but appreciated) the junctions and merges of the individual road segments and represent each junction as a vertex and each road as an edge. The starting line and the finish line can be called *S* and *F* respectively and modelled with a vertex, which has one road going away or into the vertex: a *deformed* junction of sorts. The flow of the race is specified by the game design with each road *flowing* from the starting line to the finish line, so each edge has a direction. See Image 13.2.

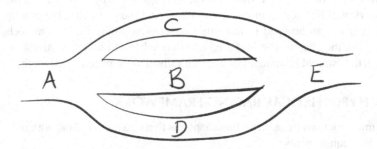

IMAGE 13.1   Example racetrack.

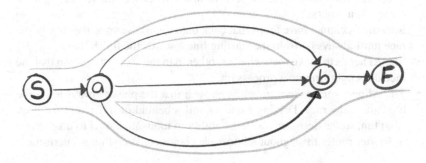

IMAGE 13.2   Road segment directions from starting line to finish line.

A set of vertices and a set of edges connecting the vertices is called an Undirected Graph. Given each road's *flow* implies that movement can happen from one junction towards the other, but not in the reverse direction on that road, this is now a Directed Graph (Cormen et al., 2009a). Conceptually, if you were modelling a street network in a city, it would have been possible for roads to come back on themselves and merge into roads in the opposite direction, or to go in a loop, but given that the racetrack does not have any loops (or "cycles"), you do not have to worry about this scenario. A Directed Graph without loops is called a DAG (Cormen et al., 2009b). Unlike its cousin, the undirected graph, the lack of cycles and the direction introduces valuable constraints, which can make reasoning about operations and movements on a DAG cheaper and simpler.

The above first-pass construction is a good start to show a more abstract representation of the racetrack and to introduce some terminology, but it has some weaknesses when thinking about implementation details. Junctions, conceptually, do not carry information about individual routes but are rather a concept for describing rudimentary racetrack topology. For example, there are three ways to traverse the track in Image 13.1, so if you were to have to store information about each path, you would need to implement a mechanism for tracking each path in the *Junction* data structure. The cost for this would be the addition of code complexity and a high cognitive load for anybody reading the code in the future. This translates to high man-hours for debugging and maintenance, resulting in delays and everything else that comes with it. Following the mantra of every good algorithm designer "can we do better?" (Roughgarden, 2017) and using the *Discovery Method* (Madu, 2014), while scribbling edge cases on a piece of paper, there is another approach that can be taken, which preserves the general idea of the DAG structure. Instead of having junctions as my vertexes, you can focus on the roads (or rather road endings) themselves being the vertexes. The rationale behind this is that if you had a simpler situation with a two-way split, as shown in Image 13.3, you could associate a path with each sleeve.

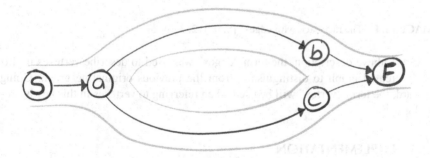

IMAGE 13.3   Racetrack with a two-way split and end-of-road association.

Conceptually, this is the case with three splits (three paths) or multiple splits at different locations. A useful observation here is that because the structure has a direction and no cycles, you can argue an upper bound on the total number of paths. If the graph was fully connected (i.e., there is a connection from every node upstream to every node downstream without introducing cycles), you would have at most $2^{(n-1)}$ paths (Liu, 1968), meaning that you can use this number to pre-allocate or reserve memory or assert for any inconsistencies in the implementation later on. It is worth noting that if the graph had cycles and/or was not directed, the maximum-paths estimation would not be as robust. There can be an unlimited number of paths when one gets caught in a loop.

Assuming the Tools Department did not give us the individual roads, but just gave us junction data, it is possible to build the road-end DAG as follows:

1. Take every edge in the previous graph and create a vertex ("edgex") where each edge used to be.
2. Take the vertex that each edgex's original edge was pointing to, enumerate the edgexes that are coming out of it and connect the previous edgex to the outcoming edgexes that you are enumerating.
3. The resulting graph is the graph of road ends that was described earlier. Except that you are missing the starting line, so you can simply add a dummy edgex "s" to denote where the starting line is.

See Image 13.4 for the original racetrack but reframed using the above steps.

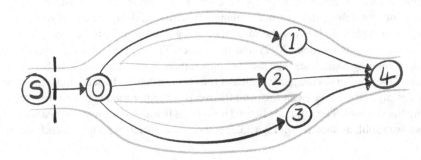

IMAGE 13.4   The racetrack with edgex' {S, 0, 1, 2, 3, 4}.

In the above description, the term "edgex" was used to describe vertexes in this newly created graph to distinguish it from the previous originating graph. Going forward, the term "vertex" will be used when referring to vertexes in this newly created graph.

13.4   IMPLEMENTATION

Having built a more robust representation of the racetrack, the next step is to pregenerate information about it. This will allow us to build heuristics and metadata that the catch-up/fallback system can use to make the AI more interesting. Now is the time to start thinking about how to distinguish between roads and how to associate different roads in the world with nodes on the graph. If the road data from the Tools department was not preconditioned as separate roads, you would apply the above procedure to break it down. Otherwise, the expectation is that the road data from the Tools department will be some list of roads in an array (or some container), since storing them this way assigns a unique "ID" to each road. For the purposes of this chapter, the index of each road in the container will be assigned to the corresponding vertex and assume they are indexes, instead of the output of some hash function. This is handy, as the road connections can be stored as a multimap of integers mapping to integers. In other words, a map<int, array<int>> or a dictionary<int, array<int>>. This can be seen in Table 13.1.

TABLE 13.1

Example Unique ID for Roads with Adjacent Roads Listed

Vertex ID/Road Index	Adjacent Roads
0	1, 2, 3
1	4
2	4
3	4
4	None

The benefit of taking this DAG approach is in a very central property, specific to this type of graph. Unlike the other types of graphs, where searching and pathfinding involves heavy-handed heuristics and cycle-braking techniques (A* and its cousins), while querying a complex, sometimes multidimensional container, nodes in DAGs have the mathematical property of having an order. This powerful property can be exploited by performing an operation called a topological sort and storing the sorted information in a linear container – an array (Cormen et al., 2009a).

There are multiple algorithms for performing a topological sort (Dasgupta et al., 2008; Cormen et al., 2009a) and while each has intrinsic benefits over the other, one relatively straightforward technique is to piggy-back on depth-first search (DFS). The high-level concept of DFS is that, starting at a vertex, you perform an operation on the current vertex and then recursively repeat this on adjacent vertices. Piggybacking on this idea is shown in Code Listing 13.1.

Code Listing 13.1: Recursive TOPO_SORT depth-first search.

```
function TOPO_SORT(array<int> vertices, multimap<int, array<int>> adjacent):
{
        stack<int> sorted = { empty }

        array<bool> visited = { all false };
        lambda onTopoSort(int vertex):
        {
                foreach(int otherVertex : adjacent[vertex])
                {
                        if(!visited[otherVertex])
                        {
                                onTopoSort(otherVertex);
```

```
                                    }
            }
                        visited[vertex] = true;
                        sorted.push(vertex);
            }
            foreach(int vertex : vertices)
            {
                    if(!visited[vertex])
                    {
                            onTopoSort(vertex);
                    }
            }
    }
```

The onTopoSort lambda is used to drive the recursion. By calling onTopoSort post-iteration, it is ensured that the forward track makes its way down the graph depth-first, while the backtrack marks where it has just been. The topological order of the DAG is then contained inside the sorted stack: {4, 2, 3, 1, 0, S}. While this ordering initially looks unnatural, if you choose a vertex ("2") and ask any of the vertexes to the right of it ("1") in the DAG, 'are you before or parallel to the chosen vertex?', the answer would always be yes. Canonically, when the sort is completed, it is prudent to pop the stack into an array, so that it would be arranged in *forward* order. The resulting array would then be: {S, 0, 1, 3, 2, 4}.

A reader with a keen eye for detail will notice that the topological sort looks like it is at the mercy of however the adjacent vertexes were sorted in the map. For example, vertexes "2" and "3" could have been swapped. This is fine, as the topological order property (before or parallel) would still be preserved. As a matter of fact, a DAG can have multiple valid topological sorts. The reason for this is that some vertexes could have the same set of dependencies, meaning that they can be ordered arbitrarily with respect to each other.

13.5 SHORTEST AND LONGEST PATH TECHNIQUE

Up until this point, a representation of a racetrack has been defined and a linear order of the roads in it produced. This section will outline a technique for taking advantage of this linear ordering. A good initial example is in relation to finding the length of the longest path, as this is usually a difficult problem for non-DAGs (Garey et al., 1976). This example will use an imaginary dataset of a different racetrack with the following road lengths, which was kindly provided by the Tools department and shown in Table 13.2.

TABLE 13.2
Road Segment Lengths

Road	0	1	2	3	4	5	6
Length	0.0	1.0	2.5	1.5	3.0	4.0	1.0

S is now called 0, hence the 0.0 length.

Because the Road IDs are not hashes, you can use them as indexes in an array, where lengths[x] is the length of said road. For example, lengths[2] is 2.5. The adjacency multimap from earlier will be used, which will be called *adjacent*. For example, adjacent[0] is {1,2,3}. And will be using the topological order contained in an array and call that *ordered*.

Using the above, you can proceed as follows:

1. Create an array of length *ordered*.size() called maxLengths and populate it with –INF.
2. The longest path to the first node is 0.0, so set maxLengths[ordered[0]] to 0.0.
3. For every vertex *V* in *ordered*, for every vertex *W* in *adjacent*[*V*] set maxLengths[*W*] to max(maxLengths[*W*], maxLengths[*V*]+lengths[*W*]).

When step 3 completes, the element in maxLengths[*ordered*[*ordered*.size()–1]] will be the length of the longest path. The reason why this works is because iterating over *ordered* ensures that the DAG is visited from predecessor towards successor and because no element in *ordered* is before any successive element in the DAG. This means that you are always iterating towards the finish line and the max() call ensures that longer path lengths are recorded if you had previously come from a parallel path.

You can also find the length of the shortest path with a slight modification:

1. Create an array of length *ordered*.size() called minLengths and populate it with +INF.
2. The shortest path to the first node is 0.0, so set minLengths[*ordered*[0]] to 0.0.
3. For every vertex *V* in *ordered*, for every vertex w in *adjacent*[*V*] I set minLengths[*W*] to **min**(minLengths[*W*], minLengths[*V*]+lengths[*W*]).

When step 3 completes, the element in minLengths[*ordered*[*ordered*.size()–1]] will be the length of the shortest path.

Conceptually, to find the actual longest/shortest path (the roads to take), all it would take is an extra map from int to int and a modification of the above algorithm, but instead of calculating min/max there would be a branch that checks if {min/max} Lengths[*V*] +.

Lengths[*W*] is smaller/bigger than the existing value at {min/max}Lengths[*W*] and if it is, the map and the {min/max}Lengths[*W*] value should be updated.

When the procedure completes, the {min/max}Lengths container will contain the corresponding length values as before, but the new map will contain a chain of vertexes/roads taken to reach the finish line, which can be extracted in a manner similar to Dijkstra or A* (Cormen, et al., 2009b).

13.6   ALL PATHS

Having generated the shortest and longest paths, our AI can choose one of two paths based on the player's performance in the game. While this is a good first step, this quickly becomes a problem in more intricate racetracks with multiple junctions. The AI will take one of the two paths, ignoring the rest. One approach to improving this would be to enumerate all of the possible paths and give the designers the ability to vary the choices based on how behind/ahead the player is.

The technique outlined in finding the shortest/longest path is extremely versatile as it can be applied to other types of problems on a DAG and will be leaned on for the enumeration problem as well.

The first thing you need to determine is how many paths in total there are in the racetrack. The same technique will be applied but with some modifications. Instead of the lengths, how many times the current road was visited will be accumulated with how many times the successor has been visited so far:

1. Create an array of length *ordered*.size() called numPaths and populate it with 0.
2. The number of paths through the first road is 1, so set numPaths[*ordered*[0]] to 1.
3. For every vertex V in *ordered*, for every vertex W in *adjacent*[V] I set numPaths[W] = numPaths[W] + numPaths[V].

The addition in step 3 is the key component. As the iteration progresses through the numPaths array, adding the current vertex's value to the *adjacent* vertexes means that parallel path's counts will get propagated and then get added together when two parallel *beams* of paths merge after a split. When the procedure finishes, numPaths[*ordered*[*ordered*.size()−1]] will contain the total number of paths from the start vertex to the final vertex and the number of paths in the entire DAG in total.

Finding the total number of paths (three) allows us to enumerate all the paths. You can pre-allocate an array of three empty arrays and use the topological sort to implement the following scheme:

1. Every path starts at *ordered*[0], so place *ordered*[0] in all three arrays;
2. For each vertex V in *ordered*:
   a. Consecutively add every vertex W from *adjacent*[V] to every array that finishes with V.
   b. Sort the array of arrays by the last element of each array topologically.

At the end of the scheme, you will have a linear path in each array. You can then run over every array or path in the array of arrays and use the lengths data from earlier to calculate the lengths of each path. As a finishing touch, you can sort the array of arrays by path length which might make querying a bit easier.

13.7   CONCLUSION

This chapter presented some key concepts of DAGs and culminated in an applicable method which combines different aspects of the key concepts. While the overall theme was to do with racetracks, the concepts directly apply to other areas like broader systems architecture, data parsing with dependencies, scheduling and more esoteric applications like sparse matrix multiplication.

REFERENCES

Cormen, T., Leiserson, C., Rivest, R. and Stein, C. (2009a) Elementary graph algorithms. In: *Introduction to Algorithms*. Cambridge: MIT Press, pp. 549–584.

Cormen, T., Leiserson, C., Rivest, R. and Stein, C. (2009b) Single-source shortest paths. In: *Introduction to Algorithms*. Cambridge: MIT Press, pp. 604–645.

Dasgupta, S., Papadimitriou, C.H. and Vazirani, U.V. (2008) Algorithms. Boston, MA: Mcgraw-Hill Higher Education.

Garey, M.R., Johnson, D.S. and Stockmeyer, L. (1976) Some simplified NP-complete graph problems. *Theoretical Computer Science*, 1(3), pp. 237–267.

Liu, C.L. (1968) *Introduction to Applied Combinatorial Mathematics*. New York: Mcgraw-Hill.

Madu, T. (2014) Effective methodology in teaching mathematics: The way forward. *Journal of Resourcefulness and Distinction*, 8(1). Available Online at: https://globalacademic-group.com/journals/resourcefulness/Effective%20Methodology.pdf.

Roughgarden, T. (2017) *Algorithms Illuminated: Part 1: The Basics*. New York: Soundlikeyourself Publishing.

14 Navigating Broken Data

Jonas Gillberg

14.1 INTRODUCTION

We have all seen it. Non-player characters (NPCs) standing still when they should be moving. Sometimes, it completely breaks their behaviour and they become unresponsive, whereas other times, they retain some basic functionality. For example, they continue to shoot at targets in the distance. It can be caused by the NPC standing in a place that has no nav-mesh, the exact position where they want to go has no nav-mesh or some similar problem. Throughout production, this is a common problem – content is updated, sometimes it is not flagged correctly for navigation, more often the nav-mesh is out of date, or some features are simply missing. This is to some degree to be expected. To have to wait for data to be fixed robs us of additional playtesting quality that could be had throughout production. This can be addressed by making the NPC navigation a bit more robust and fault-tolerant. This chapter will present a few ways in which this can be done: local resolution, relaxed navigation constraints, high-level goals, and feedback between these systems such that the right decision can be taken at the right level. These techniques have been successfully applied for test bots on titles such as *Battlefield 2042*, *Plants vs. Zombies: Battle for Neighborville* and *Dead Space*. A common counter-argument for making the system robust with internal fallbacks is that if the AI does not completely break down, the content will never be fixed. However, this depends on your development process. Detected errors and chosen fallbacks can be tracked. If those events also track positional information, they can be used to generate potentially very useful heatmaps to indicate the navigation quality at certain times or in certain parts of the game, with subtleties that may be lost if the only error response from the agent is an inability to function.

14.2 LOCAL RESOLUTION

14.2.1 DETECTION

While navigating sections of the game without a nav-mesh, or with an out-of-date nav-mesh, or simply an environment containing dynamic obstacles not represented on the nav-mesh, the agent might get stuck. This applies especially to the area of bot testing where the bots try to navigate the game to the best of their ability even during very early stages of development. To be able to handle this, it must first be detected. One way to do this is to track the distance to the next waypoint, then if no progress has been made for a certain amount of time conclude that the agent is stuck. The amount of time that is considered being stuck, as well as the minimal move distance to reset this timer, is contextual. The time needs to be short enough to allow the agent to quickly resolve issues but must not be so short as to trigger during expected slow

 DOI: 10.1201/9781003323549-14

movement such as a smoothly animated U-turn. In this scenario, the agent is either on what is thought to be a valid nav-mesh path or outside of the nav-mesh, so this cannot be resolved by repathing.

14.2.2 TELEPORTATION

Teleportation is a potential solution to the problem of an agent being stuck. It is a very powerful and easy-to-implement approach, but one that can produce some highly undesirable results. It is worth remembering that the agent is potentially in a situation where it is stuck without a reasonable way of extricating itself. If you do decide to teleport, where should that agent go? Teleportation can be handled at the path-following level by moving the agent to the next waypoint or even to the end of the path. Another reasonable teleportation target location is to a known good location. For example, where a friendly agent is located or straight to the target hostile. A hostile NPC that teleports to the exact location of the player can be very frustrating so it is something to avoid if possible. The value of teleportation depends greatly on how much you trust that the position the agent would teleport to is valid for what it is trying to accomplish. What if the agent is stuck because the next waypoint is blocked by a solid object which it will now teleport inside? Or if teleporting to the end of the path means that it would teleport outside of the currently loaded physics and fall through the world? Teleporting is also likely to cause the agent to skip important triggers in the world. Teleportation should be considered as a last resort. There are other approaches we should try first.

14.2.3 LERPING

Some situations might allow you to linearly interpolate (lerp) the agent's position towards a goal. One important advantage of this approach is that it greatly reduces the risk that the agent misses important world triggers. Another advantage is that it is slower giving other systems (such as loading) enough time to respond. A major drawback is that it is even more likely than teleportation to put the agent in a state inside of or intersecting with another object, at least temporarily, given a likely reason for lerping would be that the agent is blocked by the object we are about to lerp through.

14.2.4 AGENT RESET

The worst-case scenario and very last resort is to simply de-spawn or kill off the agent. However, this does allow for a restart of the scenario, or perhaps to spawn in another agent, or if the agent being removed was insignificant, do nothing.

14.2.5 INPUT SPAM

For input-driven test bots, it has worked surprisingly well across many titles to simply press some combination of Jump, Sprint, Vault, Interact, Open Door, or whatever similar actions are available. This allows the agent to deal with obstacles in a way very similar to how a player would. It might be worth trying to detect the specific type of obstacle the agent is attempting to navigate around, either with ray casts or other types of world queries, and this can potentially be done pre-emptively to avoid getting stuck in the first place. Depending on the situation, this pre-emptive scanning might cost more than it is worth and still might not detect the situation in time. If an agent becomes restuck in a short time period, you can cycle through different inputs depending on how many times in a row it has become stuck. Consider walking backwards or strafing whilst triggering the available actions. Sometimes, simple input spam will not be enough, and more complex or powerful methods need to be applied.

14.2.6   RAY CAST NAVIGATION

It is also possible to build alternative ray- or shape-cast-based solutions for local workarounds when the navigation mesh is not reliable or as an extension of some form of local obstacle avoidance. This approach works well for open worlds with lots of moving obstacles. Before creating such a system, first consider whether you actually need it. It is very likely to be less exhaustive and reliable, with higher CPU runtime costs, than including the current unknowns at the nav-mesh level.

14.3   RELAXED NAVIGATION CONSTRAINTS

Pathfinding from one exact location to an equally precise target location is needlessly restrictive. The smallest input deviation on either the start or the goal causes the path to fail, and the agent goes nowhere. This is also not exactly what usually happens. Nav-mesh solutions often have some way of adjusting input start and goal positions to the nearest valid position on the nav-mesh, often referred to as snapping. A common reason for this might be that the positions are based on the physics positions and that the nav-mesh has been simplified and no longer matches the physics world that well. Increasing the snapping distance of the goal might avoid some of the cases where the path find would fail. Some navigation solutions simply allow you to specify the goal itself as a radius. In either case, trying to define a global constant for snapping or goal tolerance is hard, as how precisely the agent needs to get somewhere depends a lot on the context. For example, if an agent needs to interact with a specific object, this places greater constraints on where the agent can go, compared to if it just needs to get to an area to investigate something. Often, in more dynamic situations, such as an agent chasing another agent, it is likely that the current goal will change long before the end of the path is reached. A similar case could be an agent chasing the player, who moves off the nav-mesh for a short while. In this scenario, it is much better to get a position as close as possible to the player and to continue chasing, rather than to fail the path find and potentially break the chase behaviour as a whole. One way to mitigate this is to allow for intermediate goals.

14.3.1   INTERMEDIATE GOALS

Intermediate goals can be used to allow for more permissive navigation snapping, followed by a more restrictive path find once the agent reaches that goal. Depending on your set-up, this could work similarly to how an agent follows a high-level navigation path or simply be tracked as a Boolean to indicate the intermediate state. In the case of the NPC chasing a player that goes temporarily off the nav-mesh, it would allow the NPC to continue towards this intermediate goal and to repath when the player moves. It is possible that even if the player does not move, the NPC could attack from such a position or something else will occur in the meantime which will render the issue irrelevant. This is different from simply keeping the last successful path until a better one is found in that it works even if the player is off the nav-mesh on the very first path find. The idea of an intermediate goal separate from the ultimate one can be beneficial in many situations as it can be more easily modified or discarded depending on the context.

14.3.2 DIRECT PATH FALLBACK

One of the things that intermediate goals do is to allow for a consistent way to manage goals that are temporarily, or permanently, off the nav-mesh. For temporary ones, the best case is for the situation to resolve itself by the time the intermediate goal is reached, and the subsequent path find is successful. However, if the goal is still unreachable from what is known to be the best possible position it can reach on the nav-mesh, it would need to go off the nav-mesh to reach it. To do this, you may need to lerp to the target position as discussed in 14.2 Local Resolution; however, if this should fail, teleportation should be considered.

14.4 HIGH-LEVEL GOALS

The high-level goal that drives an agent should be understood when determining which of the described approaches should be used. If the high-level goal of an agent is to get to an area, this should allow you to define a permissive area for the navigation goal, rather than specifying a position inside that area and relying on an otherwise defined constant for how permissive the snapping should be. On the other hand, if the agent needs to get to a very specific spot for some animation or special effect to play out correctly, teleportation might at times be the preferred option. High-level goals also have the benefit of being able to track progress independent of the current state of the agent's navigation. Some issues might cause the agent to end up in some form of navigation loop, like falling and then getting up repeatedly. In this case, the high-level goal could have an absolute maximum time allowed for navigation or completion; at such a time, it might simply teleport the agent to the destination or use some other forceful means to resolve the situation. To better illustrate this, let us have a look at how all these things can fit together.

14.5 PUTTING IT ALL TOGETHER

While these techniques all have some value on their own, the sum can be greater than their parts. If a path find fails to find a path within the navigation goal tolerance, propagating that failure upwards to the high-level goal allows for a lot more context when acting on the path failure. In the context where reaching the goal is important, the closest current known position on the nav-mesh might be used as an intermediate goal. For some other context, such as searching an area, it might make more sense to instead accept the end position of the path and make it the current navigation goal and also the high-level goal position. That way, it can be appropriately tracked at all levels and acted on accordingly. It might be that the goal itself is unimportant and if there are any issues with pathfinding, or path following, it should simply be aborted. Likewise, if the agent gets stuck following the path repeatedly, this might be what escalates the response to induce a teleport. You might also allow the local resolution failure to propagate all the way up to the high-level goal and on that level decide what to do. Once again, using the example of an area goal, it might make more sense to regenerate the navigation goal rather than to resort to some other form of resolution. Thinking about it as different levels and allowing the errors or issues to propagate up the hierarchy, and the resolution to be applied downwards can really help sort out ambiguous issues at the right level.

14.6   REQUIREMENTS FOR NAVIGATING BROKEN DATA

- Construct tolerant navigation goals.
- Allow for navigation to intermediate goals to further refine path queries later.
- Allow for off-mesh navigation.
- Handle small obstacles and divergences from known navigation locally if possible.
- Teleport is a better option than relying on perfect data.
- It is better to teleport and report it as an error than to allow the agent to get stuck and hope it gets noticed and reported manually.
- Make sure to propagate issues that need to be resolved, such as stuck events, up the control flow for context-appropriate resolution, like picking a new and better goal if possible.

14.7   CONCLUSION

This chapter has presented a few ways in which incomplete, broken or missing navigation data can be dealt with. Locally, through the use of abilities and teleportation. On a navigation level, using area goals, intermediate goals, and off-mesh navigation. And on a higher level, through the contextual generation of such area goals and appropriate handling of issues through propagation of feedback up the hierarchy. The intention has been to show how these techniques can help provide a more fault-tolerant AI implementation, especially throughout production, in the hopes that it will improve the quality of playtesting and ultimately the game.

15 Environment Steering

Rodolfo Fava

15.1 INTRODUCTION

Autonomous agent movement in a three-dimensional (3D) space can be challenging, especially when that involves handling multiple objectives at once. The games industry is constantly reinventing itself and the spearhead of innovation is, often, the necessity to push boundaries and find creative solutions to meet project requirements, without blowing the time and financial budget in which a game is allowed to thrive. This chapter aims to establish an intuitive, stateless, and efficient algorithm for implementing context-aware 3D navigation for air, space, and underwater movement, which expands upon Context Steering (Fray, 2015). The algorithm outlined in Fray (2015, p. 183) is very effective at tackling specific shortcomings of steering behaviours, being able to handle multiple conflicting objectives with much less oscillation than its predecessor.

Context Steering (Fray, 2015), despite its contributions to renowned racing titles, admittedly falls short of managing 3D navigation, which is expected since the algorithm was originally made for a standard racing-game case, that is, without vertical mobility. This work presents a different way to deal with movement on three axes by an autonomous agent that moves around a level with complex shapes, accounting for various elements of threat and interest, dynamic or static, while giving the impression of natural movement to the human player. To this end, ray casting, interest maps, and linear algebra will be combined to produce a powerful framework. The result of which is an algorithm that offers a holistic solution to 3D autonomous agent movement that is context-aware, lightweight, and scalable.

15.2 THE THEORY

The first step to tackling 3D movement is accounting for 3D space. A solution can be found by dividing this complex task into three parts. Each of the three planes intersecting the unit will have their optimal direction calculated, and later those directions should be added together to produce a resulting vector that will guide the unit each update cycle. Over time, the algorithm will reproduce a natural-looking path for the unit to traverse through the environment while being context-aware.

For starters, let us determine the three intersecting planes of the unit. The first plane, akin to Context Steering (Fray, 2015), is defined as the *Alpha* Plane see Image 15.1a. This can also be described as $z=0$. Likewise, the two other planes can be derived by taking each of the remaining coordinates equal to zero. For instance, by taking $x=0$, yields the *Beta* Plane, shown in Image 15.1b. Lastly, assigning $y=0$ yields the *Gamma* Plane, illustrated in Image 15.1c. Each plane will have its context

DOI: 10.1201/9781003323549-15

evaluated separately, then each resulting vector will be added together. The process of calculating each plane's resulting vectors is discussed in detail in Section 15.3 Applications.

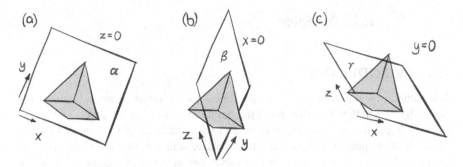

IMAGE 15.1   (a) *Alpha* plane, (b) *Beta* plane, (c) *Gamma* plane.

The basic implementation for each plane goes as follows: For a unit to get to its goal while avoiding obstacles on the way (walls, other players, and the like), as shown in Image 15.2a, the algorithm would first generate n directions based on the forward vector of the unit. For the sake of clarity, the number of directions chosen is eight. This step would represent the *alpha* plane, as described in Image 15.1a. The term "radials" is used for the shorthand of these eight directions, as depicted in Image 15.2b, bearing in mind that an amount far higher can be used if a higher level of granularity is needed and the computational resources can be easily afforded by the application.

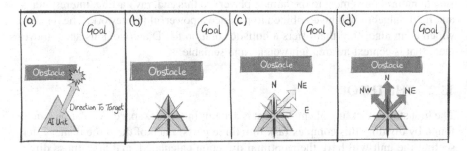

IMAGE 15.2 Algorithm Basics. (a) Situation, (b) radials of n directions, (c) Interest Processing, (d) Danger Processing.

The next step is to query for objects of interest, represented as the circle (the "Goal") in Image 15.2c in this example. The distance vector between the goal and the AI unit is then projected on each of the directions where its dot product is over zero, to determine which ones are relevant to reach the current goal.

In Image 15.2c, NE returns the greatest length as it would lead the unit to the goals more efficiently than the others. The code to implement this formula is shown in Code Listing 15.1.

Code Listing 15.1: The basic formula for increasing the size of each radial.

```
float influence = DotProduct(Distance.Normal(), Radial[n]));
if(influence > 0)
{
        Radial[n] += influence * Radial[n];
}
```

The same influence scoring for radials can be repeated for other concurrent goals and the score will be cumulative in each direction.

Following the query for objects of interest is the query for dangerous objects. The threat assessment consists of performing ray casts on objects marked as dangerous, as shown in Image 15.2d, which works well for geometry obstacles, but can also include bespoke tests for enemy units that can be cached in a pool for ease of access.

The interest processing, as well as the danger processing, will only affect relevant directions in the alpha plane radials at this time. Once both calculations are concluded, each slot of the radials can be added together as shown in Image 15.3a and b, where N and NE, although with a high-interest score, are disregarded after adding the respective danger, see Image 15.3c. This step leaves E as the most favourable direction at the end of the update cycle and should be considered the resulting vector of the alpha plane $R\alpha$, illustrated in Image 15.3d.

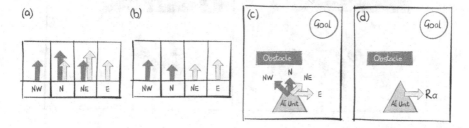

IMAGE 15.3 Calculate a context-aware result direction to move to goal $R\alpha$. (a) Interest and Danger vectors in each direction, (b) Accumulated vectors, (c) Accumulated vectors overlaid on agent in the environment, (d) The resulting vector assigned.

Once the calculations for optimal direction on the *Alpha* plane have been performed, the same process can be applied to the *Beta* plane. At first, three directions seem promising after assessing the Interest Score: *N*, *NE*, and *E*. However, after the obstacle is detected in the *NE direction* as shown in Image 15.4a, the algorithm must pick between the remaining viable radials, *N* and *E*. The latter holds the most promising score due to the dot product calculations. Therefore, E is assigned as the resulting vector for plane *Beta*, as illustrated in Image 15.4b.

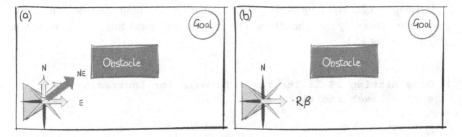

IMAGE 15.4 (a) Beta plane Interest and Danger Influence scoring, (b) Beta Result vector assigned.

The algorithm then moves on to the *Gamma* plane as shown in Image 15.5a and b, repeating the influence scoring process described previously for the *Alpha* and *Beta* planes. Notice that because the AI unit is before the obstacle, as shown in Image 15.3d, the *Gamma* plane will not intersect with the obstacle since the plane sits upright and parallel to the obstacle, as illustrated in Image 15.1c, so the ray casts will miss any threats. Since the algorithm outlines that points of interest will be treated separately, the interest projections on the plane will happen regardless of there being an intersection with *Beta*.

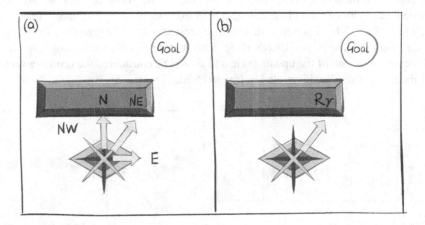

IMAGE 15.5 (a) *Gamma* plane Interest and Danger Influence scoring, (b) *Gamma* Result vector assigned.

With all three result vectors ($R\alpha$, $R\beta$, $R\gamma$) calculated, they can now be added together to determine the final resulting vector Rf (Image 15.6).

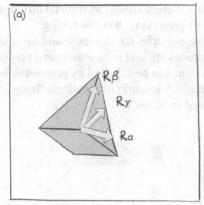 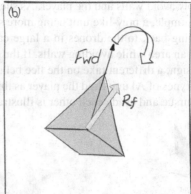

IMAGE 15.6 (a) 3D view of the AI unit. Adding together the context result vectors $R\alpha$, $R\beta$, $R\gamma$, (b) At the end of each cycle, the AI agent interpolates its rotation so that the forward vector meets the final resulting vector Rf.

A further step for the interest map is to consider the current velocity of the unit for scoring a radial, which will prevent oscillations by rewarding radials aligned with the current movement. See Code Listing 15.2.

Code Listing 15.2: Advanced interest map scoring. Adds the speed dot product to reward directions that are aligned with the unit's current movement.

```
for (TPair<int32, FVector>& RadialDirection : EnvironmentPlane.InterestPlane)
{
        FVector Dist = NextCheckpoint - OwnerActor->GetActorLocation();
        float GoalDotProduct = FVector::DotProduct(Dist.GetSafeNormal(),
        RadialDirection.Value.GetSafeNormal());
        float SpeedDotProduct = Vector::DotProduct(OwnerActor->GetVelocity().
        GetSafeNormal(), RadialDirection.Value.GetSafeNormal());
        if (GoalDotProduct > 0.0f)
        {
                RadialDirection.Value += InterestWeight * GoalDotProduct *
                RadialDirection.Value + InterestWeight * SpeedDotProduct *
                RadialDirection.Value;
        }
}
```

15.3 APPLICATIONS

The scenarios for using *Environment Steering* can range from flying units in a dog-fight game to spaceship movement in a galaxy far, far away. Perhaps even underwater movement for an autonomous agent such as an AI shark or submarine. For instance, let us take a scenario with some autonomous drones in a large, enclosed area, such as a cave. One of the advantages of environment steering is that it can easily be coupled with other systems, such as path-following, where the next waypoint is considered the target. In addition to moving toward the next point in the path, it should also sensibly avoid walls and the player. As such, different agents can respond differently. For example, a prey-like unit being more self-preserving than risk-taking.

Going back to the drones in a large cave example, the drones would be able to patrol an area while avoiding walls. If the drones are said to be evasive and prey-like by design, a different take on the flee behaviour can be achieved by processing both other types of AI units and the player as threats. A scenario with multiple flying units that pursue and evade each other is illustrated in Image 15.7.

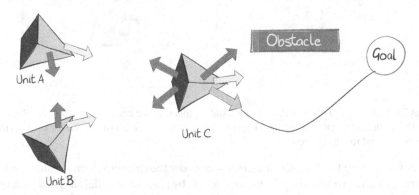

IMAGE 15.7   AI scenario. Units A and B go after C while staying clear of each other. Unit C takes A and B as threats while it avoids obstacles and heads toward its interest point (the "Goal").

The seamless combination of the described interest and danger processing across multiple entities can produce an immersive experience for the player. It strives to achieve a pattern of movement that looks natural as it pursues its goals, while self-preserving by avoiding dangerous situations. How the goals and dangerous situations are determined can be as varied as intended, which may be used by different games in bespoke settings.

The goals can also be represented by a multitude of entities. For example, path waypoints while on patrol or racing, enemy entities while engaged in combat, items to be picked up, and friendly entities if the unit has a group behaviour. A solution to easily identify the relationship between actors is to use tags for identifying the type of entity. Hierarchical tags can provide an even finer level of granularity. For a game that simulates air combat, an AI system may want to treat a health item differently from a friendly entity. Although both are interesting elements, each can have its own tweakable weight to be processed by the environmental steering algorithm.

An interesting take would be considering two or more goals simultaneously, for instance, a flying unit may want to slightly deviate from the optimal path to the next waypoint just enough so that it can pick up a consumable item like health or fuel, before resuming its path-following routine. Furthermore, the weights for each item can also be adjusted at runtime. For example, if a unit is low on fuel the interest weight might be increased for the petrol can.

15.4 AGGRESSIVENESS PROFILES

Regarding the general behaviour of the AI unit that implements Environment Steering, some overarching alterations can be made to produce a unit that is more relentless in searching for certain goals, taking more risks next to dangerous objects, or being more inclined to be defensive regardless of interest objects.

15.4.1 DEFENSIVE

A defensive profile is a more conservative take in contrast with the rather moderate approach as suggested in Image 15.3. In this instance, when there is a threat nearby, the unit's main objective will be to avoid the threat. That means ignoring the interest points altogether while the threat is still present, which could be translated into a very low tolerance for any danger, or very specific kinds of threats. This case is shown in Image 15.8.

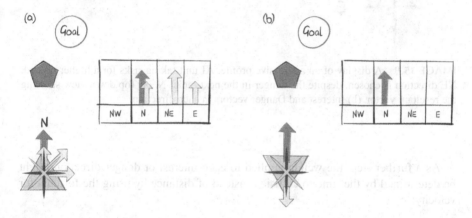

IMAGE 15.8 (a) The defensive unit is presented with both goal and threat. (b) Defensive Profile overrides all interest directions and heads in the opposite direction of danger.

15.4.2 RISKY

As part of an advanced strategy, the unit may choose a high-risk strategy. For instance, to lose another unit that is chasing it, it may still choose a potentially dangerous direction on purpose, going where another unit that is not so risk-inclined would take. This risk-taking can be mitigated by keeping the time to collision very small to still avoid objects at the last moment to ensure self-preservation. Another situation where this risk-taking may lead to higher rewards is to select a tight spot surrounded by dangerous actors that may lead to one of its goals faster. For example, a pick-up health item that is surrounded by enemies or obstacles. This risk-taking profile is shown in Image 15.9.

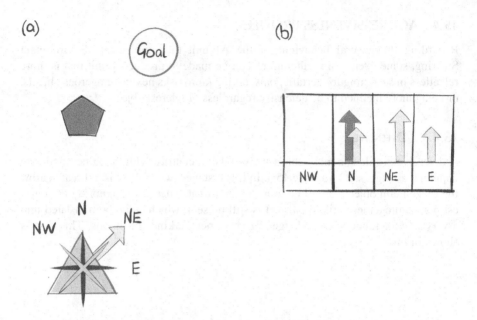

IMAGE 15.9 A display of an aggressive profile, AI unit taking risks for a higher reward. NE direction is chosen, despite the danger in the next radial N. (a) Top down view showing the resultant vector. (b) Interest and Danger vectors in each direction.

As a further step, the weight applied to each interest or danger direction might be determined by the time to collision instead of distance by using the formula for velocity:

$$^vAI\ unit = d/t$$

Both velocity (v) of the AI unit and distance (d) to interest or danger actors can be easily queried at runtime. Knowing this, the time to collision can be derived by manipulating the formula above to give:

$$^tCollision = d/v$$

15.4.3 MODERATE

A balance between both profiles described is to define a threshold value for both danger and interest scores for each radial. This can provide interesting combinations and further tweaking options to find the desired balance for the game requirements. Code Listing 15.3 explains how it can be done.

Code Listing 15.3: Radials can be filtered out following score thresholds.

```
FVector UAWEnvironmentSteeringComponent::GenerateEnvironmentPlaneMapResult(FAWEnvironm
entPlane& EnvironmentPlane)
{
        FVector Result = EnvironmentPlane.SumPlane[0]; //Init Result as first radial,
                                                        //override if needed.

        for (TPair<int32, FVector>& RadialDirection : EnvironmentPlane.SumPlane)
        {
                int index = RadialDirection.Key;
                if (EnvironmentPlane.DangerPlane[index].Size() > DangerThreshold ||
                    EnvironmentPlane.InterestPlane[index].Size() < InterestThreshold)
                {
                        //Filter out radials according to
                        //the score thresholds.
                        RadialDirection.Value *= 0;
                }
                if (RadialDirection.Value.Size() > Result.Size())
                {
                        Result = RadialDirection.Value;
                }
        }

        // (...)
        return Result;
}
```

15.5   CONSIDERATIONS

Ray casts can be quite expensive if the number of directions per environment plane is too high. There are quite a few solutions to mitigate that cost, however. One of them is to keep a reasonable amount of plane directions, a good rule of thumb is to go with 2^n since in computers everything is stored in binaries. A ballpark figure of directions is between 32 and 128 directions per plane, which renders smooth results and costs between 1 and 4 ms of processing per frame, respectively, depending on the hardware available.

Moreover, a viable option to keep ray casts to a minimum is to cache important entities, such as enemy aircraft and items, into a pool in the game director. This requires the storing of them in memory beforehand instead of querying for all objects of a certain class on every update cycle. Even so, cached units checking against each other would amount to a *Big O* of $O(n^2)$, which could be drastically reduced with the use of Space Partitions such as Binary Space Partitioning trees, quadtrees, and octrees. Consequently, cached units would only check against each other if they were in the same or neighbouring cells in the octree.

Some other practical tips for better results can be achieved by making use of sphere tracing rather than line tracing, since the former can take into consideration the dimensions of the AI unit (represented by the sphere radius) and prevent the unit from colliding unnecessarily with geometry in between the radials. In addition, another logical step is balancing each plane map processing separately before adding them together for the final resulting vector.

15.6 CONCLUSION

All in all, Environment Steering provides an innovative take on context-aware 3D movement that can easily be scaled and adapted to fit the requirements of a game. Even so, it is expected that high-quality results will still rely on appropriate balancing over many iterations. If any performance bottlenecks arise, practices such as caching and space partitioning are suitable approaches that will improve the efficiency of the approach detailed in this chapter.

REFERENCE

Fray, A. (2015) Context steering. In *Game AI Pro 2*, Edited by Steve Rabin. CRC Press, Boca Raton, FL, pp. 183–193.

16 Using Voxels for Environmental Cues

Richard Bull

16.1 INTRODUCTION

A common requirement when developing game AI is to enable non-player characters (NPCs) to reconcile the question of *"Where am I right now?"* In answering this question, you can facilitate features such as intelligent ambient conversation – *"Hey! I recognise this place, I used to play here when I was a kid!"*. You can efficiently check whether they are indoors or outdoors to see if they are safe from spying eyes (or acid rain!). You can check whether they are in a safe neighbourhood belonging to their faction, whether the space they occupy is too tight to transform themselves from a lithe robot into a giant truck, or whether they are standing dangerously close to a potential chokepoint that could be used for an ambush.

The possibilities are as endless as the environmental cues you can parse, and these cues can directly provide you with more dynamic, reactive, and immersive NPC behaviour.

16.2 THE SIMPLE APPROACH

You can achieve all of this quite easily using trigger volumes. For example, suppose you have already modelled in your game world a large building with multiple rooms, situated in a village, which itself belongs within the boundaries of a county. A level designer could come along and mark up a trigger volume encompassing each room in the building, tagging the room with its type (kitchen, bedroom, and the like). They could then place a trigger volume encompassing the entire building, tagging it as indoors and with the building type – "the Manor house". Finally, they could encompass the whole village with one huge trigger volume, tagging it with the village's name as a region type, and marking it up as outdoors.

As a rule, prioritise tag overrides hierarchically by smallest volume size. This means that if you move your avatar in this example around inside the village region volume, but they are not inside the house yet – so they are just occupying the single largest volume, then they are outdoors, and they are in the village. If they then enter the house, but they are not yet in a specifically markedup room, they now occupy the Manor house volume and the village volume. The village is outdoors, and the Manor house is indoors, so the agent is being told they are in both states, but because the Manor house volume is the smaller of the two overlapping boundaries that they occupy, they are definitely indoors. This example works even more robustly should they enter a room in the house which is exposed to the elements. For example, a little

DOI: 10.1201/9781003323549-16

courtyard space within the overall boundary of the Manor house. If this had its own room volume, marked as outdoors, and an agent stood here, they would be nested three volumes deep, and because the courtyard "room" is the smallest, they are now outdoors again.

As you can tell from the examples, this is a very simple but powerfully clever markup system that NPCs can make good use of, and if your game world is unusually small, and rarely modified, this might be enough for your game. However, "unusually small" and "rarely modified" do not apply to a large majority of games in development! You could not, for example, expect the level designers to go through and mark up every room and every building in a *Grand Theft Auto 5*-scale open world, and then realistically expect them to stay on top of the multitudes of trigger volumes as the game world inevitably changes during development. It would be nice to fall back on this manual markup system for distinctly bespoke cases, but ideally, you need to supply the design team with a system that can maintain itself as best it can when environments are tweaked, and even supply as much automated environmental markup as it can without even needing to stick virtual signposts down.

16.3   ANALYSING THE ENVIRONMENT USING VOXELS

There are multiple methods of terrain analysis you could use to aid in automating manual markup, but a robust and classic method is the octree, to subdivide the environment into voxels. It might even already be happening in your game engine, for use by rendering or illumination systems, which means you may even be able to leverage some shared technology for the AI systems.

Either way, what you need out of the octree is to subdivide the space so that you end up with a voxelised region of the environment where you have a set of voxels overlaying collision (closed voxels) and a set of voxels occupying navigable spaces (open voxels). Once you have this, you can use the current position of an NPC to query for their currently occupied open voxel and start to mark up and interrogate these voxels for spatial information.

16.4   GENERATION PHASES

The complete environmental markup process can take place offline, and the data generated can be saved and stored as a binary data file. However, there may be situations where some or all of the data would need to be regenerated at runtime if the environment is modified.

A generation phases look like this, and each of these stages will be explored in more detail next:

1. Generate the octree, and all open and closed voxels, using user-defined seed bounds.
2. Cull any voxel that ends up fully outside the seed bounds after generation.
3. Perform interior tests on open voxels.
4. Propagate markup seeds throughout the voxel space.
5. Inherit the tagging of any markup bounds into the voxel space.

16.4.1   GENERATING THE VOXEL SPACE

To begin the generation process, place an oriented bounding box into your environment, which defines the region in which you want to generate voxel markup space. During the octree generation, this region is extruded to be uniform across the three dimensions (if it is not already), and then any generated voxels that completely escape the original bounding region can be culled at the end.

The octree generation is a recursive function, called initially with the extruded seed bounding region, then subsequently with octant bounds, and at a simple algorithmic level looks something Code Listing 16.1.

Code Listing 16.1: Recursive function for octree generation.

```
private void GenerateOctree(Bounds boundingBox)
{
        bool containsCollision = CheckCollisionInside(boundingBox);

        if (boundingBox.size.sqrMagnitude <= m_MinVoxelSizeSqr)
        {
                // Reached minimum voxel size
                CreateVoxel(boundingBox, !containsCollision);
        }
        else if (containsCollision)
        {
                // Break up octant into 8 pieces to isolate the collision further
                var min = boundingBox.min;
                var center = boundingBox.center;
                var halfHeight = new Vector3(0.0f, 0.0f, boundingBox.size.z *
                0.5f);
                var octantSize = (boundingBox.size / 2.0f);
                var octantHalfSize = octantSize * 0.5f;

                // Bottom row 34
                // 12
                var octants = new Bounds[8];
                octants[0] = new Bounds(min + octantHalfSize, octantSize);
                octants[1] = new Bounds( new Vector3(center.x, min.y, min.z) +
                octantHalfSize, octantSize);
                octants[2] = new Bounds( new Vector3(min.x, center.y, min.z) +
                octantHalfSize, octantSize);
                octants[3] = new Bounds( new Vector3(center.x, center.y, min.z) +
                octantHalfSize, octantSize);

                // Top row 78
                // 56
                octants[4] = octants[0];
                octants[4].center = (octants[4].center + halfHeight);

                octants[5] = octants[1];
                octants[5].center = (octants[5].center + halfHeight);

                octants[6] = octants[2];
                octants[6].center = (octants[6].center + halfHeight);

                octants[7] = octants[3];
                octants[7].center = (octants[7].center + halfHeight);

                for (int iOctant = 0; iOctant < octants.Length; ++iOctant)
                {
                        GenerateOctree(octants[iOctant]);
                }
        }
        else
        {

                //Fully open space voxel - potentially larger than the minimum
                // voxel size.
                CreateVoxel(boundingBox, true);
        }
}
```

The first check in this function is to determine if the bounding area of the supplied octant contains any collision. It then subsequently checks to see if the bounds are at least as small as our smallest defined voxel size, and if so, create an open or closed voxel at this position and make no more recursive calls from here. Otherwise, if the bounding area did contain collision, it subdivides the next eight octants and calls recursively on each one. If it did not contain collision, you can create an open voxel, which could potentially be any size between the minimum voxel and the original seed octant bounds, and this particular branch is complete.

What is being done here is to mark up all of the empty space within the original bounds, using the largest possible voxels it can, and at the same time marking up the collision with a density equivalent to the smallest allowed voxel size. This is a fast and effective method of determining what voxel is occupied by a world position, what connections this voxel has within the octree and a map in which to apply metadata related to the voxel for the NPCs to query.

The next phase of the generation process is to cull any voxels that exist completely outside of the original seed boundary area. This can happen if the boundary must be extruded to fit in a uniform shape. Any voxels that overlap the boundary edges will be maintained, so the voxel space can bleed outside of the original boundary but only so far that they intersect.

16.4.2   Interior Tests

In the manual approach to placing environmental markup trigger volumes, the level designer is tagging the space as being indoors or outdoors. This is something that can easily be automated now with the voxel approach, using a simple series of upward ray casts from each open voxel.

A reasonably effective and simple test for this is to take each open voxel and cast a ray to an apex height position from the top centre and each top corner. If a threshold of these five rays (say 50%) collides with a polygon, this voxel is indoor or at the very least under cover from the sky. Image 16.1 depicts this process.

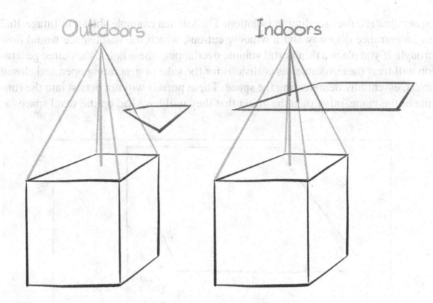

IMAGE 16.1 Testing to see if a voxel is indoor or outdoor.

You now have an octree that can query a world position and be told whether that position is indoor or outdoor.

16.4.3 MARK-UP SEEDS AND PORTAL BOUNDARIES

In the simple trigger-based volumetric approach to marking up rooms and regions, if you wanted to mark up a room interior as being a kitchen, you would extrude a trigger volume to fill the space and set that volume with a *room:kitchen* tag. As mentioned, this is fine until an artist modifies this room during development and the designer then has to keep on top of these changes, rebuilding their trigger volume to match. Using voxel space generation, you can now make this process more robust by simply having the designer place a markup seed – merely a world space position – instead of volumes.

During the *"Propagate markup seeds throughout the voxel space"* (Phase four) of the generation process, you locate each seed placed within the octree boundary, find the octant/voxel within which it is placed, and mark this voxel with the seed tagging. You can assume that if this seed is tagged as *room:kitchen*, it will have been placed within an open voxel inside the kitchen interior space. Now you perform a flood-fill algorithm across all connected open voxels, and mark each of these connections as *room:kitchen* as well. The obvious issue with this flood-filling routine is that it will more than likely also leak out of doorways, and even if it did not because of the way the collision layers is sorted, you still might want to demarcate the kitchen room space to completely isolate the voxels used by the tag markup in a more controlled fashion. This is where portal boundaries come in handy.

A portal boundary is simply a volume that can be placed during the level design markup process, at the same time as placing seeds, to block off entrances and exits to a space that requires seeding in isolation. The kitchen example shown in Image 16.2 has an entrance doorway and a window cut-out, which the voxel space would flow through. If you place a thin portal volume overlapping these holes, the octree generation will treat these volumes as collisions for the sake of generating open and closed voxels, essentially demarcating the space. These portals will not persist into the runtime of the game, other than the effect that they will have had on the voxel space.

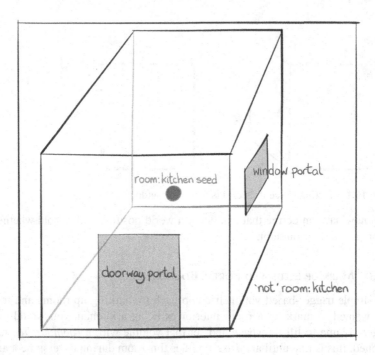

IMAGE 16.2   Portal boundaries.

16.4.4 Inherit Markup Bounds

This final stage is the simplest. You simply need to perform a pass over all of the manually placed markup bounds that a designer may have placed and propagate the tags onto the open voxels contained within them. Any existing type tags already autogenerated in previous phases should be stored hierarchically with precedence, as manual markup should trump automation. For example, if you have seeded your kitchen, and a designer has placed a manual boundary inside the room marking up a pantry inside it, then the kitchen room tag would be stored on the open voxel, but so too would the pantry tag with higher precedence. A point occupying said voxel would be, in terms of room occupation, "primarily inside the pantry, and also within the kitchen". This precisely mimics the occupying volume size order-of-precedence rule specified in the simple volumetric approach to markup described earlier.

16.5 CONCLUSION

An octree is a powerful tool to use in your game engine for fast positional look-ups for all kinds of purposes, from rendering to game logic. Leveraging and sharing that technology for AI environmental querying, particularly when much of that data markup can be automated as part of the voxel generation, makes a lot of sense and can provide supplementary richness to AI behaviour and response. This markup could be used for simple 'where am I' querying, provide voxel-based environmental pathfinding for breadcrumbing, or even to make very high-level movement decisions based on region-type traversal, and it is always an 'easy sell' if you can reuse core game engine data for multiple purposes in your project development

17 The Creature Believability Scale

Dr Nuno Vicente Barreto,
Dr Fernando Penousal Machado,
and Dr Licínio Roque

17.1 INTRODUCTION

To experience world-driven video games, players must believe, or at least accept, the information that they are provided with, even though it might challenge, or even contradict, their concept of reality. It becomes the developer's goal to make the world feel believable – a concept that plays an integral part in improving player experience through engagement (Warpefelt, Johansson, & Verhagen, 2013). One of the elements responsible for that are the actors, or agents, inhabiting these worlds.

When studying the production of content, the importance of evaluation becomes clear. To create believable creatures, the proper tools are required to both evaluate a creature's behaviour and look beyond its visual representation. First, creatures are more than their individual elements and evaluation should take this into account. Second, they exist within a context. The latter defines their role, and any detraction may cause a creature to be perceived poorly.

While, in the context of believability, humans have a predefined set of criteria, including showing personality, emotion, self-motivation, change and social relationships (Thomas & Johnston, 1995), creatures interact with humans differently. For example, they lack a human-understandable language, so the same criteria might not hold true.

This chapter proposes an architecture-agnostic tool capable of measuring creature believability so that at the design stage (automated or otherwise) developers can maximise a creature's perception. A set of heuristics, or rules, can be derived from such a tool, to inform and guide the process and to help design creatures who support the suspension of disbelief mediated by the fictional worlds of video games.

17.2 UNDERSTANDING BELIEVABILITY

Before introducing the evaluation instrument, an understanding of what is meant by 'believability' is required. In the media, it is tightly coupled with the concept of suspension of disbelief. This was first introduced by Coleridge and Shawcross (2001), in their autobiographical reflection, when they state that believability is an act people must be willing to do (even at a subconscious level), framed within the medium's bounded veracity (only requiring a 'semblance of truth'), happening in

DOI: 10.1201/9781003323549-17

a contextualised environment, or 'moment.' In short, when experiencing media, humans are willing to believe in something that is unbelievable, for the sake of context.

In psychology, 'presence' encompasses how this phenomenon manifests itself in technology-based media. Defined as 'the perceptual illusion of nonmediation' (Lombard & Ditton, 2006), it is a phenomenon which causes a person to stop acknowledging the existence of a medium, responding as if it is absent. For example, acting as a window to its content. In both the games industry and its academic counterpart, it is argued that 'presence' plays an important role in improving the player's experience (Warpefelt, Johansson, & Verhagen, 2013). It then becomes one of the goals of a development team to help create and maintain it.

This then raises the question of how developers can provide players with a 'semblance of truth' to help them 'suspend their disbelief'? This is where believability comes in. Fogg and Tseng (1999) state that in computer software, information corresponds to the mental model created by the user. This is also true in video games as players also create mental models when they play, leading them to accept in-game agents as 'alive and thinking' (Rosenkind, Winstanley & Blake, 2012). This is further supported by studies that not only show that believable agents are perceived to be more engaging than non-believable ones (Warpefelt, 2016) but also how to craft them.

However, possibly due to the way people tend to anthropomorphise media content (Reeves & Nass, 2003), they overwhelmingly focus on humans (Reynaud, Donnart, & Corruble, 2014) despite the existence of other animals. Even video games focusing more on animals follow this anthropomorphic trend (Frank, Stern, & Resner, 1997). Nonetheless, they, as autonomous agents, are also meant to support the immersion of these virtual worlds. So, it then becomes important to provide the means by which to create them.

For AI programmers tasked with designing, and developing creatures, having a tool that helps them evaluate content around a concept potentially as vague as believability, in a contextualised manner, becomes invaluable.

17.3 THE CREATURE BELIEVABILITY SCALE

The Creature Believability Scale (CBS) is a design tool to help developers assess and potentially produce their creations. It relies on characteristics meant to convey believability and takes the form of a 5-point rating scale containing twenty three statements divided into four categories. Participants can answer with one of the following agreement values: 'Not At All', 'Slightly', 'Somewhat', 'Moderately' and 'To a Great Extent'. The statements are as follows:

Relation with the Environment: Items related to environmental interactions, ranging from reactions to environmental cues and directed behaviours to biological systemic exchanges.

1. The creatures interact with the surrounding environment.
2. The creatures have motor coordination.
3. The creatures direct their movement towards/away from targets.

4. The creatures can find objects in the environment.
5. The creatures can expel organic waste.
6. There are signs of previously expelled organic waste, such as faeces, urine, goo, and the like.
7. The creatures' actions are appropriate to their circumstances.

Biological/Social Plausibility: This category relates to a creature's plausibility as a biological organism; for example, showing autonomy, reactivity to its surroundings and the ability to interact with other creatures.

8. The creatures can move independently.
9. The creatures' agility reflects their volume.
10. The creatures react to environmental triggers.
11. The creatures can perform tasks by coordinating with other creatures or humans.
12. The creatures audio-visually communicate with other creatures or humans.
13. The creatures engage in reproductive acts.
14. There are signs of previous reproductive acts, such as eggs, cubs, pregnancy, and the like.

Adaptation: This category relates to how a creature's body and mind adapt to the environment and biological changes. For example, growing.

15. The creatures learn from past events.
16. The creatures use past experiences to overcome novel situations.
17. The creatures change the way they look with age.
18. The creatures change the way they sound with age.
19. The creatures change the way they behave with age.
20. The creatures can imitate others to develop their own behaviours.

Expression: The elements in this category refer to how a creature uses its body as a means to communicate, learn, or survive.

21. The creatures' body language anticipates their actions.
22. The creatures show signs of emotional reaction to objects, events, and other creatures.
23. The creatures' bodies seem adapted to their habitat.

While this scale was designed to fill in the gap of an evaluation process, it can also be incorporated during the creation phase. This allows developers to produce content to maximise believability and, subsequently, assess if their interpretation of the scale aligns with the players. As such, a workflow can then be derived:

- During the creation phase of a creature, the scale's items can be viewed as heuristics.
- These heuristics can be incorporated into its design and architecture.

- During the evaluation phase, playtesting and expert evaluation can be used, with the CBS as a measuring tool, to validate the previously produced artefact.
- This process can be repeated until developers are satisfied with their end result.

With this scale, additional evaluation tools could be derived. One such tool is the CBS.

17.3.1 THE CREATURE BELIEVABILITY SPECTRUM

Though the CBS can output a believability index to help assess individual creatures, this can be supplemented by a more visual framework – a referential list to help compare video game creatures. Such frameworks can help designers understand not only how to improve pre-existing designs and interpreting how each dimension, and statement, contribute to its overall believability perception but also to compare their own designs against other elements.

Thus, the CBS consists of an axis ranging from 0 (non-believable) to 10 (believable) where creatures are sorted according to their perceived believability index.

Indexes can be calculated by summing the rates obtained after applying the CBS (or the median of each of its items' ratings, if several players are used during data gathering). They can either be used to represent their overall 'believability', in which case all the items are used, or, to represent a specific category, in which case, only its items are considered.

As mentioned, from a game design perspective, the CBS can provide additional insights. For instance, creatures from similar video games (or having similar roles/ screen time) can be compared and categorised, through the spectrum, to allow developers to set baselines for their own creatures' requirements, from either their overall perceived believability or from specific categories. Moreover, it can help us to understand how different approaches in both development and design may be perceived and assist in identifying potential pitfalls.

17.3.2 EXAMPLE OF USING THE CREATURE BELIEVABILITY SCALE

To illustrate how the scale could aid the design of creatures, imagine the following scenario: A team is developing a science-fiction exploration game where players take on the role of an astronaut tasked with bio-surveying an uncharted planet. During their research, they find a companion creature, nicknamed Loncey, who ends up helping them throughout the course of the game.

For this practical example, the development team wants to assess the believability of three types of creatures the player encounters. They are as follows:

- **Blarma**: These Armadillo-like creatures roam some of the areas of the environment. They appear individually, or in a line formation, and move by hopping around on alternate sides. Players can try to interact with them, but the Blarma do not react. Their on-screen presence can be small.

- **Loncey**: A docile lion/coyote hybrid the astronaut meets early in their adventure. Outside of cutscenes, it is always near the player albeit it only wanders around and can be knocked unconscious by other creatures. Its onscreen presence is large.
- **Raptar**: These are weak reptilian creatures that are hostile to the player. Players are forced to kill Raptars to proceed with their survey. They stay idle but will pounce at players as soon as they see them. They will keep pouncing until they are killed. Unlike the previous two creatures, these have a medium onscreen presence.

With the creatures deployed in a demo build, an evaluation test can be conducted, following the workflow described earlier.

1. Beta-testers are prompted to play through the build and evaluate the three creatures, using the CBS.
2. With the data collected, the agreement values of each item can be converted to a scale of 0–4, and the median of each of the scale's items ratings can be calculated. This allows us to calculate a Believability score, first across all of the scale's categories then individually.
3. The data can then be analysed to compare each creature and allow the team to reflect on their strengths and weaknesses, in terms of believability, and subsequently theorise potential solutions.

For this example, the results of undergoing the hypothetical test are depicted in Tables 17.1 and 17.2. As can be observed, Table 17.1 shows Blarma, Loncey and Raptar scored an overall total of 2.39, 4.35 and 5.65, respectively, well below the scale's maximum score of 10 (believable). It is also evident that Blarma was considered the least believable of the group.

TABLE 17.1
CBS Results, Normalised to a 10-Point Semantic Scale.

Scale	Blarma	Loncey	Raptar
1	0	2	4
2	0	4	3
3	3	4	4
4	2	3	4
5	0	0	0
6	0	0	0
7	0	1	4
8	4	4	4
9	2	2	4
10	0	2	2
11	0	1	0
12	2	1	0
13	0	0	0
14	0	0	0
15	0	1	1
16	0	1	1
17	3	2	4
18	2	2	4
19	1	2	4
20	0	1	0
21	1	2	4
22	0	1	1
23	2	4	4
Total	2.39	4.35	5.65

TABLE 17.2
CBS Results by Scale Category, Normalised to a 10-Point Semantic Scale.

Categories	Blarma	Loncey	Raptar
Relation with the environment	1.79	5	6.79
Biological/Social plausibility	2.86	3.57	3.57
Adaptation	2.5	3.75	5.83
Expression	0.32	0.75	0.96

With these values, developers can then attempt to maximise the believability of any/each of the creatures by taking into account a predefined goal score (either established by the developers themselves, or obtained by scoring creatures, from similar games, using the same methodology) or improve the score of one/two creatures using the third one's score as a baseline.

In an ideal world, developers would improve every aspect of their creatures until they achieved maximum believability; however, as resources are limited, this might not always be possible. In this example, this was assumed and, using only the tested creatures' scores, developers would concentrate on improving Loncey because (a) it is not as believable as Raptar and (b) its onscreen presence is the greatest of all the creatures.

Focusing on Loncey, more in-depth information can be garnered by calculating normalised scores of the scale's categories as depicted in Table 17.2. This helps identify which areas Loncey lags behind Raptar. These can also be prioritised by taking into account the game's design goals. For example, given that Loncey is meant to accompany and help the player, improving its believability in both relations with the environment and expression should be the first step.

There are other conclusions that can be drawn from the data which we'll leave as an exercise for the reader. Each one will help to identify ways to iterate on Loncey and improve the believability in this creature. Finally, after iterating, developers can rerun a similar test and iteration process until they are satisfied with the overall results.

17.4   CONCLUSION

Creatures can play an integral part in world-driven video games. They provide audio-visual feedback over time which players can perceive. This lets them understand what creatures do and how they do it. And when done right, it may promote 'presence' in the player.

The CBS was presented as a tool to aid AI programmers when developing creatures. It works on a 5-point scale and catered towards evaluating creatures through the lens of believability.

Because content creation is a two-phased iterative process (creation followed by evaluation), the scale aims to complement existing architectures and algorithms. In particular, it is meant to help developers shift their mindset to reflect upon this to maximise creatures' believability, through a set of guidelines, and, subsequently, assess their results in a contextualised environment. By itself, the CBS can assess individual creatures, providing an idea of which areas need additional work. However, several evaluations can be combined to produce a CBS which allows developers to compare creatures and identify their strengths and weaknesses.

ACKNOWLEDGEMENTS

This work was partly supported by the CISUC ICIS project CENTRO-07 -0224-FEDER002003 and the FCT Ph.D. Grant SFRH/BD/100080/2014.

REFERENCES

Coleridge, S., and Shawcross, J. (2001) *Biographia Literaria*. London: Electric Book Co.

Fogg, B., and Tseng, H. (1999) The elements of computer credibility. *Proceedings of the SIGCHI Conference on Human Factors in Computing Systems the CHI is the Limit – CHI '99*, New York.

Frank, A., Stern, A., and Resner, B. (1997) Socially intelligent virtual petz. Socially Intelligent Agents. *AAAI Fall Symposium*, [online] pp. 43–45. Available at: <https://alumni.media.mit.edu/~benres/verbiage/Socially%20Intelligent%20Virtual%20Petz.htm#:~:text=Socially%20Intelligent%20Virtual%20Petz&text=We%20have%20developed%20a%20series,layered%203D%20animation%20and%20sound.> [Accessed 7 August 2022].

Lombard, M., and Ditton, T. (2006) At the heart of it all: The concept of presence. *Journal of Computer-Mediated Communication*, 3(2). Available at: https://academic.oup.com/jcmc/article/3/2/JCMC321/4080403

Reeves, B., and Nass, C. (2003) *The Media Equation: How People Treat Computers, Television, and New Media Like Real People and Places*. Center for the Study of Language and Information Publication, Cambridge University Press.

Reynaud, Q., Donnart, J., and Corruble, V. (2014) Evaluating the believability of virtual agents with anticipatory abilities. *Proceedings of the 2014 International Conference on Autonomous Agents and Multi-Agent Systems*, Paris, pp. 1533–1534.

Rosenkind, M., Winstanley, G., and Blake, A. (2012) Adapting bottom-up, emergent behaviour for character-based AI in games. *Research and Development in Intelligent Systems*, XXIX, pp. 333–346.

Thomas, F., and Johnston, O. (1995) *The Illusion of Life*. New York: Hyperion.

Warpefelt, H. (2016) The Non-Player Character – Exploring the believability of NPC presentation and behaviour. Ph.D. Stockholm University.

Warpefelt, H., Johansson, M., and Verhagen, H. (2013) Analyzing the believability of game character behaviour using the Game Agent Matrix. *Proceedings of DiGRA 2013: DeFragging Game Studies*, Atlanta, GA.

18 Automated Testing Using AI Planning

Dr Bram Ridder

18.1 INTRODUCTION

As games are growing ever larger and more complex, the need for testing, and the time it takes to test a game, has increased. There are many well-established types of automated tests like unit tests, functional tests, and smoke tests. These tests gather performance metrics like frames per second, memory usage, loading times, bandwidth usage, and many more. They also perform code coverage, detect crashes, fire asserts, and create error logs, amongst a plethora of other functions. This data is invaluable for development teams to optimise and stabilise their games.

This chapter will focus on automated testing i.e., tests that play the game as a player by simulating keyboard, mouse, and game controller inputs. Most solutions that are used to test games like this use a combination of pre-generated scripts, behaviour trees (BTs), finite-state machines (FSM), and reinforcement learning agents. They load a level and test it for a certain amount of time and then quit. Taking this a step further, an AI framework will be described that is capable of consistently completing entire games from start to finish. The benefits of such a system are manyfold. Not only does it provide more extensive code coverage and metrics that better reflect the game, but it can also detect game and level design issues. If the framework is unable to complete a game, then this is usually due to a coding bug or issue with the level or game design. The system described in this chapter has been successfully utilised to complete games such as *Zombie Army 4*, *Evil Genius 2*, and *Sniper Elite 5*, amongst others.

18.2 AI PLANNING

The roots of planning can be traced back to STRIPS, a planning language that defines an initial state and goal as propositional values and a set of actions. Each action has a precondition, which dictates when an action can be executed, and an effect which details how a state is updated after applying the action. A solution to such a planning problem is a sequence of actions that, when applied to the initial state, leads to a state where all the goal conditions are true. The most notable application of AI planning systems in the games industry is Goal-Oriented Action Planning (GOAP). This was first popularised by *FEAR* and has since been used in various other projects like *Tomb Raider*, *Assassins Creed*, and *Middle-earth: Shadow of Mordor* games. One of the main benefits of such deliberate systems, compared to reactive systems like BTs,

 DOI: 10.1201/9781003323549-18

is that it allows for smarter AI that can reason how their actions affect the world state and future actions.

18.2.1 SIMPLE NUMERICAL PLANNING

Simple numerical planning problems are deterministic, fully observable, and can reason about numbers but do not deal with time. The framework described is expressive enough to model and find solutions to complete all campaigns of *Evil Genius 2*, *Sniper Elite 5*, *Zombie Army 4*, and many others.

18.2.1.1 Domain

A planning system needs an abstract model of the game that it needs to play, a so-called Domain. This includes the following information:

- The type of things that can exist in the game. For example, Player, Enemy, Location, Door, Key, and the like. Each type can also be a supertype of other types, for instance, you could define a Type Actor that is the supertype of Player and Enemy.
- The properties between these types. These denote their relationships using first-order predicate logic. Each predicate has a name and a sequence of types. For example:
  - (at Actor Location), an *Actor* can be **at** a *Location*;
  - amount Item Actor), an *Actor* can have an **amount** of *Items*. Numerical predicated are prefixed with a #.
- And finally, the actions the player can perform in the game. Each action has a name, a sequence of named types, specifies when it is applicable (its preconditions), and how it affects the world state (its effects). For example, for a player to move from location A to location B, the player must be at location A and there must be a valid path from location A to B. The effect on the world of this action is that the player is no longer at location A but is now at location B, see *Code Listing 18.1* for the full definition using PDDL notation.

```
Code Listing 18.1: A Move action.

(:action Move
        :parameters (?p — Player ?from ?to — Location)
        :precondition (and
        (at ?p ?from)
        (connected ?from ?to))
  :effect (and
        (not (at ?p ?from))
        (at ?p ?to))
  )
```

18.2.1.2 The Problem

During runtime, an *instance* of the domain is created, which consists of the initial state, a representation of the current game world, and the goal we are trying to achieve. This is a problem that the AI Planner is tasked to solve.

18.2.1.2.1 The Initial State

The initial state consists of all *Objects* that are part of the world. Each object has a unique name and is of a certain type that is defined in the domain. For example:

- p – Player, object *p* of type *Player*.
- blue_key – Key, object *blue_key* of type *Key*.

It also contains all *Facts* that are true. A *Fact* is an instance of a predicate, where each *Type* is instantiated with an Object of the correct type or subtype. For example:

- (at p player_loc), the *Player* object p is at the *Location* object *player_loc*,
- amount blue_key p) = 2, the *Player* object p has two *blue_key* objects.

For boolean predicates, you only declare those *Facts* that are true. This is the so-called closed world principle which means that all *Facts* that are not declared are assumed to be false. For numerical facts, their numerical value is declared.

18.2.1.2.2 The Goal

The goal is a logical expression of what value *Facts* must have. For numerical facts, the following expressions are allowed: equal to, less than, greater than, less or equal to, and greater or equal to. For example, a goal could be:

- (and (at p finish_loc) #(amount reactor_cores p) > 3)

18.2.2 FINDING A SOLUTION

Once the initial state and the goal are defined, the AI planner creates all the possible facts and actions that can exist. In a process called *grounding*, all possible facts and *grounded* actions that can exist are constructed by enumerating all possible sets of objects that match the predicate's types defined in the domain.

For example, starting with the following objects:

- p1, p2 – Player
- loc1, loc2, loc3 – Location

Six Facts will be generated:

- (at p1 loc1)
- (at p1 loc2)
- (at p1 loc3)

- (at p2 loc1)
- (at p2 loc2)
- (at p2 loc3)

Then 18 *grounded* Move actions will be generated:

- (move p1 loc1 loc1)
- (move p1 loc1 loc2)
- (move p1 loc1 loc3)
- (move p1 loc2 loc1)
- (move p1 loc2 loc2)

An AI Planner's job is to find a sequence of grounded actions that transition from the initial state to a state where all the goals are satisfied. One of the major problems with AI Planning is the complexity of the problems; simple numerical problems are semi-decidable, which means that the search space can be too big for these techniques to find a solution in a reasonable amount of time. Even worse, if no solutions exist, then this cannot be proven. Even classical planning problems, which do not reason about numbers, are PSpace-Complete.

18.2.3 State-Based Planning

One of the search techniques developed to solve planning problems is to explicitly explore the search space. Searching can start at the initial state and the search space is explored by generating successor states from any state that has been generated until a goal state is found. This method is called Forward-Chaining Planning.

You need a good heuristic to guide the AI planning system; given a state, which of the possible successor states should it explore first? The general way to formulate a heuristic is by abstracting the given planning problem and solving the simplified problem. The plan length of the solution to the simplified problem is used as the heuristic for the original problem. The approach used in this framework was the so-called Numerical Relaxed Planning Graph heuristic (nRPG).

18.2.4 Numerical Relaxed Planning Graph Heuristic

You relax a planning problem by adding negative effects to successor states, instead of deleting them, and using lower and upper bounds to capture the possible range of numerical facts. An nRPG is constructed by creating alternating fact and action layers as follows:

1. The initial fact layer is the initial state of the AI planning problem.
2. All actions whose preconditions are satisfied in the previous layer are added to the next action layer.

4. The effects of the actions in the previous action layer are applied as follows:
   - All positive and negative boolean effects are added to the next fact layer.
   - All numerical effects expand the upper or lower bounds, accordingly.
   - A special No-Op action for each fact in the previous fact layer is added, whose precondition and effect are that fact.
5. Is the goal satisfied in the current fact layer?
   - If so, we are done.
   - Otherwise, go to step 2.

An example of an nRPG is depicted in Image 18.1. All No-Op actions and facts that were true in a previous fact layer are omitted for clarity. You may never reach a fact layer where the goals are valid. You stop the construction of the nRPG when you reach a fact layer whose facts are identical to the previous one. At this point, you can conclude that no solution exists for the original planning problem. After all, if no solution exists for the relaxed planning problem, then no solution exists for the original one. The reverse is not true though. If you can construct an nRPG, then you cannot conclude that a solution exists to the original planning problem.

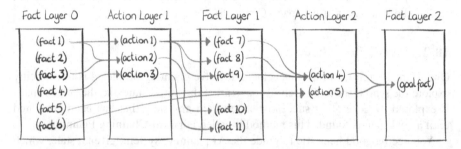

IMAGE 18.1   An example of an nRPG with a single goal fact.

After an nRPG is constructed, the search for a solution to this relaxed problem as follows:

1. Mark goal facts in the last *Fact* layer.
2. Select an action in the same action layer as a marked fact that achieves that fact. Unmark the achieved fact and mark all the action's preconditions in the previous fact layer.
3. If there are no marked facts, or all marked facts are part of the initial state:
   - Then you are done, and the number of selected actions is the heuristic.
   - If not, go to step 2.

Sadly, finding the optimal solution is an NP-Complete problem. To determine which action to pick for each marked fact, you use a heuristic. The cost of each action is the sum of the fact layers where each of its preconditions was first achieved. No-Ops have a cost of 0, so they are always chosen over other actions if possible.

A solution to the RPG in Image 18.1 is depicted in Image 18.2. The solution for this nRPG requires three actions so the heuristic we have calculated is 3. Note that the optimal solution is 2, by picking *action 1* and *action 4*. *Action 5* is preferred over *action 4*, because its heuristic is 2, whereas *Action 4*'s heuristic is 3.

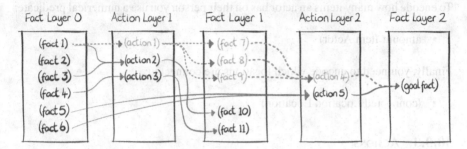

IMAGE 18.2   A solution to the nRPG depicted in Image 18.1.

18.3   A WORKED EXAMPLE

This example will use a domain for a *Sniper Elite*-like game, where the player needs to acquire special items, kill enemies, and eventually reach a location to exfiltrate.

18.3.1   TYPES

The types in this domain are:

- *Locatable* – the supertype of:
  - *Item* – That might be necessary to collect or to open Doors with, and
  - *Actor* – the supertype of: *Player* and *Enemy*.
- *Location* – A position in the world.
- *Door* – A door obstacle that might need to be interacted with to proceed.

18.3.2   PREDICATES

First, you define the predicates, which tell us where the actors and items are located. This notation can be simplified by utilising the supertype Locatable:

- (at Locatable Location)

To open a door, you need to define what keys a door needs to be opened. A location is included in this predicate as well, to encode where an actor needs to stand to open the door with a key. This allows a door to be set up such that different keys could be used at different locations:

- (requires Door Key Location)

Second, we need to define which two locations a door blocks. You will have one location on either side of a door:

- (blocks Door Location Location)

To encode how many items an actor has on their person you use a numerical predicate:

- amount Item Actor)

Finally, you need to encode which locations are connected:

- (connected Location Location)

18.3.3 ACTIONS

18.3.3.1 Move

The move action determines where a player is and where they want to move to. If the action is possible, it returns the modified state of the world. This was depicted in Code Listing 18.1.

18.3.3.2 Pickup

The pickup action is depicted in Code Listing 18.2. A Player can pick up an Item if the player and the item are both at the same location. After picking up the item, the item is no longer at the location and is added to the player's inventory.

```
Code Listing 18.2: A Pickup action.

(:action Pickup
          :parameters (?p - Player ?item - Item ?loc - Location)
          :precondition (and
          (at ?p ?loc)
          (at ?item ?loc))
   :effect (and
          (not (at ?item ?loc))
          (increase #(amount ?item ?p) 1))
)
```

18.3.3.3 Steal

The steal action is depicted in Code Listing 18.3. With this action, players get to steal an item from an enemy. The player is required to be at the same location as the enemy and that the enemy has at least one item of the type you are trying to steal.

Code Listing 18.3: A Steal action.

```
(:action Steal
           :parameters (?p — Player ?enemy - Enemy ?steal_loc - Location ?item — Item)
           :precondition (and
           (at ?p ?steal_loc)
           (at ?enemy ?steal_loc)
           (> #(amount ?key ?enemy) 0))
     :effect (and
           (decrease #(amount ?key ?e) 1)
           (increase #(amount ?key ?p) 1))
)
```

18.3.3.4 Open

The open action is depicted in Code Listing 18.4. With this action, players use the items that they have in their inventory to open doors. A player is required to be at a location where it can interact with a door, (interaction_loc). This location also informs what key they need to use. It also determines what location is on the other_ side of the door that can be moved to after opening the door.

Code Listing 18.4: An Open action.

```
(:action Open
           :parameters (?p — Player ?door - Door ?interact_loc ?other_side - Location
           ?key — Item)
           :precondition (and
           (at ?p ?interact_loc)
           (blocks ?door ?interaction_loc ?other_side)
           (requires ?door ?key ?interaction_loc)
           (> #(amount ?key ?p) 0))
     :effect (and
           (not (blocks ?door ?interaction_loc ?other_side))
           (not (blocks ?door ?other_side ?interaction_loc))
           (connected ?other_side ?interaction_loc)
           (connected ?interaction_loc ?other_side)
           (decrease #(amount ?key ?p) 1))
)
```

18.3.4 EXAMPLE PROBLEM

The objects that are part of this problem are depicted in Image 18.3. The connectivity between the locations is depicted with solid lines. The dotted lines depict locations that are blocked by a door.

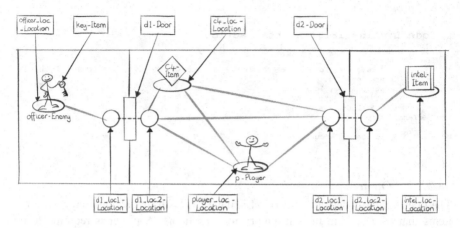

IMAGE 18.3 Example problem, solid lines show the connectivity and dotted lines show locations blocked by doors.

The list of facts, apart from the connected ones, that are part of the initial state is:

- (at p player_loc)
- (at officer officer_loc)
- (at c4 c4_loc)
- (at intel intel_loc)
- amount c4 p)=0
- amount key p)=0
- amount c4 officer)=0)
- amount key officer)=1)
- (requires d2 key d2_loc1)
- (blocks d1 d1_loc1 d1_loc2)
- (blocks d1 d1_loc2 d1_loc1)
- (blocks d2 d2_loc1 d2_loc2)
- (blocks d2 d2_loc2 d2_loc1)
- (requires d1 c4 d1_loc2)

The goal in this problem is simply:

- amount intel p)>0

In other words, the player wants to have acquired the intel.

18.3.5 EXAMPLE PLAN

When you ask the AI planner to solve this problem then it will produce the following plan:

1. (move p player_loc c4_loc)
2. (pickup p c4 c4_loc)

3. (move p c4_loc d1_loc2)
4. (open p d1 d1_loc2 d1_loc1 c4)
5. (move p d1_loc2 d1_loc1)
6. (move p d1_loc1 officer_loc)
7. (steal p officer officer_loc key)
8. (move p officer_loc d1_loc1)
9. (move p d1_loc1 d1_loc2)
10. (move p p d1_loc2 d2_loc1)
11. (open p d2 d2_loc1 d2_loc2 key)
12. (move p d2_loc1 d2_loc2)
13. (move p d2_loc2 intel_loc)
14. (pickup p intel intel_loc)

An important characteristic of an AI planning system is that all you have to do is describe the world and goals. The AI planning system will reason what needs to be done to reach the goals, there is no need to leave breadcrumbs to *guide* the planning system.

18.3.6 PROBLEM GENERATION AND PRUNING

Care needs to be taken so that you do not create a planning problem that is too big. You need to make sure that the branching factor is not too large. In large worlds, we do not want to expose all the items, enemies, doors, and the like. Use an iterative approach and only expose what is necessary to find a solution. To illustrate this in more detail, the previous example is used to show how this can be achieved.

The planner starts at the goal and creates a location from which to pick up the intel. Next, it finds a path from the player's location to the pickup location of the intel and checks if the player will pass through any doors to get there. If so, an object for each door is created, the locations on both sides of each door are generated, and it checks what items can open these doors. Next, it iterates through all these items and finds a path from the player's location to these items, performs the same checks, and generates the necessary objects. The planner finds that the player needs items of type C4 and Key. An item of type C4 is at a location, whereas the item of type Key is held by an officer, so you need to expose that to the planner as well.

The number of grounded actions can be pruned by removing all grounded actions that are as follows:

1. Do not have any relevant effects. For example, the grounded action (*move p loc1 loc1*) does not change a state when applied to it.
2. Will never contribute to reaching any goals. This is done by labelling all grounded actions that can achieve any of the goals or any precondition of a grounded action that has been labelled. Any grounded action that is not labelled will never contribute to reaching the goals or enable an action that can.

Reducing the planning problem and pruning useless grounded actions decreases the branching factor and increases planning time. These two simple pruning strategies can reduce the number of grounded actions by over 90%.

18.4   EXECUTION

Now, with an understanding of how to create a domain, planning problems, and how AI planning works, the framework that has been used for automated testing on *Zombie Army 4*, *Evil Genius2*, and *Sniper Elite 5* will be explained. The overall framework is depicted in Image 18.4.

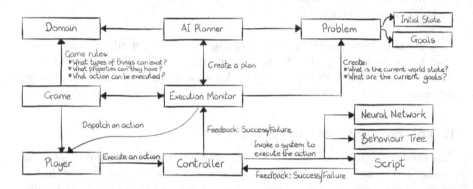

IMAGE 18.4   Execution framework.

The driving component is the execution monitor. When the game is running, it will assess the current game state and use the predefined domain to create an AI planning problem. How this is handled is game-specific for example *Zombie Army 4* needed a very different problem-generation algorithm than *Evil Genius 2* did. The AI planning system is invoked once a problem has been generated. If a solution is found, then the execution monitor will dispatch one action at a time to the player. The player uses a controller to invoke an AI system to execute this action. After the action has been executed, the system will return whether it succeeded or failed to execute the action. If the action is successful, then the next action in the sequence is dispatched. When all actions have been executed, or when an action fails to execute, the execution monitor reassesses the current game state and creates a new AI planning problem to be solved.

One benefit of this architecture is that the AI planning system takes care of most of the complexity (causal reasoning, making sure enough resources are available when it comes to executing an action, and the like), which leaves the execution behaviours relatively simple.

The BTs used in *Zombie Army 4*, *Evil Genius 2*, and *Sniper Elite 5* never had more than three nodes. However, it is important to make the systems that execute actions robust. If the execution of actions is brittle, then the system will spend most of the time replanning. For example, the *move* behaviour in *Zombie Army 4* and *Sniper*

Elite 5 has combat capabilities to destroy enemies that got in the way by performing melee attacks.

18.5   CONCLUSION

This chapter described a novel automated testing framework that has been successful in completing the games: *Zombie Army 4*, *Evil Genius 2*, and *Sniper Elite 5*. An actual player is mimicked as closely as possible by making the executing behaviours set the key, mouse, and/or controller inputs. For these games, the only cheat used was invulnerability, which is common for automated testing purposes. Due to its ability to complete entire games, it has great code coverage and was able to find a good number of bugs. Furthermore, it has helped developers to find bugs such as out-of-world issues and soft locks. It has also helped designers find issues with the game design. For example, in *Evil Genius 2*, this system turned out to be a great tool to fine-tune and find bugs in the tutorial section. It even prompted the designers to change some aspects of the tutorial.

The overall planning time was usually a few milliseconds and took around 25MiB for *Evil Genius 2*. The longest planning time was 1.5 seconds, which was on *Sniper Elite 5*. The highest memory usage was 180MiB on *Evil Genius 2* for problems that could not find a solution with 1,000 explored nodes, which was the limit imposed before abandoning planning.

The time it took for this system to play through a mission in *Zombie Army 4* and *Sniper Elite 5* ranged between 20 minutes to an hour. An *Evil Genius 2* campaign took between 64 and 75 hours, depending on which genius was picked.

While this framework was used to perform automated testing with great success, it is not limited to that role. It can be used to create more intelligent non-player characters that are not just reactive but deliberate about how to achieve future goals. This enables designers to create more believable environments where non-player characters do not just follow scripted behaviour, or only react to what the player is doing, but have goals that they can actively pursue. Other applications include multi-agent storytelling and making a game more accessible by playing part of a game autonomously or guiding a player through a game.

19 Dumbing Down AI
The Art of Making Intelligence Stupid

Sarah Cook

19.1 INTRODUCTION

Every programmer wants to make their artificial intelligence (AI) perfect, responding to events in the way we expect a human to, but this usually results in a game where the player can never win. So how can we make the AI less intelligent without it looking unconvincing? This chapter looks at some of the approaches used in real games, and how to use them successfully in yours.

Establishing how intelligent an AI should be is an important step in this process, and this chapter briefly discusses some of the salient considerations for determining the level required. Next, it gives some tips on which areas are likely candidates for decreasing the skill of your AI. It then moves on to looking at common methods for reducing the intelligence of non-player characters (NPCs) such as randomisation, encouraging movement, and counter-intuitive responses. Finally, it gives examples of how smoke and mirrors can make these measures more believable.

19.2 DETERMINING HOW INTELLIGENT YOUR AI SHOULD BE

The first step in dumbing down your AI is to determine how intelligent your AI should be. This can be affected by several different considerations, such as the role of the AI, the intended players, and what you can sensibly vary. In general, you need to answer five main questions:

19.2.1 QUESTION 1: WHAT IS THE FORMAT OF YOUR GAME?

Is it turn-based, a shooter, or a simulation? The more immersive and realistic your game, the more intelligent your AI is going to need to be.

19.2.2 QUESTION 2: WHAT IS THE ROLE OF AI IN YOUR GAME?

This is likely to be determined by the type of game you are developing, although there are some overlaps. Different AI roles can suggest options for dumbing them down (these will be discussed in more detail later in the chapter), as well as indicating how stupid you can make them.

 DOI: 10.1201/9781003323549-19

Do the AI agents attack the player? What form do these attacks take? Do they have weapons such as guns and other projectiles? Are they restricted to melee attacks? Do the attacks vary between agents? In much the same way as animals that use tools are perceived to be more intelligent, so are agents with weapons when compared to those without, but any form of AI attack can have its effectiveness varied to lower its skill level.

Are the agents trying to beat the player in another way? Are they restricted to simple interactions with the player, or are they there just to be killed? AI designed to outmanoeuvre the player, such as reaching a target destination first, blocking player movement, or stealing items from the player, would be perceived as more intelligent than those limited to simple behaviours such as running away.

Are they supporting characters? Is your AI a friend rather than a foe, who provides information, objectives, and items to the player? The need and options for dumbing down AI in this case are smaller and the variations are likely to rely on the extent of the information made available or the usefulness of the items.

Alternatively, are your agents simulated AI versions of teammates, designed to mimic the actions and responses of human players? In this case, you can consider them in the same way as NPC enemies, as only their targets vary.

Do different types of AI have different roles? For example, do you have *cannon fodder* agents that would be expected to be dumb combined with bosses that have more refined behaviour? If so, each type of agent should be considered separately, and their skill levels compared to achieve the desired effect.

19.2.3 QUESTION 3: WHAT LEVEL OF PLAYER IS YOUR GAME AIMED AT?

Understanding the players that you are trying to reach is critical in determining how intelligent your AI really need to be. In general, AI aimed at casual gamers can be a lot more stupid than AI aimed at more serious players, as casual gamers tend to be a lot more forgiving than hardcore ones. For the casual market, you would also expect a lower player skill level, so they will need more help to beat the AI.

In addition, you need to consider player expectations. More realistic game environments will encourage players to expect more realistic AI behaviours. Humanoid AI are usually assumed to be more intelligent than non-humanoid, so give thought to what the player will expect from the type of AI you have chosen.

Do your research and look at what other games do. Remember to consider the type and target audience when choosing games to review.

19.2.4 QUESTION 4: WHAT VARIABLES CAN YOU CHANGE?

What attributes affect the skill levels of your agents? This will normally be decided by the role of your AI, so consider this when choosing variables that you would like to vary. There is no point considering options that are not relevant to your chosen game type, such as projectile spread, for games that have only melee attacks, or route variation where only one route is possible.

Having lots of attributes to choose from sounds like it would be advantageous, but more often than not you will find that only a handful of variables will give you more than enough flexibility.

Could you completely disable part of the AI, rather than adjusting values? It is going to take time to understand and balance the AI data, so keep the variables independent where possible, and only change one variable at a time.

19.2.5 SHOULD THE AI HAVE VARIABLE SKILL LEVELS DEPENDENT ON THE DIFFICULTY SETTINGS?

If your game has multiple difficulty settings, should this affect the AI? If so, you will need to define the minimum and maximum skill of the AI, and which attributes can be varied to change this. Do not be tempted to change all the possible variables for all levels, if only changing one or two would work equally well.

There are alternatives to varying AI skill levels to affect the difficulty. For example, increasing the number of agents, or replacing existing agents with their more intelligent counterparts, or varying the environment.

How far you can dumb down the AI is determined by their believability. When do they stop being convincing? If your agents are not believable there will be an impact on the playability of the game, but it can be useful to find that point. This can be a very fine line, so be prepared to spend some time working out what is, and what is not, convincing. However, remember that believability is subjective, so it is likely to vary between players. Some players will always say that the AI is stupid, so make sure you get multiple opinions, and try to get them to explain their decision.

19.3 METHODS FOR REDUCING AI SKILL

Having established how intelligent your agents need to be, the next stage is to consider which approaches are the most appropriate for reducing the AI skill level. Again, the answers to the previous five questions will give you an idea of the available options, with different formats and AI roles having the biggest influence. In the majority of cases, skill variation will depend on some kind of randomisation, as is often the case with AI behaviour in general.

The methods for reducing AI skill mostly fall into four categories:

19.3.1 CATEGORY 1: ROUTE VARIATION

Randomisation of the target destination or variation of the route itself can be used to vary how fast an AI can reach a destination. The purpose here is to allow the player to reach the goal first. Also, the AI can deviate from the ideal line in driving games, bringing an agent into attack range, or determine if an agent successfully intercepts the player to attack.

19.3.2 CATEGORY 2: RESTRICTING AI KNOWLEDGE

By its very nature, a game will have access to all of the information all of the time, from player location to available resources, and even the results of randomised equations. Should the AI have access to all this information? At the opposite end of the scale, you could make the AI blind and deaf, with no access to the player and world information to make intelligent decisions.

Obviously, neither of these approaches will make AI believable, so the trick is to find a reasonable level between the two. In addition, the passing of knowledge between AI, known as propagation, can also be controlled. Finding the correct balance for this can be difficult, but limiting what the AI knows about the player and the world is a must.

19.3.3 CATEGORY 3: COUNTER-INTUITIVE BEHAVIOUR

Counter-intuitive behaviour is where the AI does something substantially different to what would be expected of a human player. This can take many forms, from encouraging agents to move regardless of threat level or location, or searching for the player, to increased messaging of intentions. For example, agents that move out of cover only a short time after being attacked or the use of animations to telegraph an agent's attack before they happen.

19.3.4 CATEGORY 4: VARYING THE EFFECTIVENESS OF ATTACKS

The AI should be prevented from delivering attacks with pinpoint accuracy every time. In many ways, this approach is related to the level of knowledge made available to the AI. Knowing the player's location even when they are not visible leads to levels of attack accuracy above what would be believable, as does the ability of an agent to land a headshot every time. As with counterintuitive behaviour, there are many different approaches to reducing the effectiveness of attacks, from projectile spread and intentional misses to limiting player's position prediction and targeting.

Each of the methods described can be used individually or combined, although the specifics of how they are applied relies on factors such as game format and AI role. Route variation and restricting AI knowledge are common across many game types and genres, but even these will need to be adapted to the individual AI types and environments.

Turn-based games, such as those where agents seek to take over a map, usually have more basic AI. This therefore offers fewer options when it comes to dumbing them down, but route variation and restricting AI knowledge are two approaches that can be used. This might include limiting information on player's position, varying how effective attacks are using a randomised outcome, and changing routes to determine which areas of the map are uncovered over time.

As the game environment becomes more realistic, and the roles of AI become more complex, the options for reducing skill level increase. In driving games, the AI could have inbuilt slowdowns and randomised crashes. Similarly, capture-the-flag-based games would rely heavily on route variation but could also limit the amount of player information available to effectively mask the player's position.

Games requiring highly complex NPCs, such as those where the AI can attack the player with guns, give the highest number of possible approaches. Suggestions might be to restrict information on the player location and inventory, projectile spread, encouraging movement, and randomisation of routes between locations. These are only a small proportion of those which may be appropriate, and there are many other possible combinations, some of which will be discussed in more detail later in the chapter.

Whatever the format and style of your game, it is important to remember to keep it simple wherever possible. With a huge number of possible approaches and combinations, it is advisable to start small with just one or two that are the most applicable. You can include more reductions in skill as you go, but understand why you are adding them, and remove any that are no longer in use.

19.4 COMMON APPROACHES TO DUMBING DOWN NPCs WHO ATTACK THE PLAYER

With many different options available, this section will look in more detail at one example – Humanoid AI, in realistic environments, who attack the player with weapons such as guns. This example has been chosen because it gives us many approaches to discuss, but the individual methods and combinations outlined are only a small number of the options available to reduce the AI's skill level. Despite this, agents in such a scenario can be difficult to balance, as there is a fine line between them being believable to the player and just looking dumb.

The most obvious place to start is by limiting the amount of player information made available to the AI, as this will also affect other aspects such as route variation and attack effectiveness. The game will always know the location of the player, and all information pertaining to inventory and the like, but you can restrict how much of this you make available to the AI.

19.4.1 AI AWARENESS

First, you need to decide a sensible range at which the NPC should be able to *see* or *hear* the player. In reality, the majority of AI systems rely mostly on sound to convey information, due to the expensive overhead of using line-of-sight tests, so most reactions will be triggered by this alone. This can also be used to our advantage, as a specific destination becomes less obvious compared to a general direction.

Another consideration is how this distance affects weapon usage? For example, the firing of a gun would be heard much further away than a footstep, and the use of remote sounds such as explosives can be used to feed the AI false information.

19.4.2 AI MEMORY

How fast should the AI *forget* about player info? This is regularly controlled by cooldown timers, which makes it an easy way of adjusting AI behaviour. However, this can be difficult to balance and still have your NPCs believable. Typically using times equivalent to those of a player prove to be too long, keeping the AI in cover or searching for much longer than feels appropriate, but decaying knowledge too quickly will make them appear stupid and unrealistic.

19.4.3 WORLD KNOWLEDGE

Another thing to consider is how much game information should be made available to the AI? Should they just be informed of player location, or is passing on knowledge of the inventory they carry important too? Will this change over the course of the game, or be gained gradually as they encounter the player more frequently? In many cases purely knowing where the player is at any given time, possibly along with their movement speed and direction, should suffice.

19.4.4 SHARED AI KNOWLEDGE

Propagation is the passing of knowledge from one AI to another, which can be a powerful tool. However, careful thought should go into what information is propagated, at what distance, and how fast. Not enough and the AI looks unresponsive, too much and the whole map suddenly knows the player's location. This leads to another method for dumbing down AI skills. By reducing this passage of knowledge, or restricting its type, less information is known by the AI and they cannot respond to what they don't know.

19.4.5 COUNTER-INTUITIVE RESPONSES

Encouraging movement, for instance forcing an agent out of cover after a player attack, is a common form of counterintuitive behaviour employed for this type of game. Although it would be odd for NPCs not to hide for at least some time after being shot at or otherwise attacked, AI hiding behind cover is virtually impossible to shoot, so you need them to move regularly. This does not necessarily have to involve moving agents to completely different locations repeatedly but may use smaller movements such as peeking out to give the player more chance for an attack. Rather than immediately switching back to their prior behaviour, a de-escalation, first to moving between cover locations is likely to be more convincing. Using timers and randomisation to encourage movement provides a way to balance the effects.

Moving towards threating sounds rather than away from them is another form of counterintuitive behaviour that is regularly used in these situations. A good example of this is with search behaviours where agents can be seen scouring an area, trying to pinpoint the exact location of the sound that was heard. Although this may be expected in certain circumstances, such as the incidental noise made by player movement, it can be used widely to dumb down the AI. Searching can be used to lure AI into a trap, or to distract them from the players themselves, which makes it a powerful tool for many situations, as well as its use in reducing AI skill level. In addition, allowing de-escalation from defensive behaviour to searching allows NPCs to wander into player range without it looking like they were intentionally sent to be killed.

19.4.6 ROUTE VARIATION

Route variation is widely used in games to make AI movement more believable. By extending and exaggerating this behaviour, it can also be employed to make NPCs appear less intelligent.

By varying routes, an agent can be encouraged to pass through more dangerous areas, without being perceived as unrealistic by the player. Choosing paths that avoid cover, use narrow bottlenecks, or intentionally pass within range of the player makes agents more vulnerable to attack. Achieving this may be as simple as ignoring knowledge of player location when generating routes or deliberating weighting areas without cover as more desirable.

Destination offsets or using longer or more complex routes can also be used to slow down NPCs, leading to them reaching a goal later or reducing the likelihood of them intercepting the player. This in turn can be used to affect the effectiveness of an attack or limit how much knowledge can be gained along the way.

Also, limiting how often routes are updated can be used to make AI look less intelligent. Without regularly adjusting routes to follow a moving player, the precision of the original path generated rapidly becomes irrelevant. However, updating too frequently would allow the AI to accurately target the player for each attack.

19.4.7 ATTACK VARIATION

Varying the effectiveness of attacks offers a wide range of options for dumbing down AI. The type and variety of attacks will affect which approaches are the most likely to be appropriate, but there are methods that are common regardless.

19.4.8 TELEGRAPHING AI INTENTIONS

Telegraphing the intention to attack by deliberately messaging the player that an attack is about to begin can be used to make an assault less effective, leaving the player time to react or avoid the encounter. This could be as simple as a shout from an agent which advises the player that NPCs are closing in or using animations to taunt or announce the direction and type of attack about to be performed. Other than controlling how often these cues occur, it is a difficult approach to balance. Cues are either triggered or not, but a simple solution is to vary the magnitude of when they will occur.

19.4.9 INTENTIONAL MISSES

AI with knowledge of the player's location, and a clear line-of-sight, should be able to land a maximum damage attack every time. Allowing this to happen, however, would lead to a game where the AI are very difficult to defeat, and therefore create a negative player experience. Intentional misses are a technique used to control the effectiveness of an attack, by allowing the AI to fail to land the attack at all, or by reducing the damage done when one does hit the player.

This is one of the few options available to an agent that only has melee attacks, but intentional misses can be easily applied to agents with weapons. Generally, they are achieved by varying target locations or delaying the attack, although these variations can in turn take several forms. Possible options include small adjustments to the direction of the attack or delaying the attack until the player is out of range, making the agent overshoot or completely miss without looking unconvincing. In addition, limiting the use of position prediction, where the speed and direction of a player are taken into consideration when launching an attack, can also be used to create believable misses.

19.4.10 Projectile Spread

The spread of projectiles is a slight variation on the theme of intentional misses and can be applied to any projectile, not just bullets. It is not only a believable way of limiting the effectiveness of an attack but would in many cases occur in a similar real-world situation. This is achieved by applying a slight offset to the target location of the projectile or the path along which it travels. You should restrict the corresponding offsets to be small enough to be realistic.

Applying spread means that not all shots will hit the player, and high-value impacts such as headshots can be reduced in frequency. The size of the spread and whether this should vary over time will normally be dependent on the type of projectile and weapon used to launch it. Common factors that are normally considered include weapon recoil, increased accuracy over time, the number of simultaneous projectiles, and the distance from the target.

Whether you use one or many approaches to dumb down your AI, there are several ways that you can make their behaviour appear more intelligent than it is. The following section describes some hints and tips to achieve this.

19.5 USING SMOKE AND MIRRORS TO MAKE AI MORE BELIEVABLE

When trying to make dumbed-down AI more convincing, you generally have two options – try to deflect attention from the AI behaviour or call attention to it. Experience suggests that a combination of the two tends to work best, where this is possible. The following are just some of the ways in which this can be achieved.

19.5.1 Calling Out Mistakes Rather than Trying to Hide Them

Although it seems illogical, calling out intended or even unintended mistakes, can make AI seem more intelligent. A good example of this might be animations or audio cues used as responses to intentional misses. Having an agent shout something like "Oh no I missed!", "That didn't work, run!", or "Where did they go?" can be remarkably effective. In the same way, using animations showing frustration at having missed, or confusion about why the attack failed, can also be very convincing.

19.5.2 Using Speech to Explain Why the AI Are Acting in a Certain Way

Speech can be a very good way to give believable reasons for counter-intuitive behaviour. It messages the intention of the AI if it is not immediately clear to the player, or can be employed to indicate why an agent's behaviour has suddenly changed. An obvious example of this is using speech to announce the de-escalation of a threat, which can be used to deflect attention from how fast this has happened. Shouts between nearby AI can also be used to propagate knowledge about player location, which can be very effective to encourage teammates to retreat when under attack, or to search an area in which a sound has been heard.

19.5.3 Varying Animations to Make the AI More Believable

Using variations of animations is a common way of making AI behaviour more believable, not just when dumbing down AI. Even slight changes in idle animations can make NPCs more believable or enhance the differences between contrasting AI roles. When trying to deflect attention from reductions in AI skill, they can be used to hide near misses, add delays to attacks, or even just message the agent's intention to the player. More specifically, an agent could taunt the player before an attack or slightly offset a melee designed to miss. Using a range of animations can also allow more control over some of the skill reduction approaches, or more easily accommodate randomisation.

19.5.4 Behaviour that Implies that the AI Does Not Know Where the Player Is

Investigation and searching behaviours are regularly used to imply to the player that their location is not known, regardless of what information the AI has access to. Rather than alerting agents on the first sighting of the player, or even an incidental noise, having them investigate the relevant location allows a delay in acquiring player knowledge that looks believable. On the flip side, having NPCs search the area in which a player was last seen can make them appear to forget the player's location fairly quickly, a lot more convincingly.

19.5.5 Emergent Behaviour

Although not technically the correct usage of the term, here *emergent behaviour* refers to any seemingly intelligent behaviour, which has not been programmed or scripted. Often by not scripting exactly what AI should do in a given situation, and instead using more general rules allows AI to combine behaviours in ways that are not always expected. This in turn can lead to humorous situations and responses that would not have been convincing otherwise. Examples may be NPCs diving off bridges to avoid grenades or kicking projectiles as they dive to get out of the way. It would be virtually impossible to program these scenarios outside of a scripted cutscene or similar, but both appear realistic when encountered by accident.

19.6 CONCLUSION

Every programmer wants to make their AI perfect, responding to events in the way we expect a human to, but this rarely leads to a good player experience. This chapter has looked at a variety of ways in which AI can be dumbed down, to make them easier to attack, or less lethal to the player.

First, it laid out some guidelines for establishing how intelligent the AI should be, given the type of game, AI roles and a few other considerations. Next, it looked at several approaches that can be used to reduce the AI skill levels and applied them to give specific examples for use in a game with NPCs that attack the player with weapons. Finally, it gave a range of examples of how smoke and mirrors can make these measures more believable.

20 Race Director

Andy Brown

20.1 INTRODUCTION

The most crucial element of racing AI is making the AI as competitive as possible without resorting to what some players would consider *cheating*. Sometimes, cheating is not even really cheating, but the AI not appearing human-like, such as making mistakes and doing their task too well can be perceived as such. For all the good things the AI does in a game, it will often be the weak points that get a mention in a review, so it is important to focus on the player experience and making the game accessible to your target audience.

Sonic & All Stars Racing Transformed brought together a range of techniques to deliver an AI experience that allowed the design team to deliver a game that could grow in difficulty whilst providing all players with a satisfying experience. This chapter will cover the system that managed the race as a whole – the *Race Director* whose job it was to manage the race from a high level.

20.2 KART RACING

The most important element of any AI racer is getting the AI to be as competitive as possible before resorting to any kind of additional aids. The key to this is getting the AI to race around each of your circuits as quickly as possible, maximising corner speeds and taking the best racing line. Ideally, you want to have an AI that is so good that you can then just scale things back to reduce the difficulty. Each track on *Sonic & All Stars Racing Transformed* was made up of either driving, boating, or air sections, but the basic premise was the same – ensuring maximum speed around the entire circuit. To get the AI to this level requires a process focused primarily on racing line modifications and maximising corner speeds to allow it to take each corner at the absolute limit. This is a manual process that involves watching the AI race around continuously whilst making small tweaks to each corner in turn. Obtaining metrics from the best human players is also essential to working out where you can shave time off a lap. These metrics can be obtained by either watching the QA department play the game in real time or by studying recordings of great lap times. This will be an ongoing process for the entirety of the project, but it becomes easier once the handling models are locked down. However, there will always be a hundredth of a second to be found by making small modifications.

Most tracks in karting games will have shortcuts which not only give tracks variety but is one of the many levers available to modify the AI difficulty. The more difficult AI can take the shorter routes, whereas the easier AI would take the longer routes. To complicate matters slightly, in *Sonic & All Stars Racing Transformed*,

DOI: 10.1201/9781003323549-20

following the racing line, or taking all the shortcuts, did not always result in the fastest route around the track since the game also featured boost pads, which were often placed away from the racing line with an element of risk in taking them. The AI needs to consider these to ensure they remain competitive.

Part of the AI following logic in karting games is the ability for the racing line to be semi-dynamic. In other words, it continually looks at the track ahead and patches in additional sections of the racing line for things to avoid or pick up. This means that boost pads can be taken if desired. This gives another lever for adjusting AI difficulty.

With competitive racers in place, the next area to look at is pickups and weapons. Since *Mario Kart*, these have been a staple of karting games. *Sonic & All Stars Racing Transformed* featured a variety of pickups with most of them requiring some skill to use. No Mario-style blue shells for Sonic. For each weapon, the AI was given a unique behaviour which could be scaled to their skill level and depended on the difficulty settings. Tweaking these values created an engaging player experience. The game itself had a standard race option with easy, medium, and hard difficulties, but it also had a world tour where you would be introduced to the game with progression getting increasingly more difficult. Designers will undoubtedly require the ability to script the desired outcome of a race. This is where the *Race Director* comes in.

20.3 RACE DIRECTOR

The basic concept of the *Race* Director is that each AI racer has a profile which allows you to define the following:

20.3.1 THE WEAPONS PROFILE

The weapons profile contains all the tweakables for an AI using weapons or pickups. You could have an unlimited number of these profiles and apply them to any AI vehicle. For simplicity, assume that you only have easy, medium, and hard. Each profile would dictate distances at which weapons would be fired, the probability of missing the target and cool-down timers. You can even have separate values to distinguish between AI attacking other AI and human racers. All of these subtleties give you the ability to adjust the difficulty without it being obvious to the player.

20.3.2 THE HANDLING PROFILE

Each racer will require a handling profile. These are not necessarily tied to difficulty and are simply a way to dictate the various driving parameters for an AI racer and the various vehicle types. *Sonic & All Stars Racing Transformed* had three types – Land, Sea, and Air. These profiles include such things as look ahead distances, drift parameters, and the like and featured twenty four different characters. Handling profiles gave the ability to tweak individual vehicles if required. For vehicle types using the same handling model, a default set-up can be sufficient, but the option is still there if needed. Always better to have flexibility in a system!

20.3.3 THE ZONE PROFILE

Each racer is designated a zone profile. A zone is an area on the racetrack where attributes can be manipulated. A zone does not necessarily need to be a static location. It can be an area around another AI vehicle.

This profile contains attributes for defining their pure driving skill. This boils down to three values. The main being a skill percentage which essentially gives you the ability to scale up or down the default maximum speed a vehicle can travel at. The remaining two values are a start and end distance, and these were defined when the zone was in operation. The distance itself is the distance from the racer they are tracking. An example of this can be seen in Table 20.1.

TABLE 20.1

Example Zone Profiles

Zone Name	AI Skill Multiplier	Start Distance	End Distance
IN FRONT OF RACER	0.9	300	500
AROUND RACER	0.9	−300	300
BEHIND RACER	1.0	−600	−300

To briefly go through the details in Table 20.1, it states that if the AI can get 300 metres in front of the car they are tracking, then the zone "IN FRONT OF PLAYER" is activated, likewise if the AI drops behind the tracked player, then the "BEHIND PLAYER" zone would kick in. You can see that the behind-player zone would increase the skill of the AI, thus giving the AI a chance to catch up.

A general rule for any of these zones is that if a human player is within close proximity, then there should be no cheating going on. The whole idea behind this is to mask the fact that the AI is dynamically adapting to how a human player is performing.

The AI Skill Multiplier can also be greater than 1! This will technically allow the AI to *cheat* but it gives the design team the flexibility to increase the top speeds within reason – if the human players do not notice of course!

20.3.4 ASSIGNING PROFILES

The final piece of the puzzle is assigning these profiles to each racer. To do this, you need a table with a column for each racer. In *Sonic & All Stars Racing Transformed,* rather than assigning a profile to a specific racer, it was decided to assign them to races in certain positions which allowed for a shuffled-up starting grid and also provided more variety. This system is also dynamic in that the profile for each racer can be assigned based on their position. If the best AI at the time is hit and therefore drops down to last place, rather than them suddenly trying to regain first place, they can inherit the last place profile.

A typical race profile for an easy race would look something like Table 20.2. The most important row that underpins the logic is "TargetPlayer". This is the player that each AI will use as reference for their zone profile. You can see that the AI in first would track the best human player, the others would track the best AI player, the idea being that the best AI will dictate the pace for the rest of the AI to achieve some semblance of order. Should an AI come off track or be hit, then they will just slot into the relevant profile based on their position. This gives the design team a fair degree of control over how a race will pan out.

TABLE 20.2

A Typical Race Profile in *Sonic & All Stars Racing Transformed*

Attribute	AI Position 1st	AI Position 2nd	AI Position 3rd	AI Position 4th	AI Position 5th
Weapons profile	Easy	Easy	Easy	Easy	Easy
Default car skill	0.8	0.7	0.6	0.5	0.4
Default boat skill	0.8	0.7	0.6	0.5	0.4
Default aircraft skill	0.8	0.7	0.6	0.5	0.4
Default zone profile car	Easy	Easy	Easy	Easy	Easy
Default zone profile boat	Easy	Easy	Easy	Easy	Easy
Default zone profile aircraft	Easy	Easy	Easy	Easy	Easy
Handling profile	Default	Default	Default	Default	Default
Target player	BestHuman	BestAI	BestAI	BestAI	BestAI
Pick shortest route probability	0.2	0.1	0.1	0	0

20.3.5 Race Segmentation

There are a couple of important things missing – these being the behaviour at the start of a race and behaviour during a race. When developing *Sonic & All Stars Racing Transformed*, the design team had expressed an interest in making the race difficulty dynamic, so that even an easy race might begin with the AI being more difficult to race but on the final lap they could ease off and give the human player the satisfaction of just beating the AI as they cross the finish line. To achieve this, a simple concept was added to the race profile. The race itself could be split into segments, these segments would define a percentage of the overall race distance and would allow zone profiles and weapons profiles to be altered. No two tracks will be the exact same length, so using percentages allowed for a race profile to be applied to any track and reduced the game data required. These segment profiles can be applied to all racers or specific racers as required. An example is shown in Table 20.3.

TABLE 20.3

Segments of a Race that Could Produce Override Profiles

Segment Name	Percentage	Override Zone Profile
StartLine	10	StartLine
MidRace	50	Default
EndRace	40	EndRace

Using the example values given in Table 20.3, you can see that the race has been split into three sections. The first being the *StartLine* segment. This allows all of the AI to go flat out at the start of the race, until 10% of the race distance is completed, where the *Default Profile* will be applied, followed by the *EndRace Profile* for the last 40% of the race. There is no limit to the number of segments. It is a design decision, but realistically you will only need three or four segments for most scenarios.

20.4   CONCLUSION

As stated at the beginning of the chapter, the key aim for the AI in *Sonic & All Stars Racing Transformed* was to make an enjoyable and competitive experience with a minimum of negative callouts in reviews. The Eurogamer, IGN & Gamespot reviews of the game either fail to mention the AI (a positive!) and where it is mentioned it was with comments such as "surprisingly competent AI rivals". To this end, it can be concluded that the goals set out to achieve were met. On top of this, it gave the design team the ability to script the overall feel of a race from start to finish, was entirely data-driven, and was highly customisable. Variants of this code were also used in subsequent titles due to its success and flexibility.

21 SB-GOAP
Self-Balanced Goal-Oriented Action Planner

Michele Condò

21.1 INTRODUCTION

There are several solutions to implement behaviours for non-player characters (NPCs) in games. One of these approaches is to use an automated planning architecture to solve the problem of decision-making and to execute the best strategy. The most famous automated planner is Goal-Oriented Action Planner (GOAP) (Orkin, 2003).

GOAP is a simplified STRIPS-like planning architecture (Fikes & Nilsson, 1971) which can solve many problems relating to autonomous character behaviours in games. Although GOAP is powerful, it has some disadvantages, and two of these limitations usually lead to AI coders adopting other solutions instead. These limitations are that GOAP has less control over the plan compared to other solutions, and has the potential for repeating plans, which can break the player's immersion. Normally, to solve these two problems, GOAP is placed side by side with other systems. To improve the control over the plan, a finite-state machine (FSM) can be used, while to solve the repetitiveness, some sort of randomness can be added. Although the GOAP might be implemented using algorithms such as A*, it is usually done as a decision tree-based approach only, which does not give much room for randomness (Millington, 2019).

To overcome these limitations, you can use a strong path search algorithm-based approach, with custom action-related cost/estimate functions and use more detailed prerequisites and effects.

If you put all this together, you get a Self-Balancing Goal-Oriented Action Planning architecture. This chapter details the Self-Balancing GOAP architecture (SB-GOAP), which gives more flexibility and plan variation, removes repetitiveness, gives more control, and limits the need for other systems to support the planner.

21.2 SB-GOAP OVERVIEW

SB-GOAP aims to solve some of the problems highlighted in the introduction. The advantages this architecture brings can be summarised as follows:

1. It creates more variations when planning, breaking the repetitiveness, and reducing the chance of a plan reusing the same set of actions over time, without the need to create different or more actions with different or more prerequisites. This is because of its deep connection with the search path algorithm.
2. It gives more control over the plan, by explicitly marking a prerequisite as "false" it can be excluded from an A* search.
3. It needs to communicate with the gameplay code to determine if an action of a plan was performed successfully.

SB-GOAP implements two cores of logic. The first is working within a path-searching algorithm and taking advantage of it (since it is tightly knitted to it), driving the decision-making. Actions require functions to compute cost, estimate cost, get neighbours, and determine if a goal is reached. The second is the logic handling the connections between the planner and the gameplay code.

In short, the first part exploits the search path algorithm in order to drive the plan, not only by prerequisites but also by the cost of the actions, while the second part aims to adjust such cost if the agent gets interrupted while actually performing the action.

In fact, even if a plan can be computed in one frame, the actual execution by the agent can last seconds, minutes, or longer. For instance, an action such as "Create Axe" might take anywhere from 5 to 30 seconds. So, if something happens to the agent while performing this action, it should be flagged as "not optimal" for this goal.

21.3   PATH SEARCH EXPLOITATION

This section will define what an action is in SB-GOAP as it is slightly different from the GOAP version. Image 21.1 shows a classic implementation of a GOAP action with preconditions and effects. Preconditions are used to determine if an action fulfils the requirements of the current state for it to be considered for the plan. The effect is how this action will modify the world state. The effects and preconditions are Boolean, which if they are present means they are considered "true", otherwise "false", although an effect can exist and be set to "false".

This sort of action works well with a decision tree-based approach or for any approach that does not require the searching of a path. This is because without a cost, the planner can only reason with preconditions which results in repetitiveness (Orkin, 2003).

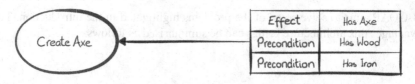

IMAGE 21.1   Action in the classic GOAP.

Image 21.2 depicts the same action shown in Image 21.1 using GOAP, but this time using a cost. In this version, the plan can be driven by the path search algorithm. Some sort of randomness can also be added to these types of actions but can result in worse plans.

	Effect	Has Axe
	Precondition	Has Wood
	Precondition	Has Iron

IMAGE 21.2   Action in GOAP with a cost.

Image 21.3 depicts the same action, but this time using SB-GOAP. As can be seen, it has a cost, which is the "default" cost of the action. It is defined as a default cost because it is not the one that is going to be used. SB-GOAP externally defines two other fields – a "hitch" value, which is defined on a per-user basis, and a normalised multiplier, which is defined on a per-agent or per-type of agent basis. The first can be seen as the "obstacle" cost added to the action, if the actual execution gets interrupted, which will increase the traversal cost, and the multiplier, which scales the "hitch" cost (values between 0 and its maximum value).

The preconditions and effects also have values. These can be Boolean or numerical, as the functions used in the path search algorithm are the ones dealing with them. For example, if the preconditions and effects were implemented as Booleans, you will have something like this:

- Effects → Has Axe: TRUE, Has Wood: FALSE, Has Iron: FALSE
- Preconditions → Has Wood: TRUE, Has Iron: TRUE

If instead they were implemented as numerical values, you would have something like this:

- Effects → Has Axe: +1, Has Wood: −2, Has Iron: −3
- Preconditions → Has Wood: +2, Has Iron: +3

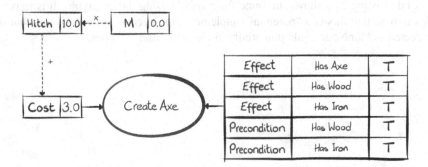

	Effect	Has Axe	T
	Effect	Has Wood	T
	Effect	Has Iron	T
	Precondition	Has Wood	T
	Precondition	Has Iron	T

IMAGE 21.3   Action in SB-GOAP.

SB-GOAP has the following classes which the path search algorithm needs to handle directly:

- **Action**: Contains cost, effects, and prerequisites.
- **WorldState**: Contains an identifier and a map of state identifiers and state values which, during traversal, will be created, updated, and added to a new PlanNode.
- **PlanNode**: Encapsulate for the world states for searching purposes. Contains a pointer to a world state and a pointer to the action that led to this node.
- **PlanRequest**: Encapsulates the initial world state, goal world state, and all the actions taken into consideration. It can contain all the possible actions or a subset depending on the context. The latter is obviously better for performance reasons.

It is important to discuss how SB-GOAL modifies A*, but only the custom functions needed will be covered. It is worth mentioning without going into too much detail that the functions *FindInOpenList* and *IsInClosedList* compare an array of PlanNodes against the current node, where the comparison is if the current node world state is equal to the PlanNose's world state.

Code Listing 21.1 presents the *IsGoal* function that checks if the current node is the goal node. This implementation simply checks to see if every state (Boolean) of the node passed in matches the value (Boolean) of the current node, and if so, it is the goal state.

Code Listing 21.1: The *IsGoal* function within PlanNode, using Boolean type.

```
function CurrentNode.IsGoal with CurrentNode is C has
       input: PlanNode with OtherNode is O
       output: Boolean with true if w of O same of w of C
       with: w is World State pair(state is s, value is v)

       for each pair(s, v) in w of O do
                 if Ow(s, v) ≠ Cw(s, v) return false
       return true
```

Code Listing 21.2 shows the same function but using integral types. It is important to note that this is a "potential" implementation because it depends on what is expected as PlanNode could potentially implement different types.

Code Listing 21.2: The *IsGoal* function within PlanNode, using integral types.

```
function CurrentNode.IsGoal with CurrentNode is C has
        input: PlanNode with OtherNode is O
        output: Boolean with true if w of O same of w of C and Cw(s, v) ≥ Ow(s, v)
        with: w is World State pair(state is s, value is v)


        for each pair(s, v) in w of O do
                if Ow(s) ≠ Cw(s) return false
                else if Cw(s, v) < Ow(s, v) return false
        return true
```

The *GetNeighbours* function is core to SB-GOAP because it is where an action determines if it can "work" on the world state. If so, it creates a new world state with prerequisites and effects on the current frame. Code Listing 21.3 shows the algorithm behind checks for Boolean types.

Code Listing 21.3: The *GetNeighbours* function, using Boolean type.

```
function CurrentNode.GetNeighbours with CurrentNode is C has
        input: PlanRequest with Request is R
        output: Array<PlanNode> with Neighbours is N
        where Niw := Cw and Niw(s, v) := ∀e(s, v); e ∈ Ai in A
        with: Niw is World State pair(state is s, value is v) of Ni, Ni is new
        PlanNode
        where preconditions are p and effects are e of An | {Ai} is Action in R
        where p(s, v) = Cw(s, v), Cw is World State pair(state is s, value is v) of C
        where Nia is Ai in Ni led to Cw

        N := ∅
        for each A in R do
        for each pair(s, v) in p of Ai do
                for each pair(s, v) in w of C do
                        if p(s, v) = Cw(s, v) then
                                new Ni
                                Nia := Ai
                                Niw := Cw
                                for each pair(s, v) in e of Ai do
                                        Niw(s, v) := e(s, v)
        return N
```

Code Listing 21.3 also showed how to create a new PlanNode containing a WorldState, based on the world state of the current node processed (if the action fits the prerequisites of the world state of the current node). Any new state, or existing state, is updated with the effect of each action in PlanRequest.

Code Listing 21.4: The *ComputeCost* function, using Boolean type.

```
function CurrentNode.ComputeCost with CurrentNode is C has
          input: PlanRequest with Request is R, PlanNode with OtherNode is O
          output: Float with Cost is T

          where T := (if   (Ca ≠ 0)  ⟹  TCa else 0)  + ∑_{Ai=1}^{An} TOa

          with: TCa is cost of A led to Cw or 0 if no A led to Cw,
          where preconditions are p of An | {Ai} is Action in R
          where p(s, v) = Ow(s, v) and Ai = Oa
          where TAi is cost of Ai
          where Oa is Ai led to Ow, Ow is World State pair(state is s, value is v) of O
          where Ca is Ai led to Cw, Cw is World State pair(state is s, value is v) of C
          T := if  (Ca ≠ 0) ⟹ TCa else 0
          for each A in R do
                    for each pair(s, v) in p of Ai do
                              for each pair(s, v) in w of O do
                                        if p(s, v) = Ow(s, v) and Oa = Ai
                                                  T := T + TAi
          return T
```

The *ComputeCost* function shown in Code Listing 21.4 occurs for each neighbouring node being expanded. Because the nodes generated by the *GetNeighbours* function (in Code Listing 21.3) contain both the world states and the action that led to it, the *ComputeCost* function can use this information to determine a cost.

The last function to be explored is one to estimate a cost. *EstimateCost* is shown in Code Listing 21.5 and is used to estimate the cost from the current node to the goal node. It returns a cost of 1 for any not-identical world state between two nodes.

Code Listing 21.5: The *EstimateCost* function, using Boolean type.

```
function CurrentNode.EstimateCost with CurrentNode is C has
        input: PlanNode with OtherNode is O
        output: Float with HeuristicCost is H
        where H := if   (Cw(s, v) ≠ Ow(s, v))  ⟹ 1 else 0
        with: w is World State pair(state is s, value is v)

        H := 0
        for each pair(s, v) in w of C do
                  for each pair(s, v) in w of O do
                            if Cw(s, v) ≠ Ow(s, v)
                                      H := H + 1
        return H
```

21.4   BALANCING THE PLAN

The second core concept of SB-GOAP is balancing, or to be precise, the self-balancing of actions. Since the SB-GOAP has a deep connection with A*, by adjusting the cost of an action, you can affect the result of the planning process.

But why would you want to do that? You might want to adjust costs as the "optimal" plan is not always "optimal", especially in terms of game design. As mentioned previously, a plan can be calculated in a single frame, but the actual execution (by an agent), for each action could take several seconds or even minutes to enact and, in this time, anything could happen to the agent.

This means a plan towards a goal might be optimal on paper, but not optimal in the current environment/context. Also, the "optimal" plan might be the same plan towards the same goal repeatedly, breaking the player's immersion.

When a plan is issued, SB-GOAP does not directly use the cost associated with an action. It adds it to another cost called a "hitch" cost. The "hitch" cost looks like an obstacle cost for a nav-mesh: When patched, the cost of the new nav-mesh generated is altered by the obstacle cost. The implementation details may vary, but what you have is an altered cost, an increased one, and SB-GOAP adds the "hitch" cost, multiplied by the multiplier, to the action cost.

Table 21.1 lists some possible actions along with their ID, multiplier and "hitch" cost used by agents to build a plan to complete a goal.

TABLE 21.1

Storage of the Multiplier Per Agent Per Action and the "Hitch" Cost Per Action

Action	Pairs {Agent/Agent Group/Agent Type, Cost Multiplier}	"Hitch" Cost
Chop Tree	{{ID:0, M:0}, {ID:3, M:0.4}, {ID:7, M:0.8}, {ID:.., M:..}}	8
Mine Ore	{{ID:1, M:0.4}, {ID:3, M:0.2}, {ID:7, M:1}, {ID:.., M:..}}	8
Smelt Ore	{{ID:1, M:0.7}, {ID:2, M:0.6}, {ID:3, M:0.5}, {ID:.., M:..}}	5
Work Wood	{{ID:0, M:0.1}, {ID:1, M:0.9}, {ID:9, M:0.1}, {ID:.., M:..}}	5
Create Axe	{{ID:3, M:0.2}, {ID:6, M:0.5}, {ID:8, M:0.3}, {ID:.., M:..}}	10
Sell Axe	{{ID:1, M:0.5}, {ID:3, M:0.2}, {ID:5, M:0.2}, {ID:.., M:..}}	10
Steal Gold	{{ID:0, M:0}, {ID:3, M:0}, {ID:7, M:0.1}, {ID:.., M:..}}	20

When an agent issues a plan, the cost of an action (C) passed to PlanRequest is the default cost of the action (c) plus the multiplier (m) multiplied by the "hitch" (h) cost: $C = m * h + c$. Taking the example action from Image 21.3, an agent with ID 6 is assessing "Create Axe" which has a default cost of 3.0, a multiplier of 0.5, and a "hitch" cost of 10.0, so the actual action cost in this very moment is:

$$C = m * h + c = 0.5 * 10 + 3.0 = 8.0$$

This agent can be found on the "Create Axe" row of Table 21.1 – the second pair in the Pairs List.

The last row in Table 21.1 has an action called "Steal Gold" and is a valid action for accumulating gold, but if such an action has a default cost which is far more than the sum of the other costs in the plan, it is unlikely to ever be triggered, even if it has no prerequisites and the effect is "Have Gold", which is the goal state.

The reason for this is that you do not want civilians to steal gold, so the action is costed accordingly. But what if you do want a civilian to start stealing? Without the need to make any new custom actions for the civilian, or to use another system with SB-GOAP, you can simply adjust the cost.

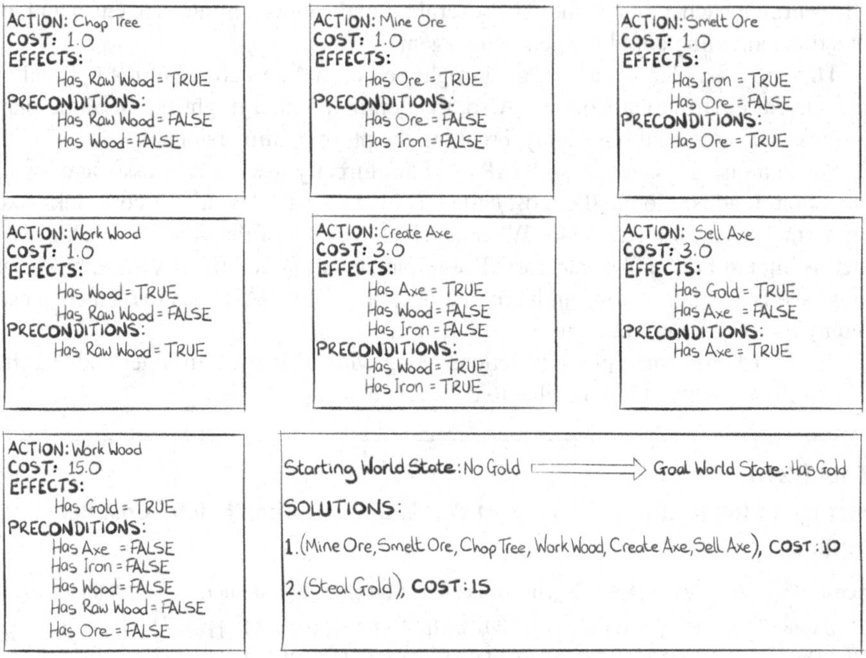

ACTION: Chop Tree
COST: 1.0
EFFECTS:
    Has Raw Wood = TRUE
PRECONDITIONS:
    Has Raw Wood = FALSE
    Has Wood = FALSE

ACTION: Mine Ore
COST: 1.0
EFFECTS:
    Has Ore = TRUE
PRECONDITIONS:
    Has Ore = FALSE
    Has Iron = FALSE

ACTION: Smelt Ore
COST: 1.0
EFFECTS:
    Has Iron = TRUE
    Has Ore = FALSE
PRECONDITIONS:
    Has Ore = TRUE

ACTION: Work Wood
COST: 1.0
EFFECTS:
    Has Wood = TRUE
    Has Raw Wood = FALSE
PRECONDITIONS:
    Has Raw Wood = TRUE

ACTION: Create Axe
COST: 3.0
EFFECTS:
    Has Axe = TRUE
    Has Wood = FALSE
    Has Iron = FALSE
PRECONDITIONS:
    Has Wood = TRUE
    Has Iron = TRUE

ACTION: Sell Axe
COST: 3.0
EFFECTS:
    Has Gold = TRUE
    Has Axe = FALSE
PRECONDITIONS:
    Has Axe = TRUE

ACTION: Work Wood
COST: 15.0
EFFECTS:
    Has Gold = TRUE
PRECONDITIONS:
    Has Axe = FALSE
    Has Iron = FALSE
    Has Wood = FALSE
    Has Raw Wood = FALSE
    Has Ore = FALSE

Starting World State: No Gold $\longrightarrow$ Goal World State: Has Gold

SOLUTIONS:

1. (Mine Ore, Smelt Ore, Chop Tree, Work Wood, Create Axe, Sell Axe), COST: 10

2. (Steal Gold), COST: 15

IMAGE 21.4 Actions, costs, and possible solutions.

Image 21.4 depicts a list of actions taken into consideration for an agent desiring to make gold (the goal). For an agent to get gold, there are only two possible solutions within such actions, one with a total cost of 10 and the other with a total cost of 15. The "Steal Gold" action explicitly requires all preconditions to be false (this is not mandatory), otherwise the agent might end up stealing gold right after having chopped a tree or mining ores.

First, take a look at the first solution in Image 21.4. The order of the actions will be exactly that based on preconditions and effects. This is important to mention because not only can SB-GOAP balance the actions based on something "bad" but can also balance them based on some predicates. For instance, it is possible to check before issuing the plan if the agent is mining in open space, like on some rocks in a forest, which makes sense for the agent to mine and then chop wood. And after those actions, going to work the wood and smelt the ore. Checking the distance of a player to the wood and the forge will help SB-GOAP to decide on a plan of actions. Say P_0 is the agent position, P_1 is the wood centre area, and P_2 is the forge, and they are respectively as follows:

$$P_0 = (5,5,10), P_1 = (7,7,11), P_2 = (9,9,8)$$

Checking the distance between these gives:

$d_{01} = |P_0 \cdot P_1| = 3$ is the distance from the agent to the closed tree in the wood.
$d_{02} = |P_0 \cdot P_2| = 6$ is the distance from the agent to the forge.

You can then use any sort of algorithm you want to get a normalised value between 0 and 1. In this case, using a SoftMax function and passing in 3 and 6, you get: $\sigma(d)_i = \{0.04742, 0.9525\}$.

You can use these two values as temporary multipliers without passing anything from memory, since it is a "one shot update based on distance", giving the following:

"Work Wood" action cost updated to $= 0.04742 * 5 + 1 = 1.2371$
"Smelt Ore" action cost updated to $= 0.9525 * 5 + 1 = 5.7625$

If you run the same plan with these two actions having the costs updated, you will have the following result: {Mine Ore, Chop Tree, Work Wood, Smelt Ore, Create Axe, Sell Axe}, which is a believable way to deal with the plan in a different spatial context.

There is no difference between the logic just described and for balancing. Everything is dependent on the type of game, the design, the implementation, and many other factors. Compared to the first core concept of SB-GOAP, which can be any well-defined path search algorithm, the second core concept (balancing) can be whatever implementation works – there is no strict approach. The only requirement is that it follows these rules:

1. It needs to be stored as shown in Table 21.1. It does not need a data storage table strictly speaking as shown, but it needs a place where it can be kept. This is because (in the case of balancing due to external factors, during the execution of the actions of the plan), the multiplier must be updated over time.
2. It needs a way to bring back the multiplier to 0 over time. This can be done after every plan issued if a multiplier does not equal zero, by just dropping it by a constant value or by a result of a decay function to reset to zero after some time has passed.
3. The multiplier should be between 0 and 1 to have more control over the hitch cost, but the implementation can also decide to not clamp it. If this is the case, the "hitch" cost will have a value more than its maximum value.

21.5 INTERRUPTIONS

Keeping with the same example as previously described, the agent is concocting a plan to make gold. It has the following default solution: {Mine Ore, Smelt Ore, Chop Tree, Work Wood, Create Axe, Sell Axe}.

Imagine that during the actions "Smelt Ore" and "Create Axe" something happens – the agent gets killed twice, once during each action.

To keep the example short and to the point, the order of the actions does not change during the step, even if they might change because the cost changes. Remember, you do not decrease multipliers at every step, but all multipliers do start with a value of 0.0. Because the change can be very small, the following example will use SoftMax and the Sigmoid function to have an average increment with a small variation to show the change over the two issued plans.

So, this is what happens:

1. Plan(P):{Mine Ore, Smelt Ore, Chop Tree, Work Wood, Create Axe, Sell Axe} = 10
   a. Killed at "Smelt Ore": (Cost (c) 1.0, Multiplier (m) 0.0, Hitch (h) 5)

$$\sigma(x)_i = e^{z_i} / \sum_{n=1}^{N} e^{z_k} \text{ for } i = 1,\dots,N \text{ where } N = \#P(0,0,0,0,0,0)$$

$$\sigma(x)_i = \{0.1667,\ 0.1667,\ 0.1667,\ 0.1667,\ 0.1667,\ 0.1667\ \}$$

   b. $m_2 = m_2 + \varsigma_\alpha\left(\sigma(x)_2\right) = 0 + \varsigma_\alpha(0.1667) = 0.5415$

   c. New "Smelt Ore" Cost is $C = 0.5415 \times 5 + 1 = 3.707$

2. Plan(P):{Mine Ore, Smelt Ore, Chop Tree, Work Wood, Create Axe, Sell Axe} = 12.707
   a. Killed at "Create Axe": (Cost (c) 3.0, Multiplier (m) 0.0, Hitch (h) 10)

$$\sigma(x)_i = e^{z_i} / \sum_{n=1}^{N} e^{z_k} \text{ for } i = 1,\dots,N \text{ where } N = \#P(0,0.5415,0,0,0,0)$$

$$\sigma(x)_i = \{0.1488,\ 0.2558,\ 0.1488,\ 0.1488,\ 0.1488,\ 0.1488\ \}$$

   b. $m_5 = m_5 + \varsigma_\alpha\left(\sigma(x)_5\right) = 0 + \varsigma_\alpha(0.1488) = 0.5371$

   c. "Create Axe" Cost is $C = 0.5371 \times 10 + 3.0 = 8.371$

3. Plan(P):{Mine Ore, Smelt Ore, Chop Tree, Work Wood, Create Axe, Sell Axe} > 15

So, the cost of the plan (Plan 3) is now over 15 (to be precise it is 18.078), which means it is not a good choice for the plan considered for the goal of making gold. In fact, with a cost of only 15, the "Steal Gold" action will be the result of the new plan SB-GOAP has computed and returned to the agent.

As we have seen in the two examples, the one based on the distance of the agent between two different locations where actions should take place, and the one where it gets killed twice, SB-GOAP is able to change behaviour and adapt without the need for any other external help. You just need to keep in mind that the cost and the hitch cost need to be well-designed for the type of agent and the type of game.

21.6   CONCLUSION

This chapter has shown how SB-GOAP is deeply driven by a path search algorithm. This allows it to not only look at the preconditions and effects, but it can use a cost proactively in order to decide "which route" the plan can take depending on variations. These variations can be achieved without the need of having another system on top, they can be "one shot" without the need of any memory storage, or the multiplier can be accumulated over time whenever something external happens to the agent during the actual execution of the actions.

The balancing part of SB-BOAP can include a huge range of algorithms of any sort, from the simplest approach to the most complex. Also, emergent behaviours will be seen over time, which is within the control of the designers.

The takeaway of using the SB-GOAP approach is that by having more control over the plan, and over a single action, it reduces the overhead of actions through to its reusability and the removal of supporting systems.

SB-GOAP can be easily expanded to use neural networks. For instance, reinforcement learning could adjust the multipliers of the costs directly, since world states can be seen as nodes of the neural network and actions as connections (using the cost as weight).

In short, how SB-GOAP is designed can be extended in many ways.

REFERENCES

Fikes, R. E. and Nilsson, N. J. (1971) Strips: A new approach to the application of theorem proving to problem solving, *Artificial Intelligence*, 2(3–4), pp. 189–208.

Millington, I. (2019) *Artificial Intelligence for Games*, Boca Raton, FL: CRC Press.

Orkin, J. (2003) Applying goal-oriented action planning to games, *AI Game Programming Wisdom*, 2, pp. 217–228.

22 Generalised AI Planners

Andrea Schiel

22.1 INTRODUCTION

In the field of game AI, planning is most often found in solving the problem of AI agent navigation – path planning. Outside of path planning, only a few games have implemented a full-order planner as part of their agent decision-making. Planning is unique in that it can deal with highly complex problems that involve solving for multiple constraints. Planners can be developed to coordinate multiple agents or to solve more abstract problems such as planning the build order in a real-time strategy game. Even when such a need exists in a game, planners are often not implemented, and this is partly because they are expensive to implement, they tend to have an inherently higher run-time cost, and authoring the data for the planners takes both time and expertise.

As a result, in games, planners have been hardcoded for the domain (domain-specific) that they were designed to solve. *F.E.A.R.*, a first-person shooter game (FPS) released in 2005, utilised an approach known as Goal-Oriented Action Planning (GOAP) for its full-order planning (Orkin, 2006). GOAP has since been used in many games including *Shadow of Mordor, Shadow of War, Tomb Raider*, and the *Assassin's Creed* series (Conway et al., 2015). Even A*, typically a navigation solution, was specialised to work as a planner for AI control in *Super Mario Brothers* in 2009 (Karakovskiy & Togelius, 2012). Several variants of hierarchical task networks (HTNs) have been used in titles such as *Killzone 2* and *Killzone 3* (Straatman et al., 2013), *Transformers: War for Cybertron* (Humphreys, 2013), *Left Alive* (Hasegawa, 2019), *Blue Protocol* (Yoshimoto, 2020) and many others. HTNs tend to be domain-specific as they can be optimised with gameplay-aware tasks and actions to plan with. For example, *KillZone 3* had weapon-specific methods such as *use_missiles*. *StarCraft* started with a highly domain-specific scripted AI but was later outfitted with a specialised AI planner technique combined with machine learning (ML) (Deneke et al., 2020). Unity now provides a GOAP implementation which allows the user to specify the actions and goals for their game. This allows the planner to be used for any game, but it is useless without the actions and goals. As soon as the actions are authored and use game-specific knowledge, the planner is no longer generalised.

22.2 GENERALISED PLANNERS DEFINED

22.2.1 DOMAIN-SPECIFIC PLANNERS

There is a hidden cost to being domain-specific. Planners like these require an expert to author all of the data. How much expert knowledge is required to author the data

DOI: 10.1201/9781003323549-22

for a given planner depends on the domain (the problem space) that the planner was designed to solve and the type of planner. Planners that solve very specific problems in a game, such as the build order problem, require domain-specific data such as available agents, resource costs, resource availabilities, and so on. The tasks or actions that make up the plan would contain specialised actions of the various gameplay elements such as performing an assassination or executing a build order. That the planner is built to know what problem it is solving is what makes it domain-specific. Some approaches naturally lend themselves to being domain-specific such as HTNs. HTNs are authored by their goals and/or tasks that they use to build a plan. These planners need to resolve conflicts and constraints during or after the planning phase which also tends to require domain knowledge.

22.2.2 Domain Free Planners

Domain-free planners are more generalised, making them more suitable for solving a wide range of problem types. These planners require the ability to handle and act at a much more fundamental level. They are generally more adaptable and deal well with new situations. Having an adaptable planner would be ideal for games that involve a level of unpredictability and are less structured. Their lack of domain specificity reduces the development time in the long run, as experts do not need to spend a vast amount of time encoding domain-specific tasks, goals, or actions. They also do not require domain experts. While this may not seem to be a strong point, consider that this would free up designers for game balancing and higher-level work. It also frees up the UI or tools programmer needed to develop the editor for the designer to work with. In larger studios, a generalised planning system could be used across multiple titles.

In stark contrast to their specialised counterparts, generalised planners can also plan across disparate areas of the game. For example, in a FPS, instead of having one planner for path planning and another planner to work out the targets for a given agent, imagine a planner that could plan out where the agent needs to go, add in actions to shoot along the way, and even plan to reload, possibly even grabbing that med kit. In most games, this is currently simulated using influence maps, weighted pathfinding, or the use of a utility system. As game systems become more powerful, this approach, once only enjoyed by researchers and thought too slow, could become a powerful approach for the AI game programmer. The catch, of course, is to build a domain-independent planner usable for a game.

22.3 APPROACHES TO GENERALISING PLANNERS

Attempts have been made to generalise HTNs (and other planners) with the introduction of abstraction of how the planner's problem (domain) is represented. In 1998, the Planning Domain Definition Language (PDDL) was presented to the AI Planning Systems (AIPS) competition (Ghallab et al., 1998). PDDL is now on its 4th variation, but still, the core idea is a common, general planning syntax for classical planners. The hope was that if the language was expressive enough, and generalised enough, a planner could solve any sort of problem. In other words, the ideal domain-free planner would have no knowledge of the type of problem it was solving. Prior to PDDL, problems had to be expressed in a domain-specific way. The support for PDDL by a planner does not make it necessarily domainless, but it does allow for the abstraction of the problem space which is a good first step. Many off-the-shelf planning systems, both domain-independent and domain-specific, support PDDL to some extent. In the context of game development, having a domain-free way to express planning problems would extend the ability of the planner to solve for different areas of the game. For example, the same planner could solve a resource-building tree as well as solve for unit deployments. Arguments have been made that PDDL could be of use in games (Bartheye & Jacopin, 2019), but at the time of writing, there has not been widespread adoption of such in the industry.

Another approach is to abandon the pure domainless planner and utilise either domain knowledge or more specialised planners in areas requiring a certain level of performance. This is referred to as the portfolio approach. This is a strategy that utilises more than one planner. For example, a game may leave the base path planning to an A*-based system but combine that with a more generalised planner for solving another area of the game. The idea behind a portfolio approach is to leverage the strengths of various planning methods to improve overall performance, robustness, and adaptability when dealing with different types of planning problems. It could be argued that many games with planners are somewhat already doing this. However, the portfolio approach is a little more involved as the system needs to choose which planner(s) to apply and implement strategies on how to merge the different plans. The planners in a portfolio can be all domain-independent, all domain-specific, or a mix. The planners would all be different in how they plan. Optimisations in portfolio approaches tend to be in how it chooses between plans and there have been some recent advances with the portfolio approach applied to generalised planners (Rizzini et al., 2015). Note that the execution of the various planners chosen can be in parallel, offering another opportunity for optimisation. While the use of the portfolio approach in games is not new (Churchill & Buro, 2017), its use with full-order planners to offset the cost of domain-independent planners is still under active research. The detractor here is that now multiple planners need to be implemented and maintained. However, having a portfolio could also be a risk mitigation strategy against a lot of plan failures or spikes in performance.

Possibly a more pragmatic approach would be the one taken by goal and task Pyhop or GTPyhop (Nau et al., 2021). This is the latest incarnation of a HTN that has been made to be as generalised as possible. GTPyhop is a goal-oriented variant of HTN – much like GOAP or goal decomposition planners (Shivashankar et al., 2012). As PDDL abstracts the problem domain, making it possible to describe many different types of planning problems, GTPyhop abstracts the goal and action space. Goals are decomposed into subgoals, and tasks are decomposed into subtasks. The generalisation is that GTPyhop provides a set of primitive methods that can be reused across different domains. These methods perform basic actions and can be combined in various ways to achieve higher-level objectives. Any game that currently uses an HTN could do the same. It does allow for the definition of new operators and methods, which could bring in some domain knowledge if the implementor is not careful. To guard against this, GTPyhop separates the planning system from its knowledge.

This allows the planning itself to be generalised while still allowing some injection and optimisation of specific knowledge. Other planners, such as Fast Downward, also utilise this modularisation to achieve domain independence. There are variants that use the portfolio approach, allowing Fast Downward to choose the best search approach at the time. Unlike GTPyhop, Fast Downward also supports PDDL. Both systems offer off-the-shelf planning systems that could be utilised in games.

22.4 CHOOSING TO BE FREE

Choosing the right planner, generalised or not, is going to be highly dependent on the types of problems being faced by the game's AI. Assuming that the problem is a good planning problem, there are advantages and disadvantages to each type of planner. Spatial problems, such as path planning, tend to do well with a variant of A* search because these plans involve a small action space (walk), a large search space (the area the agent can walk), and a simple heuristic (cheapest cost). Research trees are not dissimilar from path planning as they too involve optimisation of costs. On the other hand, problems that involve timing or coordination do not do so well using a simple graph search. These sorts of problems usually fall to planners like GOAP or HTN. The choice between GOAP- and HTN-based planners can be determined by whether there are a few goals to choose between (GOAP) or multiple methods to solve the same goal (HTN). SPARK is a planner that deals in probabilities, which is useful if there is some ambiguity in assessing the outcome. If the problem space involves a lot of conflicts and constraints between possible actions, outside of pruning or optimisation of the search space, using a planner combined with a constraint solver may be required. Temporal constraints may require the use of a HTN like SIADEX which is better at expressing time. Table 22.1 gives an overview of the different planners discussed in this chapter.

If the flexibility or reusability of a domain-free approach is needed but there is a pre-existing planner, then there is the option to convert the planner to become more generalised. This could involve the integration of PDDL, the further abstraction of its tasks or actions, and the separation (modularisation) of its data and its planning. The planners in Table 22.1 that are not naturally domain free, or support PDDL, could be converted to do so. If there is a specific subproblem that requires optimisation, the portfolio approach might be the solution. Further optimisations can occur by parallelising the planning and the use of pruning or heuristics to speed up the search.

TABLE 22.1
Comparison of Planners Discussed

	GOAP	HTN	SIADEX	GTPyhop	Fast Down	FF Planner
Approach	Search through action space	Decomposition of tasks	Partial decomposition of tasks (and NLP)	Decomposition of goals (and tasks)	Heuristic search through world state	Forward chaining heuristic state space planner
Problem types	Choosing between multiple goals; simple actions	Complex actions	Natural language dialogue; tasks; forest fire combat	Supports choosing of goals and task breakdowns	Cost optimal planning	Cost optimal planning
PDDL?	N	N	N	N	Y	Y
Ordered plan?	Y	Y	Partial	Y	Y	Y
Problem complexity	Handles moderate levels of complexity	Handles high levels of complexity with mod constraints	Handles high levels of complexity with high constraints; temporal	Handles high levels of complexity	Applied to simpler problems so far	Applied to simpler problems so far
Optimal plan?	Y	N	N	N	Y	Y
Domain free?	N	N	N	Y	Y	Y

22.5 ADVANCES IN GENERALISED PLANNERS

22.5.1 MACHINE LEARNING AND PLANNERS

Integration of ML, or the use of ML with planning, is nothing new. DeepMind is arguably the most well-known example. While it showcased the powerful results achievable by combining planning with ML, the goal was more to enhance planners' efficiency, adaptability, and scalability by leveraging learned models for action outcomes, state transitions, and value functions.

There is also a field of study called Generalised Planning which is very distinct from the concept of a generalised planner. It is important to note that in Generalised Planning, ML is used to *find* generalised plans as opposed to *creating* generalised planners (Rivlin et al., 2020).

ML has also been used as a planner itself such as with TDDP-Net, a 3D-pathfinding planner that uses a deep neural network (DNN). While the resulting DNN model could be domain-specific due to the nature of the training data, the approach showcases the potential of using learned models to directly generate plans (Wu et al., 2019). In the broadest sense, using DNNs could be considered a generalised approach, in that the resulting planners can adapt to different environments without manual encoding of rules or heuristics.

Others have used DNNs and reinforcement learning techniques to optimise classical planners by improving the search heuristic using the predictive nature of ML (Groshev et al., 2018). Creating a general set of actions or tasks to support a generalised planner could also be achieved via reinforcement learning.

22.5.2 HYBRID PLANNERS

With respect to domainless planners, a common hybrid approach involves using a non-planning method to abstract the planning problem. Abstracting the problem either using PDDL or through some other means is required by a generalised planner. If the problem domain is not abstracted in some fashion, the planner will need domain-specific information to understand the problem it is trying to solve.

As previously discussed, ML can be combined with planning. In particular, for generalised planners, using ML to optimise the search can make generalised planners more performant.

By its very nature, a portfolio approach is a hybrid strategy as it involves combining multiple planners or algorithms to tackle the same problem. This hybrid strategy aims to benefit from the strengths of different methods and improve overall planning performance.

There have also been attempts to automate the abstraction of a classical planner which requires a hybrid of a classical planner with an abstraction heuristic (Srivastava et al., 2011).

In the field of robotics, there has been some success using probability methods to enhance exploration which is then fed into a generalised planner. This hybrid approach combines probabilistic reasoning with planning to enhance exploration and decision-making in uncertain environments.

Hybridising a generalised planner with a more domain-specific execution module is an effective way of getting the best of both worlds. It leaves the planner to generate more generalised, higher-level plans, while a more practical execution module provides an efficient and domain-specific plan following.

22.5.3 MULTI-AGENT PLANNING

Multi-agent planning is a sub-field of planning that specifically deals with planners coordinating many agents. Recently, the use of generalised planners has allowed multi-agent planners to reduce the amount of communication between agents and increased plan reuse (Borrajo & Fernández, 2019).

Recently, more attention has been paid to a related field – multi-agent pathfinding. Most of the focus here has been optimisation, such as improving the runtime efficiency by improving the algorithm selection used by the planner (Kaduri et al., 2021).

22.5.4 PROBABILISTIC PLANNING

The use of probabilities, either in the form of Bayesian networks or a DNN with planning is not new. It is particularly applicable in the field of robotics where execution of a plan can fail, and the planning environment is unstable. There are specific planning systems such as HYPE and GOLOG to incorporate the concept of probabilities into planning. Prediction has also been used with temporal reasoning planners and to optimise action selection.

22.6 CONCLUSION

As planners find broader applications in games beyond pathfinding, it will become increasingly important to cultivate their evolution towards enhanced efficiency, ease of implementation, reusability, and adaptability. Capitalising on the increasing abilities of modern game systems, generalised planning should inevitably become more accessible, lowering the barrier for their integration. Incorporating generalised planners into games is particularly compelling due to their ability to tackle problems that are nigh unsolvable for classical planners. Combined with a portfolio approach, generalised planners could be introduced alongside more traditional approaches, mitigating risks. Notably, major game engines like Unreal Engine (with HTN) and Unity (with GOAP) are progressively integrating classical planning systems alongside conventional tools, mirroring the industry's recognition of the value which planners bring. Although the incorporation of PDDL into Unity (Pellegrin, 2020) is presently unofficial, this strategic move signals an industry-wide trend towards embracing generalised techniques. With the potential to reduce development time, free up designers, reduce the need for experts, adapt to unforeseen game scenarios, and facilitate reusability, it is foreseeable that these game engines will adopt more comprehensive generalised strategies. These distinct advantages make a compelling case for considering and integrating generalised planners within the realm of game development.

REFERENCES

Bartheye, O., and Jacopin, E. (2019) A real-time PDDL-based planning component for video games. *Proceedings of the 5th Artificial Intelligence for Interactive Digital Entertainment Conference*, available online: https://cdn.aaai.org/ojs/12370/12370-52-15898-1-2-2020 1228.pdf.

Borrajo, D., and Fernández, S. (2019) Efficient approaches for multi-agent planning. *Knowledge and Information Systems*, 58, 425–479. https://doi.org/10.1007/s10115-018-1202-1.

Churchill, D., and Buro, M. (2017) Hierarchical portfolio search in prismata. In Game AI Pro 3, Edited by Steve Rabin, CRC Press, Boca Raton, FL, pp. 361–368.

Conway, C., Higley, P., and Jacopin, E. (2015) Goal-Oriented Action Planning: Ten Years of AI Programming, [online talk] https://www.youtube.com/watch?v=gm7K68663rA, presented at GDC 2015.

Deneke, W., Barger, T., Carter, M., Lokken, C., and Peterson, D. (2020) VikingBot: Towards a Hybrid Artificial Intelligence for Starcraft. Western Washington University, available online: https://american-cse.org/sites/csci2020proc/pdfs/CSCI2020-6SccvdzjqC7bKup ZxFmCoA/762400b521/762400b521.pdf.

Ghallab, M., Howe, A., Knoblock, C., McDermott, D., Ram, A., Veloso, M., Weld, D., and Wilkins, D. (1998) PDDL - The Planning Domain Definition Language. AIPS-98 Planning Competition Committee.

Groshev, E., Tamir, A., Srivastava, S., and Abbeel, P. (2018) Learning generalized reactive policies using deep neural networks. *28th International Conference on Automated Planning and Scheduling*, Volume 28, Delft.

Hasegawa, M., (2019) What is the HTN-based Game AI used in left alive? Game Business article, available online: https://www.gamebusiness.jp/article/2019/10/28/16360.html.

Humphreys, T. (2013) Exploring HTN planners through example. In *Game AI Pro*, Edited by Steve Rabin, CRC Press, Boca Raton, FL, pp. 149–167

Kaduri, O., Boyarski, E., and Stern, R. (2021) Algorithm selection for optimal multi-agent pathfinding. *Proceedings of the 30th International Conference on Automated Planning and Scheduling*, Guangzhou, pp. 161–165.

Karakovskiy, S., and Togelius, J. (2012) The Mario AI benchmark and competitions. *IEEE Transactions on Computational Intelligence and AI in Games*, 4(1), 55–67.

Nau, D., Bansod, Y., Patra, S., Roberts, M., and Li, R. (2021) GTPyhop: A hierarchical goal+task planner implemented in python. *ICAPS Workshop on Hierarchical Planning (HPlan)*, University of Maryland, available online: https://www.cs.umd.edu/~nau/ papers/nau2021gtpyhop.pdf.

Orkin, J. (2006) Three States and a Plan: The A.I. of F.E.A.R., MIT Media Lab, available online: https://alumni.media.mit.edu/~jorkin/gdc2006_orkin_jeff_fear.pdf.

Pellegrin, E. (2020) PDSim: Planning Domain Simulation with the Unity Game Engine. Association for the Advancement of Artificial Intelligence.

Rivlin, O., Hazan, T., and Karpas, E. (2020) Generalized Planning with Deep Learning Reinforcement. Association for the Advancement of Artificial Intelligence.

Rizzini, M., Fawcett, C., Vallati, M., Gerevini, A., and Hoos, H. (2015) Portfolio methods for optimal planning: An empirical analysis. *IEEE 27th International Conference on Tools with Artificial Intelligence*, available online: https://ada.liacs.nl/papers/RizEtAl15.pdf.

Shivashankar, V., Kuter, U., and Nau, D. (2012) A hierarchical goal-based formalism and algorithm for single-agent planning. *AAMAS '12: Proceedings of the 11th International Conference on Autonomous Agents and Multiagent Systems*, Volume 2, Valencia, pp. 981–988, available online: https://www.ifaamas.org/Proceedings/aamas2012/ papers/1F_3.pdf.

Srivastava, S., Immerman, N., Zilberstein, S., and Zhang, T. (2011) Directed search for generalized plans using classical planners. *Proceedings of the 21st International Conference on Automated Planning and Scheduling*, pp. 226–233.

Straatman, R., Verweij, T., Champandard, A., Morcus, R., Kleve, H. (2013) Hierarchical AI for multiplayer bots in Killzone 3. In Game AI Pro, Edited by Steve Rabin, CRC Press, Boca Raton, FL, pp. 377–390

Wu, K., Esfahani, M., Yuan, S., and Wang, H. (2019) TDPP-Net: Achieving three-dimensional path planning via a deep neural network architecture. *Neurocomputing*, 357, 151–162.

Yoshimoto, Y. (2020) Y Hase, Morikatron.ai article, available online: https://morikatron.ai/2021/03/blue-protocol_aiphilosophy.

23 Unleashing Mayhem
The Demolition Derby Game Modes of DiRT: Showdown

Dr Nic Melder

23.1 INTRODUCTION

Dirt Showdown is a racing game developed and published by Codemasters as a spin-off to the main *DiRT Off Road* series. The game focused on a more arcade-style experience compared to the simulation-focused nature of the main *DiRT* series and featured both competitive circuit-based and arena-based events where you competed directly against the AI. There were also various single-player events (Hoonigan Events) as well as multiplayer-only events (Party Modes). Business reasons dictated the release date which necessitated that *Showdown* was designed to be an easy and quick game to make (the terms "reuse" and "reskin" were said a lot). From start to final submission, there were only around five months! In this time scale, it was necessary to create an entirely new arena-based vehicle AI system to support three new game modes: Rampage (traditional arena-based demolition derby), Knockout (think sumo wrestling but with cars) and Hard Target (everyone against the player, longest survival time wins).

This chapter describes how the arena game modes were developed, and how the short project duration directly impacted the code architecture/decisions made.

23.2 DESIGNER CONSTRAINTS

23.2.1 CAR HANDLING

The first decision that had a major impact on the design was what the handling would be like. Thankfully, it was decided that *Showdown* would be very much an arcade game and so the handling was designed to be very easy to drive and very accessible. To achieve this, the car handling designers and vehicle physics programmers created a comparatively simple driving model, which essentially had no sliding or low top speeds. In fact, the top speeds were so low (approximately 50 mph/80 kph) that they removed the speedometer from the game to hide the fact!

It was also decided that only a few selected vehicles would compete in the Arena modes. Only ten different cars needed to be controlled by the AI. Furthermore, the main handling configurations were essentially the same across all the vehicle types. Even though they had different masses, steering locks, accelerations and top speeds,

DOI: 10.1201/9781003323549-23

the same basic handling configuration meant that the same AI steering and pedal controllers could be used for all the vehicles.

The actual vehicle simulation was split into two parts, where there was an "invisible sled" that the wheels were attached to and then there was the visual body that was attached to the "sled" via springs. Doing it this way meant that the "sled" (which is essentially what the AI was controlling) could be set up and signed off early, allowing the other elements, such as body roll and damage to be built afterwards. It also meant that any changes to how the vehicle appeared visually whilst being driven could be adjusted without affecting the underlying handling, which would result in needing to rework the AI controllers. This meant that if it was decided that the truck needed more body roll, instead of adjusting the suspension to allow for the roll (which would affect the handling), instead, the connecting springs between the "sled" and the bodywork would be adjusted instead. This disconnect between the handling and the visuals allowed the AI to be developed on a stable handling system, whilst also allowing the designers to adjust and personalise the different vehicles without there being any huge impacts (or marginal impacts) on the vehicle AI's ability to control them. Because it was decided early on that the cars would be more arcade feeling, and also that the arena cars would be fully fictional, the fact that the cars were now less realistic was not an issue.

23.2.2   Arena Design

Design rules for how the arenas were to be designed also needed to be established at the beginning of the project. Essentially, there were only two rules established:

1. The arena floor needed to be a continuous height throughout. Continuous height did not mean flat, just that there could be no discontinuities anywhere in the arena. For example, you could not have a raised section separated by a wall, but with ramps on either side.
2. Any fixed/unbreakable obstacles inside the arenas needed to be containable in a circular boundary.

Of course, both of these rules were ignored by the artists, but at least the (truly awesome) level design team understood the need for these requirements so were able to rebuild them to adhere to the design specifications. In total, six arenas were designed and released, although these were further modified, by blocking off areas with barriers, to create eight distinct arenas. The final main arenas released are shown in Image 23.1.

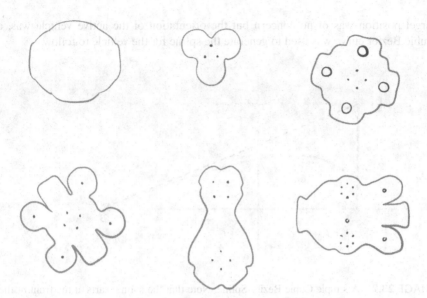

IMAGE 23.1 The six main arena designs showing the outer boundary and any obstacles that were inside the arenas (marked as circles). The vehicles would spawn outside the arenas on ramps and would drive into the arenas once the game started. The spawn points and the ramps are not shown in the image.

23.3 CONTROLLING THE CARS

When *Showdown* was developed, four racing games (three *DiRT* games and one *Grid* game) had already been released, so the engine was already mature and well-tested, with a lot of useful features that could be leveraged.

23.3.1 BASIC SPLINE GENERATION

The one thing that the AI engine did well was to follow a spline. In the previous racing games, the splines would be set up by the level designers, but since this was an open arena with no fixed "route" another approach was needed. Instead, dynamically created splines were decided upon. This was done in two parts:

1. Determine where to go.
2. Create a spline from the current position and orientation to the target.

Determining where to go was the job of the "Demolition Derby Overseer" (described later) which would provide a target position inside the arena. The current position would be the vehicle's starting point. Creating a straight line between these two points and then telling the vehicle to follow the line would have worked (it did work, as this was the first thing tried), but it is not necessarily a great solution since it did not consider the turning circle of the vehicle or any obstacles in the way of the actual driven path. This necessitated using some type of spline. As the orientation of the target position was of no concern but the orientation of the active vehicle was, a Cubic Bezier curve was used to generate the spline for the vehicle to follow.

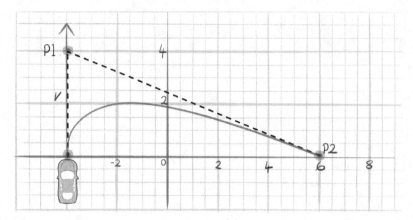

IMAGE 23.2 A simple Cubic Bezier Spline. Note that the spline starts at the front of the car and not in the middle. This is because the steering controllers would minimise the error at the front of the vehicle when calculating the steering direction.

A Cubic Bezier Spline requires three points and is depicted in Image 23.2. P0 is the vehicle's initial position and P2 is the target position. But where should P1 be placed? Since we want the spline to start with the orientation of the vehicle, P1 needs to be somewhere along a line through P0 in the vehicle's facing direction (V). But how far along this line should P1 be placed? Through experimentation, it was found that a good spline that the vehicles could follow could be created by placing P1 at a projected position along the line V, 1/3rd of the length between P0 and P2 provided that P2 was not behind P0. A minimum distance from P0 was also always adhered to and, again, this distance was determined through experimentation. This was calculated as follows:

```
float Dist = (P2-P0).Length();
float ProjectionDist = (Dist/3) < MinDist ? MinDist : (Dist/3);
Vector3 P1 = P0 + V * ProjectionDist;
```

23.3.2 SPLINE FOLLOWING

Once an appropriate path had been generated, to make the vehicle follow it requires converting the Bezier curve into a Catmull-Rom spline. Although it is possible to follow a Bezier curve directly, all the systems in the AI engine were already set up to follow Catmull-Rom splines, so converting a generated curve to this format meant that there was no need to change any of the spline following code (remember, there was less than five months development time to build these systems). One of the advantages of the Catmull-Rom spline is that it goes through every point, so converting to a Catmull-Rom spline just means sampling and storing the points along the curve (Dunlop, 2005).

The spline data curvature was then analysed to determine if the curvature was too tight and required a brake line and hold line to be added. Brake lines are used to set a speed at a point on a curve, and a hold line is the point where the vehicle could go to full throttle again. The brake lines were placed if the curvature was above a threshold (again determined by experimentation) and similarly the hold lines were placed in the same way as shown in Image 23.3. However, it is not clear what speed should be set for the brake lines? Typically, these speeds would be set manually by the level designers, or by tools that repeatedly run the vehicle through the corner whilst adjusting the speed, but since the splines were automatically generated, the level designers could not determine the speed. To generate the speed by simulating the tool (during the current frame update) is both computationally expensive and hard to implement.

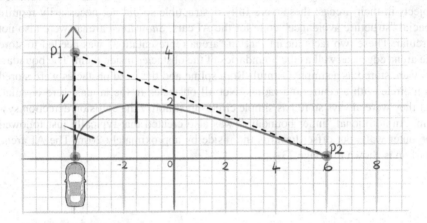

IMAGE 23.3   Spline showing where the brake and hold lines would be automatically placed.

Luckily, this was trivial on *Showdown* since one of the new features of the previously released game (*DiRT 3*) was the use of curvature statistics for determining a vehicle's speed through a corner. Each vehicle's curvature statistics were generated by driving the vehicles around circular tracks and increasing their speed until they could no longer follow the spline. This would determine the maximum speed through a given radius. When other corners of the same radius/curvature were then encountered, this speed could be read from a table and applied. In practice, on *DiRT 3*, this worked reasonably well at getting the cars to run at 90% of the target speed, so this method was used to generate the initial speeds for the brake lines. Further tools would then iterate through each brake line adjusting the speeds as appropriate to get better cornering speeds/better track times. This iterative step was required to take into account the weight shift caused by the previous corners. However, for *Showdown*, this system worked well since the handling was essentially a "sled" that had no weight shift. So, to determine the speed through the brake line, it was a matter of getting the spline curvature at that point and then looking it up in the curvature data.

There would be times though when the vehicle would fail to follow the path and would drift away from the spline. This could have been due to the generated spline being too tight for our vehicle to physically drive or because a different vehicle collided with it (or even because the steering controllers were not tuned that well), so if the vehicle was ever more than X m from the spline, it would trigger a spline rebuild request (X was between 5 and 10 m).

23.3.3   Advanced Spline Generation

One of the novel features of the arenas was that they were not all simple "bowls" but were a variety of shapes and could also have fixed, unbreakable structures in them. Although the *FlatOut* games (Bugbear Entertainment, 2004) at the time contained objects in their arenas, these were fully destructible so did not necessarily require special "structure avoidance" code for the AI cars. *Showdown* arenas were also not circular. These two facts meant that an "arena representation" was needed to store the arena edges, as well as the boundaries of the obstacles inside them. The boundaries were stored as a simple Catmull-Rom spline and the fixed obstacles were stored as a circle with a centre and radius. Not all obstacles in the arenas were circular, but they were always stored as simple circles to simplify the collision detection system. An additional "inner boundary" was also created that typically just followed the outer walls but offset towards the inside by approximately 20 m. The AI arena markup is shown in Image 23.4.

IMAGE 23.4   Arena representation showing the outer arena boundary, the inner boundary, and the obstacles' boundaries (marked as circles).

As described above, the spline was generated between the vehicle and the target. But what if the generated spline went through one of these fixed obstacles, or even outside the arena? Depending on the situation, either the spline would need to be "subtly" modified, or maybe totally regenerated.

23.3.3.1   Driving through an Obstacle

In an arena with obstacles, the generated spline may go through an obstacle. It is both possible and computationally cheap to determine the bounding box of a cubic Bezier curve, so a first pass was done to determine if the curve's bounding box intersected an obstacle's bounding circle. Assuming this was the case, a more detailed check was done to determine if the spline intersected the circle (Image 23.5). Finding the closest point on a spline (or Bezier curve) is non-trivial, iterative and involves complex maths, so instead, the generated cubic Bezier curve was converted into a series of points along the curve, and each individual point was tested against the circle. Calculating the points was required for converting the Bezier curve to the Catmull-Rom spline, so if no intersection was found then the converted spline could then be used for the path following.

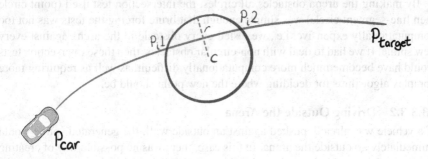

IMAGE 23.5   The initially generated spline (P_{car} to P_{target}) intersects the circle (centre C, radius r). The entry and exit intersection points are P_{i1} and P_{i2}.

However, what if an intersection had been found? In this case, you want to push the spline so that it is outside of the circle, so the entry and exit intersection points need to be found. Using the first and last points that were found inside the circle from the simple circle point test, a proper line-segment circle calculation can be done to calculate a more accurate intersection point on the circle's edge. Once the two intersection points are found, you can calculate the new point that you want the spline to pass through. This new point (M) is the midpoint between the two intersection points. As shown in Image 23.6, the new point (P_{new}) is along the vector from the circle centre (C) through the Midpoint (M) with a distance of circle radius (r) and buffer distance (b) from the centre.

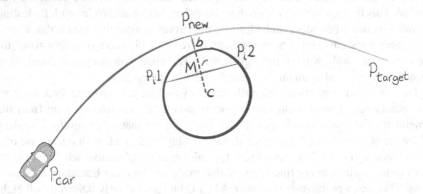

IMAGE 23.6   The two new curves created that no longer intersect the obstacle. M is the midpoint between the two intersection points, and b is the buffer distance that you want to move the new point to (outside the obstacle).

Once we had the new point, we could now create two new curves, one from the initial vehicle to this new position (P_{car} to P_{new}) and a second from the new position to the target (P_{new} to P_{target}). These two curves should then have been checked for intersections and split further as necessary, but the layouts of the Showdown arenas meant this was not needed. Although there were instances where an adjusted curve would then intersect another obstacle boundary, the chances of it happening were slim and not worth the processing to check.

By making the arena obstacles all circles, the intersection test used (point circle then line-segment circle) was simple enough that brute forcing the tests was not too computationally expensive, i.e., we tested every obstacle in the arena against every new spline. If we had to deal with non-circular obstacles, then these intersection tests would have become much more computationally difficult, as well as requiring more complex algorithms for deciding where the new point should be.

23.3.3.2   Driving Outside the Arena

If a vehicle was already pushed against an outside wall, the generated spline would immediately go outside the arena. In this case, there was no possible way of creating a meaningful curve to follow by going forward. After detecting this situation, a curve would be generated but using the opposite direction that the vehicle was facing. This generated spline, starting behind the vehicle, would automatically trigger the code for spinning cars around when they are facing the wrong direction. This was free functionality as it was in the vehicle AI systems since the original *Colin McRae: DiRT* game.

Sometimes, the curve generated would go outside the arena a little before coming back inside. In this case, the spline was repositioned in a similar way to the spline intersecting with the obstacles. First, the initial intersection between the spline and the boundary was found, and then the initial spline was cut, the point repositioned, and then two curves were created to form the path. However, during testing, it was found that just doing this with the arena boundary did not always create a spline that the vehicle could follow without hitting the boundary walls. This wasn't a big deal (it is a demolition derby after all) but happened enough times that a better fix was needed. This fix required having an inner boundary to test against instead. By testing against this inner boundary and adjusting the curves against that meant that now if there were some curves that were too tight, there was a big enough "safety zone" for the cars to run wide without hitting the wall. The inner boundary was about 10-m away from the actual boundary and can be seen in Image 23.4.

Detecting an intersection with the boundary was done using a brute force method. The generated spline was cut into segments, and then each line segment from the generated spline was tested against each line segment that made up the boundary of the arena. This brute force method was horribly inefficient, with a test case of a 200-m long spline (which was a fairly typical length of spline that would be generated) to test against every line segment that made up the outer boundary took over 1 ms. This was a problem as the entire AI CPU budget was only 0.8 ms for all eight cars! And this was a task that needed to be run every time a new spline was generated. A better algorithm could have been chosen, or spatial partitioning could have been used, but this was not functionality that was readily available (either approach would take time that just was not available – remember five months!). The thinking at the time was to optimise the brute force algorithm, and only allow the spline/ boundary intersection test to run once per frame. After optimising the code using SIMD methods (Bikker, 2017), the CPU cost dropped by a factor of over 70 to less than 0.02 ms for the same test. At that point, concerns about its performance were dispelled and it was allowed to run whenever it needed to.

23.4 CONTROLLING THE FUN: THE DEMOLITION DERBY OVERSEER

With the ability to generate splines and have the vehicles follow them, all the basics needed to build the demolition derby game modes were present. But the fundamentals of the actual game were still missing! Where should the cars drive to and who should they target? This became the primary responsibility of the Demolition Derby Overseer. As its name suggests, the Overseer was aware of all the vehicles in the game, actively assigning them targets and calculating the target points for the spline generation. For each vehicle in play, the Overseer would assign either a target vehicle to hit or a safe location to drive to. Which vehicle was targeted depended upon a number of factors that included: game mode, difficulty, the last time the vehicle was targeted, the number of vehicles targeting that vehicle, the relative position, and the orientation of the target vehicle.

When targeting a vehicle, a spline would be generated to the target vehicle. Every few seconds, the spline would be rebuilt to take into account the new position of the target and then, if a hit was successful, or after a fixed time had passed, the vehicle would then need to drive away to be able to make another attempt. Driving away meant either finding a place far away to drive to or just attacking a different vehicle that was a reasonable distance away. The distance requirement was included because the speed of collision/damage caused was an integral part of the scoring system, plus the high-speed collisions always looked so much better than low-speed ones. Since the vehicle that was being targeted was a good distance away (often over 100 metres), and was moving, the generated spline needed to be updated regularly. Also, targeting the centre of the vehicle never gave good results as it would typically result in the vehicle ending up behind the target and just following it. Instead, it was necessary to predict where the vehicle was likely to be in the future. Using a very approximate guess at how long it would take the vehicle to drive from its current position to the target's current position (just using the straight-line distance and speed), this was used as the time component in the prediction algorithm. The algorithm then took the current direction and velocity of the vehicle into account to predict where the vehicle would be at that time in the future. Using this new position as the target position resulted in much better targeting and also resulted in many spectacular T-Bones. Even though the system was very simple, because of the regular path updates, it became possible to be very precise on where to hit the vehicle. More importantly, it was possible to choose to not hit the vehicle but to get very close to it instead. This ability was used as part of the difficulty system and made for a fun gameplay experience on easier difficulties by having cars charging at the player, but then purposely missing, but not being obvious about it (it looked like they really were trying to hit the player, but they were just not quite right in their positioning).

Once all demolition derby modes were working well and were fully testable, the QA team found that they could easily outsmart the AI by just driving in a circle! This was easily fixed by incorporating the steering angle that the car was using into the prediction algorithm. In the previous racing games, this was not desirable as the AI now had access to information that the player does not have, but since it was an arcade game where realism and simulation were not the focus (unlike the main *DiRT* games), it was an acceptable solution. The "realistic" fix would have been to use the rotational velocity of the target vehicle instead, but that was a much more complex solution than just grabbing the steering angle directly.

23.5   THE DIFFICULTY SYSTEM

The difficulty system was a part of the Overseer as it was this system that decided who targeted whom and when. One aspect of the difficulty system was to control how often the player would get chosen as a target. On easy difficulties, there would only ever be a single vehicle targeting the player and there were periods of time where no one was targeting the player. On the higher difficulties, up to three vehicles could target the player simultaneously. Another element to adjusting difficulty was to modify a vehicle's prediction setting so they would actively miss the targeted vehicle. The scoring was also modified so that for easier difficulties, hitting the player would earn a reduced score (for the AI vehicles) than at higher difficulties. Finally, the maximum amount of throttle that the AI would use was also adjusted for difficulty. This would make it easier for the player to avoid collision attempts and give them a bit more time to escape from a pursuing vehicle. Further to this, if they were hit successfully, the lower collision speed would result in less damage to the player.

This system was not perfect. At times, an AI vehicle might be targeting one vehicle, but then get intercepted by another AI vehicle, or whilst chasing one vehicle, a different vehicle may get in the way and get hit instead. But because it was a Demolition Derby, it really did not matter that a vehicle was not hitting its desired targets since they were causing destruction anyway! There were also times when the AI vehicles might end up just driving into the arena wall or one of the fixed obstacles in the middle of the arenas. Again, this did not really matter since it did not happen very often, but they were also driving damaged cars around, so their steering probably did not work too well anyway.

23.6   THE DEMOLITION DERBY GAME MODES

Showdown had three different Demolition Derby game modes. These were Rampage, Knockout, and Hard Target. Each of these game modes were distinctly different, yet all used the same basic code and techniques as described in this chapter.

23.6.1 RAMPAGE

Rampage was the traditional arena-based destruction derby event where the goal was to cause as much mayhem as possible. Points were scored for the amount of damage caused, with the highest score winning. This was the base demolition derby game mode that all the systems were designed to support.

23.6.2 HARD TARGET

Hard Target was a timed event where it was everyone against the player. The longer the player survived, the higher their score. The event started with the difficulty set at 50% and the player was against four AI vehicles. After an initial delay, extra AI vehicles were added into the arena every 15 seconds. Once all eight vehicles were in the arena, the difficulty would then increase by 5% every 15 seconds. Throughout testing, nobody was ever able to survive more than 10 minutes. In one instance of testing, a place was found where you "appeared" outside the arena (due to a bad boundary definition), and if you were outside the arena, the AI would not target you. After about eight minutes (all the cars were in the arena and the difficulty was now at 70%), I picked up the controller, drove into the arena, and then survived for only seven seconds more!

23.6.3 KNOCKOUT

The Knockout game mode was essentially sumo wrestling but with cars. The events took place on a raised platform, where pushing the cars out of the arena was the goal. Destroying them also scored points of course, but knocking them out of the arena was the most optimal way to get high scores. Unlike the Rampage game mode, in this case, it was imperative that cars did not drive into the boundaries as they would fall off instead of taking damage, so extra care was taken to ensure that would not be the case. These platforms were also always empty of obstacles so there was never a need to worry about hitting things other than other vehicles. Image 23.7 shows the two arenas used for the Knockout game modes.

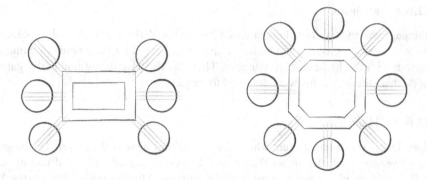

IMAGE 23.7   The Knockout arenas. Note that the outer boundary here is the actual boundary of the platform. The obstacle circles are where the ramps to get back onto the platform were located, and the lines are the "ramp splines" that the spline generation would connect to if an AI survived after falling off the platform.

One big difference between this game mode and Rampage was that whilst on the platform, instead of generating curved splines to follow, straight lines between the vehicle and its target were used. This was due to two different people working on the two game modes simultaneously. When the proper spline generation was finished and working, the straight-line system used for Knockout was working well enough that the time needed to retune the game mode to use the splines was better spent on other things (remember, less than five months development time!). Knockout also had the additional issue of how to get cars back onto the platform once they were knocked off. Originally, the plan was to just respawn the vehicles at the base of the ramps, but with the addition of some "ramp splines" and some minor changes to the spline generation/targeting code, it was possible to generate a spline from the vehicle's position to the closest ramp spline. One difference was that this time, there were two orientations needed: the vehicle's orientation and the ramp spline direction. So, using the two directions and the two start points (vehicle position and ramp spline start), a Bezier spline was created instead of a Bezier curve as was done previously. This allowed the vehicle to drive around and position itself at the base of the ramp before fully accelerating and jumping back onto the platform. From image 23.7, you should be able to see that the outer edge of the arena is not actually stored as well. This wasn't necessary as we only ever created the paths to the ramp splines, so we just made sure that the arenas had enough space that the vehicles wouldn't hit the arena walls.

23.7   RACE STARTS

As a final note, at the start of each event and after the lights changed, each vehicle would go full throttle into the middle of the arena to create a massive crash. Of course, the sensible player would just avoid the rush and then attack afterwards, so a couple of the cars were made to do the same. At every race start, a random position, mostly in the centre, was assigned to each car. By being mostly central, this added a bit of variability to how the first few seconds of the events proceeded. But for one or two vehicles, a random point in the arena was assigned instead. This meant that you would see a car drive towards the centre and then just turn away from all the mayhem. Further to this, the vehicles would sometimes delay their start and join the fray a few seconds later. This may not have been the best way to score points, but it added variety and randomness to the race starts and ensured that each event was different.

23.8 CONCLUSION

This chapter has detailed the work that went into creating the arena-based demolition derby game modes on *DiRT: Showdown*. These systems were designed and built in less than five months by just two programmers (one of whom was a junior with only one year's experience at the time!), but it was only achievable due to the existing tools and systems that could be leveraged. The tools that the level designers used were already familiar to them, even if they were now being used in a totally different way and the already existing code features could either be used directly (like the spline following system and statistics system) or copied and then updated (like the Overseer, which was based on the Race Choreographer from previous games). Given the time constraints that necessitated some of the decisions, the end result was remarkable. At the beginning of the project, the requirement was to deliver a single, empty arena with a single difficulty setting, but by the time it was completed five months later, there were multiple arenas (different shapes and with immovable obstacles inside) and three distinct game modes, with a fully working and tuneable difficulty system that featured precision driving and targeting.

REFERENCES

Bikker, J (2017) Practical SIMD Programming, available online: https://www.cs.uu.nl/docs/vakken/magr/2017-2018/files/SIMD%20Tutorial.pdf.

Bugbear Entertainment (2004) *FlatOut*. Bugbear Entertainment.

Dunlop, M. (2005) Introduction to Catmull-Rom Splines, available online: https://www.mvps.org/directx/articles/catmull/.

Index

Printed in the United States
by Baker & Taylor Publisher Services

Printed in the United States
by Baker & Taylor Publisher Services